"Msgr. Bohr's wisdom, gained during many years of experience in seminary formation, brings to life the historical and theological research contained in this important work. Informative and well-written, this book will be of great help to seminarians, priests, seminary formation personnel, and all those seeking a deeper understanding of and love for the diocesan priesthood."

—Rev. Richard J. Gabuzda
Executive Director
The Institute for Priestly Formation

"Father David Bohr's rich experience as a priest, a theologian, and a priestly formator clearly shines through the pages of his latest book, *The Diocesan Priest: Consecrated and Sent*. His insights will be a blessing to so many of us who wish the unique charism that is ours as diocesan priests to be explored and promoted for the unique calling that it is."

—Archbishop Edwin F. O'Brien
Archbishop of Baltimore

"With a compelling blend of practical insight and serious theological reflection upon the developing understanding of the ministerial priesthood from its apostolic roots in the New Testament, Monsignor David Bohr has used his own twenty years of experience in priestly formation to produce a praiseworthy study of what Pope John Paul II described as the 'gift and mystery' of diocesan priesthood. Each chapter of this work reveals Monsignor Bohr's profound love for and understanding of priestly office and priestly men. A book of this kind promotes authentic, sound, and solid doctrine in an effort to advance a theological study of diocesan priests ordained to be co-sharers with the bishops in continuing the apostolic mission of preaching, sanctifying, and shepherding Christ's flock. Monsignor Bohr has provided a rich and detailed theological reflection that should prove to be of special interest to all those involved in priestly formation."

—Monsignor Aloysius R. Callaghan
Rector and Vice President
The Saint Paul Seminary School of Divinity
of the University of St. Thomas
St. Paul, Minnesota

"*The Diocesan Priest: Consecrated and Sent* provides a thorough presentation of the historical and theological dimensions of the Catholic priesthood and is a welcome and valuable resource for anyone interested in understanding more profoundly what it means to be a priest. This study should certainly be part of any seminary formation program. Monsignor David Bohr clearly exhibits not only his expertise on the subject but also his devotion to the formation of priests from his many years as a faculty member and seminary rector."

—Most Reverend Donald W. Wuerl, STD
Archbishop of Washington

"Monsignor Bohr's years of work in priestly formation are evident in his description of the actual concerns of an often divided American presbyterate. He argues for a reappraisal of what diocesan priests *are* after demonstrating, with a rich historical sweep, what diocesan priests are *not*: not monks, not specially trained laypersons, not merely cultic functionaries, but men indelibly deputed to build up communion within the priestly people of God. Tradition teaches that diocesan priests first of all proclaim the Good News of reconciliation. Humble and solicitous like the Good Shepherd, priests seek out both those who know Christ's voice and those who have yet to hear it, and theirs, Bohr notes, is the first word in the history of Christianity: 'Rejoice! Then they celebrate that Word become flesh together with their people, empowering them to move from *missa* to mission.' Bohr notes that celibate priests should learn to enjoy communion in their own lives as well, cultivating the affective maturity that enables them to imitate Christ who engaged in 'preferential friendships' with Mary, Martha, Lazarus, and the disciple who rested his head on the Lord's chest at the Last Supper. This book would be a good companion on any priest's retreat."

—Fr. Robert Christian, OP
Angelicum University
Rome, Italy

"Msgr. Bohr has truly done a great favor for all seminarians and priests in writing *The Diocesan Priest: Consecrated and Sent*. Msgr. Bohr provides a theological reflection that is well grounded in the biblical text, while being deeply attentive to the historical development of the church's understanding of the diocesan priesthood. This book will be a great help for priests and seminarians trying to understand the priesthood as it is experienced in the years following the Second Vatican Council. In particular, Msgr. Bohr provides a profound theological reflection on the particular charism of the diocesan priest as it is lived out in relation to the baptismal priesthood of the lay faithful and their mission in the world. The theological insight of *The Diocesan Priest: Consecrated and Sent* is certainly the fruit of Msgr. Bohr's extensive experience of the diocesan priesthood. It is a book that is most relevant for the church of today."

—Philip A. Smith
Seminarian, Diocese of Toledo in America
Pontifical North American College, Europe

"As a gold mine of development and detail, Monsignor Bohr's treatment of diocesan priestly consecration and mission explores the diocesan priesthood through many phases of the exciting and fluctuating history of Christian spirituality. From the original thrust of the call and sending of the apostles to the closing ignition of priestly ministry for today, this book is a profound, stirring, informative journey. Because priestly holiness is never centered on itself, the glow of evangelization's fire always lights the way, even in periods when the fire, for various reasons, was dimmed.

"Though I was invited to give a brief recommendation, I found myself reading every word because I was learning so much. I think you will too!"

—Fr. George Aschenbrenner, SJ
Co-founder of the Institute for Priestly Formation
Author of *Quickening the Fire in Our Midst:*
The Challenge of Diocesan Priestly Spirituality

The Diocesan Priest

Consecrated and Sent

David Bohr

Foreword by Archbishop Timothy M. Dolan

LITURGICAL PRESS

Collegeville, Minnesota

www.litpress.org

Nihil Obstat: Reverend Christopher T. Washington, S.T.L., *Censor Librorum.*

Imprimatur: ✠ Most Reverend Joseph F. Martino, D.D., Hist. E.D., Bishop of Scranton, Pennsylvania, December 15, 2008.

Cover design by David Manahan, OSB. Photo © jrroman/istockphoto.com.

Excerpts from documents of the Second Vatican Council are from *Vatican Council II: Volume 1, The Conciliar and Post Conciliar Documents,* by Austin Flannery, OP, © 1996 (Costello Publishing Company, Inc.). Used with permission.

Unless otherwise noted, Scripture texts in this work are taken from the *New American Bible with Revised New Testament and Revised Psalms* © 1991, 1986, 1970 Confraternity of Christian Doctrine, Washington, DC, and are used by permission of the copyright owner. All Rights Reserved. No part of the *New American Bible* may be reproduced in any form without permission in writing from the copyright owner.

1   2   3   4   5   6   7   8   9

Library of Congress Cataloging-in-Publication Data

Bohr, David.
    The diocesan priest : consecrated and sent / David Bohr ; foreword by the Most Reverend Timothy Dolan.
        p.   cm.
    ISBN 978-0-8146-3278-9 (pbk.)
        1. Priests.   2. Priesthood—Catholic Church.   3. Pastoral theology—Catholic Church.   4. Catholic Church—Clergy.   I. Title.

BX1913.B573 2009
262'.142—dc22

                                                                    2009006632

For

Seminarians of the Pontifical North American College

Rome, Italy

2004–2007

Mater Mea, Fiducia Mea

From Jesus' prayer for his disciples at the Last Supper:

> *They do not belong to the world any more than I belong to the world. Consecrate them in truth. Your word is truth. As you sent me into the world, so I sent them into the world. And I consecrate myself for them, so that they also may be consecrated in truth.* (John 17:16-19)

Contents

Foreword by Archbishop Timothy M. Dolan   xi

List of Abbreviations   xiii

Introduction   1

CHAPTER 1: **Biblical Foundations of Priestly Office**   13

Priests and Elders in the Hebrew Scriptures   14

Jesus the Good Shepherd: A Royal Priesthood   17

Apostleship and the Development of Presbyteral Ministry
in the New Testament   23

The Universal Priesthood of the New Covenant   30

CHAPTER 2: **Priestly Ministry in Historical Perspective**   33

The Sub-Apostolic and Pre-Nicene Era
(Second and Third Centuries)   35

The Constantinian Age and the Influence of Monasticism
(Fourth and Fifth Centuries)   41

Germanization and the Feudal System
(Sixth through Eleventh Centuries)   48

The Birth of Religious Orders and Scholasticism
(Twelfth through Fifteenth Centuries)   56

The Protestant Reformation, the Council of Trent, and
Post-Tridentine Era (Sixteenth through Nineteenth Centuries)   60

CHAPTER 3: **Consecrated for Mission**   67

The Christological Context of Consecration   70

The Royal Priesthood of Believers   74

The Meaning of the Sacramental Priestly Character   77

Configuration to Christ: The Vocation to Holiness   86

CHAPTER 4: **Sent to Build Up the Body of Christ**   94

Priesthood within the Context of the Church's
Mission of Evangelization   97

The Priest as Prophet-Teacher   100

The Priest as Sanctifier   106

The Priest as Shepherd-King   113

The Mission or Apostolate of the Laity   117

CHAPTER 5: **The Spousal Meaning of Celibacy**   124

The Evolution of the Evangelical Ideal of Celibacy
for the Sake of the Kingdom   126

Celibacy: A Sign of Christ the Bridegroom's Love   134

Cultivating Affective Maturity and True Friendships   141

The Reservation of the Ministerial Priesthood to Men Only   153

Conclusion   158

Foreword

It is a given of our faith that "God can bring good from evil."

One of the "goods" that has come from the horror of the recent past's crisis in the priesthood has been a welcome abundance of solid, helpful, hopeful books on the priesthood.

We bishops and priests are "in the business of hope," and the appearance of these splendid works on the priesthood—by authors such as Howard Bleichner, David Toups, Stephen Rossetti, Mark O'Keefe, Matthew Levering, Thomas Acklin, and Justin Rigali—gives us a lot of confidence that the renewal of the priesthood longed for by Pope John Paul II might indeed be coming about.

This enticing and enlightening book by Father David Bohr is a most welcome addition to the above menu. Father Bohr's qualifications—a serious theologian, a priest of the Diocese of Scranton with long and fruitful years of service in the noble enterprise of priestly formation—make his observations timely and credible.

Far from just a "pep talk" on the priesthood, Father Bohr offers a very digestible but quality *theology* of the priesthood, using the classical methodology of Scripture, the Fathers, and an enjoyable ride through the *historical* elaboration on the theology of the priesthood.

Not to be missed is his *systematic* treatment of such pivotal issues as the Christological context, the priesthood of all believers—and how this differs from ordained priesthood—and the elusive yet essential notion of the sacramental character of Holy Orders.

Make sure you persevere to the end—a pleasant task!—because the chapter on celibacy, especially its spousal dimension, is well worth it.

Searching for a theology/spirituality of the diocesan priesthood has become somewhat of a "quest for the Holy Grail" among us. Father Bohr offers one of the more engaging considerations of this adventure that I've yet come across.

Let the renewal continue!

Most Reverend Timothy M. Dolan
Archbishop of Milwaukee
February 22, 2009
Feast of the Chair of Peter
Year of St. Paul

Abbreviations

AA   *Apostolicam Actuositatem*, Second Vatican Council's Decree on the Apostolate of the Laity, November 18, 1965.

CCC   The *Catechism of the Catholic Church*, 2nd edition, Rome, Libreria Editrice Vaticana, 1997.

CCL   *Corpus Christianorum. Series Latina*. Turnhout, 1953–.

CL   *Christifideles Laici*, post-synodal apostolic exhortation of Pope John Paul II on the Vocation and the Mission of the Lay Faithful in the Church and the World, December 30, 1988.

DCE   *Deus Caritas Est*, encyclical of Pope Benedict XVI on Christian love, December 25, 2005.

EIA   *Ecclesia in America*, post-synodal apostolic exhortation of Pope John Paul II on the Church in America, January 22, 1999.

EN   *Evangelii Nuntiandi*, post-synodal apostolic exhortation of Pope Paul VI on Evangelization of the Modern World, December 8, 1975.

FC   *Familiaris Consortio*, post-synodal apostolic exhortation of Pope John Paul II on the Christian Family in the Modern World, November 22, 1981.

GS   *Gaudium et Spes*, Second Vatican Council's Pastoral Constitution on the Church in the Modern World, December 7, 1965.

LG   *Lumen Gentium*, Second Vatican Council's Dogmatic Constitution on the Church, November 21, 1964.

NJB   The New Jerusalem Bible. New York, NY: Doubleday, 1985.

NMI   *Novo Millennio Ineunte*, apostolic letter of Pope John Paul II at the Close of the Great Jubilee Year of 2000, January 6, 2001.

OT   *Optatum Totius*, Second Vatican Council's Decree on Priestly Formation, October 28, 1965.

PDV   *Pastores Dabo Vobis,* post-synodal apostolic exhortation of Pope John Paul II on the Formation of Priests in the Circumstances of the Present Day, March 25, 1992.

PG   *Patrologia Graeca.* J. P. Minge, ed. Paris, 1857–66, 162 volumes.

PL   *Patrologia Latina.* J. P. Minge, ed. Paris, 1844–64, 221 volumes.

PO   *Presbyterorum Ordinis,* Second Vatican Council's Decree on the Ministry and Life of Priests, December 7, 1965.

RH   *Redemptor Hominis,* encyclical of Pope John Paul II on the Redeemer of Man, March 4, 1979.

RP   *Reconciliatio et Paenitentia,* post-synodal apostolic exhortation of Pope John Paul II on Reconciliation and Penance in the Mission of the Church Today, December 2, 1984.

SCael   *Sacerdotalis Caelibatus,* encyclical of Pope Paul VI on Priestly Celibacy, June 24, 1967.

SCar   *Sacramentum Caritatis,* post-synodal apostolic exhortation of Pope Benedict XVI on the Eucharist as the Source and Summit of the Church's Life and Mission, February 22, 2007.

USCCB   United States Conference of Catholic Bishops.

UUS   *Ut Unum Sint,* encyclical of Pope John Paul II on Commitment to Ecumenism, May 25, 1995.

Introduction

I will give you shepherds after my own heart" (Jer 3:15). With these words of the prophet Jeremiah, Pope John Paul II began his landmark post-synodal apostolic exhortation on priestly formation, *Pastores Dabo Vobis* (*I Will Give You Shepherds*). The pope deliberately chose this biblical image of the *shepherd*, an image that Jesus himself used to describe his own identity and ministry (see John 10:11), with the hope of showing us the way out of the crisis of priestly identity, which had developed and bred much confusion in the years following the Second Vatican Council (1962–65). The Holy Father went on to state in this document that a "correct and in-depth awareness of the nature and mission of the ministerial priesthood is the path which must be taken . . . in order to emerge from the crisis of priestly identity" (PDV 11).

While contributing factors to this priestly identity crisis may be found both within the Church and outside in the contemporary sociocultural context, it arose mainly out of errant attempts by some theologians to reinterpret Vatican II's more elaborative teaching on the nature and mission of the Church and ordained ministry. The Council Fathers had set out to explain the theological meaning of the priesthood by first reaffirming the declarations of the Council of Trent and then enlarging upon them. Trent's sole purpose had been to refute and censure the errors of the Protestant Reformers. It was never given the task of providing a comprehensive theological vision. Therefore, as a result, Trent directly countered the Reformation thesis that priesthood was simply an office of preaching by solemnly declaring that through ordination the priest is, in fact, endowed with the sacramental powers of celebrating the Eucharist and forgiving sins.

The development of the "private" Mass, accompanied by the giving of stipends and the establishment of Mass-saying benefices in monasteries of the Middle Ages, had led by the time of Trent to a commonly accepted theological understanding that it was primarily for the celebration of the Eucharist that priests were ordained. The liturgy, which in the early Church had been first and foremost a communal gathering in prayer, by now had become a privatized clerical ritual. "Altar priests" were being ordained just to say Masses for the souls in purgatory and for all manner of special intentions. The Reformation readily denounced these practices as superstitious, which Trent in turn refuted with its declaration reaffirming unequivocally the sacramental powers of the priest. This "partial" presentation on priesthood, however, in succeeding centuries would become commonly accepted as the Church's full and complete teaching on the priesthood.

In a desire to return to the biblical and patristic sources Vatican II anchors its teaching on the priesthood in the mission and ministry of Jesus Christ, as teacher, priest, and king. The office of priesthood is viewed here as "a participation in his ministry and thus includes the competence upon earth to build up the Church throughout the ages to become the People of God, the body of Christ and the temple of the Holy Spirit."[1] It is the continuation of the threefold commission Jesus entrusted to the apostles in Matthew 28:19-20—"*Go, therefore, and make disciples of all nations, baptizing them in the name of the Father, and of the Son, and of the holy Spirit, teaching them to observe all that I have commanded you.*" Vatican II deliberately based its doctrine of the priesthood upon this threefold apostolic mission "in order to retrieve this from its centuries-old restriction to the realm of cult."[2] For too long the operative image of the priest in the Church resembled more that of "the priest" found in the history of religions than it did the priesthood of Jesus Christ.

Transforming or expanding archetypes, like shifting paradigms, often precipitate a crisis because they challenge us to change and even discard those long-accepted images, which we have come to depend upon to organize and interpret our world. The process proves frightening to some, like pulling the rug out from under their feet. They resist any change that threatens their carefully constructed and comfortable worldview. Yet others revel in the opportunity to let their imaginations run wild as they explore new and exciting possibilities. As human beings, we live our lives and define reality through the use of our power of imagination. Michael Novak in one of his early works, *Ascent of the Mountain, Flight of the Dove,*

---

[1] Friedrich Wulf, "Decree on the Ministry and Life of Priests," Commentary on the Decree, Articles 1–6, in *Commentary on the Documents of Vatican II*, ed. Herbert Vorgrimler, vol. 4, 215 (New York: Herder and Herder, 1969).

[2] Ibid., 216. See *Lumen Gentium* 25–28; 34ff. (for the laity); *Presbyterorum Ordinis* 1, 4–6, 7.

observes, "Often mutual understanding depends on one's ability to grasp what is happening in the imagination of the other party in the discussion. . . . The discerning of a faulty imaginative expectation and the construction of a good one enormously raise the probabilities of insight."[3]

The renewal in biblical, liturgical, and patristic studies within the Church during the last century brought to prominence once again the fundamental role that symbols and images play in theology. The Fathers of the Second Vatican Council realized that if the Church was to have any success in effectively carrying out its mission of proclaiming the Gospel to the modern world, it needed once again to address and capture people's imaginations. Vatican II thus entitled its Dogmatic Constitution on the Church *Lumen Gentium*. Christ is "the light of the nations," whom the Church, gathered together in the Holy Spirit, is sent to proclaim (see LG 1). Presenting the mystery of the Church, the same document uses language that has recourse to images and symbols rather than to definitions. The images it employs are sheepfold, field, house, family, temple (LG 6), the body of Christ (LG 7), and people of God (LG 9–17).

Images motivate us to action. They appeal to both our cognitive and affective faculties. They present us with a vision or plan that gives us hope and motivation. Despair, on the other hand, has been described as a curtailment of the private imagination that "reaches the point of the end of inward resource and must put on the imagination of another if it is to find a way out."[4] Just as a poor or confused self-image lies at the root of a personal identity crisis, likewise uncertain or defective images of the role of the ordained priesthood in the Church have given rise to a crisis of priestly identity.

In the aftermath of Vatican II's reaffirmation of the New Testament teaching on the common priesthood of all the faithful, which the Reformation espoused as the source of ministry, a certain ambiguity began to blur the distinction between the priesthood of the baptized and that of the ordained. "There is no difference between the priest and everyone else," soon became a familiar mantra heard within the Catholic Church and was even championed by some theological circles. A number of theologians also began to advocate the Reformation notion of ordination being just an ecclesial act of delegation, ignoring or repudiating its sacramental

---

[3] Michael Novak, *Ascent of the Mountain, Flight of the Dove* (New York: Harper & Row, 1971), 18.

[4] William F. Lynch, SJ, *Images of Hope* (New York and Toronto: A Mentor-Omega Book, 1965), 19.

character as incorporation into the one priesthood of Jesus Christ, head and shepherd of the Church.[5]

Furthermore, the Second Vatican Council's teaching in its Dogmatic Constitution on the Church that only bishops possess "the fullness of the sacrament of Orders" (LG 21), and in its decree *Presbyterorum Ordinis* that the ministerial role of bishops "has been handed down, in a lesser degree . . . to the priests" (PO 2), seemed in the viewpoint of many priests to be an implied demotion of some sort. Prior to the Council seminarians were taught that ordination to the priesthood constituted the fullness of Holy Orders. Bishops were essentially priests who received the added power of governance through episcopal consecration.

Then too, in light of the Second Vatican Council's affirmation of the universality of grace,[6] some in the Church began to question the very need of explicitly proclaiming the Gospel. A few theologians even maintained that while Jesus of Nazareth was certainly the Christ, other peoples and cultures have their own christs. "Why, then, send forth missionaries?" others started to ask. A good number of Catholic educators also began to feel that the Catholic school's primary task is to offer quality education, not to evangelize. Proclaiming the Good News of Jesus Christ, they would maintain, is a direct infringement upon the freedom of personal conscience.

The proliferation of lay ministries and the restoration of the permanent diaconate in the years following the Council also added to the confusion in the minds of many priests trained in a preconciliar, neoscholastic theology. Likewise, a rapidly increasing secularism within Western society and culture itself downplayed and even showed contempt for religion. Priests, long accustomed to being accorded respect and deference in public, now not infrequently found themselves objects of scorn and derision. In a technological society that enshrines usefulness and efficiency as its main values, priesthood quickly fell to the bottom end of the scale. Func-

---

[5] See, for example, Hans Küng, *Why Priests?: A Proposal for a New Church Ministry*, trans. Robert C. Collins, SJ (Garden City, NY: Doubleday, 1972), 63–64 and 88–95; Edward Schillebeeckx, *Ministry: Leadership in the Community of Jesus Christ* (New York: Crossroads, 1981), 72–73 and 138–39; and Leonardo Boff, *Ecclesiogenesis: The Base Communities Reinvent the Church*, trans. Robert R. Barr (Maryknoll, NY: Orbis Books, 1986), 70–75.

[6] See *Lumen Gentium* 16: "Those also can attain to everlasting salvation who through no fault of their own do not know the gospel of Christ or His Church, yet sincerely seek God and moved by grace, strive by their deeds to do His will as it is known to them through the dictates of conscience." Also, *Gaudium et Spes* 22 and *Ad Gentes* 3.

tionalism as the measure of success in such a setting, moreover, cannot help but undermine and have an effect on priestly ministry.

Within the Church a growing cultural and theological pluralism led to polarizations among generations of the clergy who themselves experienced different models of formation. The growing feminist movement and persistent efforts to impose democracy upon the Catholic Church fueled a spirit of anticlericalism. This mood was further intensified by media scrutiny of clerical sexual misconduct and other errant behaviors, to which it was popularly believed priests were immune because of their "higher calling." As a result, the image of the priesthood and the priest's own self-image were thrown into confusion. The mirror was broken.

Entrusted with the responsibility of directing ministry formation in the Diocese of Scranton—lay, diaconal, and priestly—for nearly thirty years, I myself first found it necessary to have a clear understanding in my own mind of the distinctiveness of each ministry. This required my referring often to the conciliar and postconciliar documents of the Church as well as to other theological and pastoral resources. Vatican II did, indeed, provide us with a renewed perspective from which to view Church teaching. As Cardinal Joseph Ratzinger once stated, "The Council wanted to mark the transition from a protective to a missionary attitude. Many forget that for the Council the counter-concept to 'conservative' is not 'progressive' but 'missionary.'"[7] Thus it is within the context of the Church's mission of evangelization that Vatican II presented the image of the ministerial priesthood.

The Second Vatican Council's Dogmatic Constitution on the Church never treats the priesthood in isolation, as if it were a gift-apart sent down from heaven. Rather, its teaching on the ministerial priesthood is developed within the context of Christology, ecclesiology, and the apostolic ministry. *Lumen Gentium* presents the mystery of the Church, its nature, and universal mission in chapter 1. In the next chapter it speaks of the new people of God, whom Christ instituted through the new covenant in his blood (LG 9) and who "are consecrated to be a spiritual house and a holy priesthood. . . ." Yet it is careful to explain here that, "Though they differ essentially and not only in degree, the common priesthood of the faithful and the ministerial or hierarchical priesthood are none the less ordered to one another; each in its own proper order shares in the one priesthood of Christ" (LG 10). It is, then, in chapter 3 on the hierarchical

---

[7] Joseph Cardinal Ratzinger with Vittorio Messori, *The Ratzinger Report* (San Francisco: Ignatius Press, 1985), 13.

structure of the Church that the Council teaches, "Christ . . . has, through his apostles, made their successors, the bishops namely, sharers in his consecration and mission; and these, in turn, duly entrusted in varying degrees various members of the Church with the office of their ministry" (LG 28).

Many Catholics are too often unaware and confused about the origins and nature of the diocesan priesthood. While serving on the faculty of the North American College recently, I was at table with some guests from the United States, and one of them inquired if I were a Jesuit. I responded, "No, I am a diocesan priest, and the College," I added, "is a seminary for training diocesan priests." The person then asked, "Who is your founder?" I gave sort of a puzzled look and he added, "I mean, like St. Ignatius founded the Jesuits and St. Francis the Franciscans. Who founded diocesan priests?" With even a stranger look on my face I answered, "Well, Jesus Christ, and by saying that I am really not trying to be facetious."

Over the years, while endeavoring to explain the special charism of the diocesan priesthood to seminarians, I have likened the diocesan priest to the physician who is a general practitioner or in family practice, the first to take care of everyone's needs. Father Robert M. Schwartz, I believe, best explained it when he experienced a situation similar to the one I related above. Introduced once by mistake as a Jesuit, he found himself responding, "No, I am a diocesan priest. The charism of diocesan priests is the mission and spirituality of the laity." He then elaborates, "Diocesan and other parish clergy have a unique charism that places them at the heart of the mission of the Church. Not only are they called forth from the laity to be priests but they also choose to continue to live among lay people, to lead communities of lay men and women, and to focus their ministry on the mission and spirituality of the laity."[8]

When I have asked seminary applicants and seminarians why they want to be a priest, not infrequently I have heard the reply, "I want to be a priest because I want to become holy." It leaves me wondering if the respondent truly believes that he cannot possibly become holy as a layperson. Is he aware of the fact that it is first of all through one's consecration at baptism that the Christian is called to holiness? As Pope John Paul II taught, recalling the teaching of the Second Vatican Council, "We come to a full sense of the dignity of the lay faithful if we consider *the prime and fundamental vocation* that the Father assigns to each of them in Jesus Christ through the Holy Spirit: the vocation to holiness, that is, the perfection of

---

[8] Robert M. Schwartz, "Servant of the Servants of God: A Pastor's Spirituality," in *The Spirituality of the Diocesan Priest*, ed. Donald B. Cozzens (Collegeville, MN: Liturgical Press, 1997), 15.

charity" (CL 16). He reiterates this same point in *Pastores Dabo Vobis* before he describes the priest's "specific" vocation to holiness: "By virtue of their consecration, priests are configured to Jesus the good shepherd and are called to imitate and to live out his own pastoral charity" (PDV 22). Just as holiness for the layperson is found in the perfection of charity, so for the priest holiness is found in his faithfully living out the pastoral charity of Jesus Christ, the Good Shepherd.

Priests are not ordained for their own benefit but are consecrated for the sake of the laity so that they may faithfully exercise their baptismal priesthood.[9] As Pope John Paul II wrote in his 1990 Holy Thursday Letter to Priests, "The priesthood is not an institution that exists alongside the laity, or 'above' it. The priesthood of bishops and priests, as well as the ministry of deacons, is 'for' the laity, and precisely for this reason it possesses a ministerial character, that is to say one 'of service.'"[10] The spirituality of the diocesan priest finds its source not in the private or mystical vision of some founder of a religious congregation but in the priest's own personal configuration, through the outpouring of the Spirit in the sacrament of orders, to Jesus Christ "the head, shepherd and spouse of the church" (PDV 22). Through his ministry, through his exercise of pastoral charity, his faithful living out "Christ's spousal love toward the church, his bride" (ibid.), the diocesan priest is set on the right course to the perfection of life.

Pope John Paul II thus wrote, "Thanks to the insightful teaching of the Second Vatican Council, we can grasp the conditions and demands, the manifestations and fruits of the intimate bond between the priest's spiritual life and the exercise of his threefold ministry of word, sacrament and pastoral charity" (PDV 26). He then proceeded to demonstrate how each ministry contributes to the priest's growth in holiness. For instance, when preaching, the priest must first "abide" in the Word, approaching it with a docile and prayerful heart so that "it may deeply penetrate his thoughts and feelings and bring about a new outlook in him—'the mind of Christ' (1 Cor. 2:16). . . ." In celebrating the sacraments, especially the Eucharist, the priest's spiritual life is "built up and molded by the different characteristics and demands of each of the sacraments as he celebrates them. . . ." Likewise, encouraging and leading the ecclesial community "demands of the priest an intense spiritual life, filled with those qualities and virtues which are typical of a person who 'presides over' and 'leads' a community . . ." (PDV 26). The exercise and demands of ministry, when undertaken

---

[9] See CCC 1120.

[10] John Paul II, *Letters to My Brother Priests—Holy Thursday (1979–1994)*, ed. James P. Socias (Princeton: Scepter Publishers; Chicago: Midwest Theological Forum, 1992), 198.

faithfully with a sincere heart, serve to bring the priest into a more intimate communion with Christ and therefore with the Blessed Trinity, the God who is Love. The priest's identity flows from and leads back to the Triune God, who is the true source of every Christian identity (see PDV 12).

The first chapter of *Presbyterorum Ordinis* is entitled "The Priesthood in the Church's Mission." The title itself is significant. The priesthood can only be rightly understood within the context of mission, of being sent as Christ himself was sent by the Father in the power of the Holy Spirit. The Council's teaching on the priesthood, both in the Dogmatic Constitution on the Church (LG 28) and in this decree (PO 2), begins with the Johannine reference to Jesus as the one "'whom the Father consecrated and sent into the world' (Jn. 10:36)." Consecration is for mission. Indeed, we see this same connection in Luke's gospel where Jesus in the synagogue at Nazareth reads the words of the prophet Isaiah: "The Spirit of the Lord is upon me, because he has anointed me to bring glad tidings to the poor" (Luke 4:18).

In *Pastores Dabo Vobis*, Pope John Paul II reported that the synod Fathers, who met in October 1990 to discuss "The Formation of Priests in the Circumstances of the Present Day," continually returned to this Lukan passage as the starting point for their reflection upon the goal of seminary formation, that is, "the ministerial priesthood as a participation—in the church—in the very priesthood of Jesus Christ" (PDV 11). Referring to the synod Fathers again, he wrote, "It is within the church's mystery, as a mystery of Trinitarian communion in missionary tension, that every Christian identity is revealed, and likewise the specific identity of the priest and his ministry" (PDV 12). He further explained:

> In particular, "the priest minister is the servant of Christ present in the Church as mystery, communion and mission. In virtue of his participation in the 'anointing' and 'mission' of Christ, the priest can continue Christ's prayer, word, sacrifice and salvific action in the Church. In this way, the priest is a servant of the Church as mystery because he actuates the Church's sacramental signs of the presence of the risen Christ. He is a servant of the Church as communion because—in union with the bishop and closely related to the presbyterate—he builds up the unity of the Church community in the harmony of diverse vocations, charisms and services. Finally, the priest is a servant to the Church as mission because he makes the community a herald and witness of the Gospel."[11]

---

[11] PDV 16 with endnote reference to Synod of Bishops, eighth ordinary general assembly, "The Formation of Priests in the Circumstances of the Present Day," *Instrumentum Laboris* 16; cf. Proposition 7.

The ministerial priesthood finds its identity in its configuration to Jesus Christ "whom the Father has consecrated and sent into the world" to bear witness to (*martyria*) and manifest in his flesh the God who is self-giving, reconciling Love—the God who is Trinity.

While serving as academic dean at the Pontifical North American College, the American seminary in Rome, from 2004 to 2007, I was asked to present a short course on the priesthood to the second-year theologians studying for dioceses in the United States and Australia. The course was part of the College's pastoral formation program and was meant to supplement the courses on the sacraments, which the seminarians attended either at the Pontifical Gregorian University or the Pontifical University of St. Thomas Aquinas. In March 2006 the Papal Visitation of Seminaries and Houses of Priestly Formation took place at the North American College. Upon reading my outline for the priesthood course, Bishop Allen H. Vigneron of the Diocese of Oakland (now archbishop of Detroit), who chaired the visitation team, approached me about possibly developing it into a book. My responsibilities as academic dean and formation advisor, as well as conducting a first-year theological seminar for students at the Pontifical Gregorian University, made it impossible to even consider such a project. I therefore remain deeply grateful to my ordinary, Bishop Joseph F. Martino, who upon my return to the Diocese of Scranton most willingly granted me a sabbatical year to undertake the task.

Every author, of course, brings an individual and limited interpretive perspective to his or her own work, depending very much upon one's personal experiences, talents, studies, and cultural influences. I write as someone who entered a college seminary upon graduation from a diocesan co-ed Catholic high school in 1964, while the Second Vatican Council was still in session. Two years later at twenty years of age, I was sent to Rome where I attended the Pontifical Roman Major Seminary, the seminary of the Diocese of Rome, and received a PhB from the Lateran University in 1968. I was then transferred to the North American College and the Gregorian University, where I obtained an STL in dogmatic theology in 1972 after having been ordained a priest of the Diocese of Scranton in December 1971.

After two years of parochial, chancery, and Catholic high school work, I returned to Rome and earned a doctorate in moral theology, summa cum laude, at the Academia Alfonsiana in 1977 under the direction of the late Father Bernard Häring, CSsR. My dissertation was entitled *Evangelization in America*.[12] It sought to demonstrate the necessary interdependence of

[12] David Bohr, *Evangelization in America: Proclamation, Way of Life, and the Catholic Church in the United States* (New York: Paulist Press, 1977).

the major theological disciplines—Scripture, doctrine, moral and spiritual theology—within the context of the Church's primary and essential mission of evangelization. Our lived faith-response to the grace of Christ, namely, the life in the Spirit proclaimed by the Gospel, is the true foundation of the Christian moral life. It furthermore constitutes the apt subject matter for a theology of Christian living, which the Second Vatican Council for all practical purposes called for when it mandated the renewal of moral theology (see OT 16). While over the years I may not have seen eye-to-eye, nor at all times concurred with some of Father Häring's conclusions on moral issues and a few other theological matters, I shall ever remain grateful to him for his overall theological vision, depth of spiritual insight, and constant encouragement always to see, first of all, God's grace operative in our world. He also initially pointed out to me what he called "my gift" of first seeing the whole before its parts, the gift of a synthetic as opposed to an analytical mind.

For thirty years I have been primarily involved in ministerial formation, teaching, diocesan administration, and evangelization programming (both on the diocesan and national levels). My assignments have included serving as diocesan director of the Office for Continuing Education of Priests (1978–89); vice-rector/academic dean (1988–90) and rector (1990–2004) of St. Pius X Seminary, Dalton, Pennsylvania (a college, pre-theology program); founding director (1984–88) and fourth director (1995–2004) of the diocesan Pastoral Formation Institute; as well as founding director of the diocesan permanent diaconate formation program (1988–2004). I have also been teaching courses in Christian formation and moral theology in all the above venues over the same time period. It is from this perspective that I write this theological reflection on the diocesan priesthood.

The Diocesan Priest: Consecrated and Sent is intended for anyone interested in reflecting upon the historical and theological developments that underlie the contemporary understanding of the ministerial priesthood, mainly within the Roman Catholic tradition. Bishops, priests, seminarians, as well as those discerning a vocation to the diocesan priesthood, are envisioned as the prospective reading audience. Chapters 1 and 2 trace the development of the understanding of priesthood from biblical times up to the eve of the Second Vatican Council. Chapter 3 reflects upon the theological meaning of "consecration" or "anointing" as it first applied to Jesus of Nazareth—the Messiah, the Christ, God's Anointed One—and then to the Christian priesthood. As found in the Sacred Scriptures, moreover, consecration is always for "mission." Chapter 4, therefore, explores the theology of mission and its unfolding in the threefold office of diocesan priests—ordained to be co-sharers with their bishops in continuing the apostolic mission of preaching, sanctifying, and shepherding Christ's flock. In chapter 5, I conclude with a brief look at the history and theology of celibacy, a charism of the Holy Spirit that over the centuries has become an integral part of the ministerial priesthood in the Latin Rite.

Many books and articles, indeed, have been written in recent years analyzing the impact that changes within the Church and society have had upon the priesthood since the Second Vatican Council (1962–65). Some have reflected experientially upon what it means to be a priest today. Others have looked upon priests and priesthood candidates from socio-logical, cultural, psychological, and formational perspectives. Celibacy and the spiritual life of the priest also provide the focus of a number of these works. A few, in addition, have presented a history or theology of the priesthood. *The Diocesan Priest: Consecrated and Sent* proposes chiefly to be a "theological reflection" upon the developing understanding of the ministerial priesthood from its apostolic roots in the New Testament. The course I first presented at the North American College consisted largely of a blending of sources that I pulled together over my nearly twenty years in seminary formation. This book reflects that basic synthesis. At the same time, I hope it still captures a bit of the spirit of St. Bonaventure who maintained that theology exists not merely "to serve contemplation, but also to make us holy; in fact, its first purpose is to make us holy."[13]

---

[13] Bonaventure, *Prologue to the Commentary on the Book of Sentences*, 3, Quarachi ed., I, 13.

Chapter 1

Biblical Foundations of Priestly Office

Jesus said: "I am the good shepherd, and I know mine and mine know me, just as the Father knows me and I know the Father; and I will lay down my life for the sheep."

—John 10:14-15

The image of the priest that comes to us from the history of religions is that of someone whose office it is to perform religious rites and make sacrificial offerings on the behalf of the people. The priest is a person set apart or consecrated to serve as a mediator between the deity and the worshiper. Originally, such cultic functions were carried out by the head of the family. The office later became a public one, and in many instances was connected with the head of a clan or the king. Thus history provides us with numberless examples of blending political activity with religious functions, like the Pharaoh in Egypt, who fulfilled the role of a king-priest. We also find examples of shamanism in which the functions of the priest and prophet or seer are combined, as was the case with Zarathustra in Persian religion. Strictly speaking, shamans are not priests since their mediatorship is not cultic but personal by nature because of a mystical gift. For our purposes in this chapter, we shall first consider the changing images of the priest in the Hebrew Scriptures. Then we will reflect upon the New Testament's understanding of Christ's priesthood and its continuance in and through the apostolic ministry of the Church.

Priests and Elders in the Hebrew Scriptures

As we search the Old Testament for antecedents to the Christian priesthood, we need to look beyond both the Aaronic priesthood and that of the Levitical line in postexilic Judaism. Indeed, when we later move into the New Testament we never find the word "priesthood" or "priest" (*hiereus*) employed to designate the ordained ministry or the ordained minister. Only the Letter to the Hebrews will use the term and apply it to Christ alone, whom it refers to as the "great high priest" (Heb 4:14ff.). Yet, as we shall shortly see, even there the concept of priesthood is developed with exceptional originality. Furthermore, the leadership instituted by the apostles in the first Christian communities more readily resembled the college of seventy elders established by Moses through his giving them a portion of his spirit (cf. Num 11:16-17). These ruling presbyters or *zeqēnîm* continued to serve within the Jewish community during the New Testament period and beyond as representatives of the people in political and religious matters, and frequently acted as judges.[1]

Scripture scholars have identified two different forms of priesthood during the historical development of Judaism. An earlier nonspecialized exercise of priestly functions was evident in the time of the patriarchs, when religious and cultic roles were carried out by the heads of families or clans. Even later Moses himself, not a priest in the strict sense, performed the sacrificial ritual of the covenant (cf. Exod 24:3-8). David and Solomon, furthermore, exercised the activities of the king-priest following the pattern of other monarchies in the Near East. Melchizedek, to whom Jesus' priesthood will be compared in the Letter to the Hebrews, was a particular example of such a king-priest outside Judaism. His meeting with Abraham is recounted in Genesis 14:18-20. This monarchical priesthood was, in fact, more ontological than functional. It arose from the king being anointed with oil at his coronation, thus constituting him a son of God in some sense. "The priestly status itself was bestowed upon the monarch by means of an oath sworn by the deity at the king's coronation: 'The Lord has sworn and will not change his mind: You are a priest for ever after the order of Melchizedek' (Ps 110, 4)."[2] Such a royal priesthood, therefore, was considered to be more permanent and enduring than that of the ordinary priests who ministered in the many local Jewish sanctuaries.

---

[1] See CCC 1541: "The liturgy of the Church, however, sees in the priesthood of Aaron and the service of the Levites, as in the institution of the seventy elders [cf. Num 11:24-25], a prefiguring of the ordained ministry of the New Covenant."

[2] D. W. Rooke, "Jesus as Royal Priest: Reflections on the Interpretation of the Melchizedek Tradition in Heb 7," *Biblica* 81 (2000): 81.

A specialized priestly function connected with the tribe of Levi emerged during the period of the Judges. The priest, called in Hebrew *kōhēn*, was fundamentally a man attached to a sanctuary or temple, where he carried out sanctuary duties on a day-to-day basis. Until the limitation of the priestly ritual to Jerusalem, which occurred sometime just before the Babylonian exile, groups of priests also served other sanctuaries, such as at Shiloh (1 Sam 1–3) and Nob (1 Sam 21–22). They attended the Ark in the sanctuaries at Shiloh and Kiriath-jearim (1 Sam 7:11), as well as in Jerusalem. Priests alone were allowed to carry the Ark when it was moved (1 Sam 4:4-11; 2 Sam 6:6-7; 15:24-29). We do not find anywhere in Israel the idea that one was divinely called to be a priest. Priesthood was simply a job, a function that came to be hereditary once it was exclusively associated with the tribe of Levi in the postexilic period.

In addition to their ritual or cultic functions, Israelite priests in the early period also delivered oracles to disclose the will of God by using objects called Urim and Thummim inside an ephod, which was a sort of cultic instrument kept in a sanctuary or near the Ark (1 Sam 2:18; 2 Sam 6:14). They thus manifested the divine mind in terms of a yes or a no, or by indicating "this" action rather than an alternative. Later in the royal period the priests were given the further task of preserving and handing down the law, ordinarily pronouncing on questions of the separation of the holy from the profane.[3] They carried out all their functions under the authority of the high priest. After the Exile, however, the law came to be interpreted principally by legal scholars and the scribes. The priests now confined their activities to worship and the offering of sacrifices.

When men were installed as priests, they were "made holy" (in Hebrew *qiddēš*—cf. 1 Sam 7:1). Holiness was not here considered to be a moral quality, but rather referred to being set apart to serve God, who alone is holy. To make someone a priest was to separate him from the profane so that he could more appropriately approach God as a mediator on behalf of the people by bringing their prayers and sacrifices into the sanctuary or temple. Virtually nothing is known about any ritual acts utilized to initiate men into priestly service in the preexilic period. After the exile we do find descriptions of ceremonies used to consecrate or ordain priests and high priests (cf. Exod 29 and Lev 8). Indeed, it seems that the rite of royal anointing was transferred from a prophet to the high priest. The anointing of ordinary priests was a custom introduced only later. During this same period the high priest was not only the head of cult, but he also

---

[3] See John J. Castelot and Aelred Cody, OSB, "Religious Institutions of Israel," in *The New Jerome Biblical Commentary* 76:9.

became the president of the Sanhedrin and the chief representative of the people to the foreign powers ruling Palestine during these centuries.

The Sanhedrin, a council of ruling elders or presbyters (*zeqēnîm*), can be traced back to the establishment of a college of seventy elders by Moses (cf. Num 11:16-17). Both the Jewish and Christian concepts of the presbyterate are based upon this latter body. By the time of the Roman occupation of Palestine every Jewish community had its own sanhedrin or *zeqēnîm* elected by the people to administer the community's affairs. They interpreted the law, collected and distributed alms to the needy, and had charge of the local synagogues and the Temple in Jerusalem. These Jewish presbyters of the Roman era, although not of the priestly line, were ordained by the laying on of hands. This practice finds its origin in Moses' laying on of hands and sharing his spirit with Joshua, who in turn shared it with the elders of Israel (Num 27:18ff.; Deut 34:9).[4] The ritual laying on of hands thus came to denote the imparting of the divine spirit in order to carry out an assigned task or mission.

Prior to the Babylonian exile, it must be noted, the prophets also played a major religious leadership role in Judaism. Derived from the Greek *prophētēs*, literally "one who speaks before others," the prophet was someone who communicated divine revelation. Like the priests, they too were set apart or sanctified not by contact with the altar but by their possession of and by the word of God. Samuel was one of the first to appear on the scene in Israel. He was a judge as well as a prophet. At the word of Yahweh he installed Saul as king (cf. 1 Sam 7–10). Then he delivered an oracle deposing Saul (duplicate accounts in 1 Sam 13 and 15) and anointed David as king (1 Sam 16:1-13). Samuel offers sacrifice (1 Sam 16:2) as does the prophet Elijah on Mount Carmel (1 Kgs 18:18-46). Moses, moreover, came to be revered as the greatest of all the prophets. He was the supreme example of one who receives the word of Yahweh and speaks it to Israel. In the postexilic community, however, the written word of the law replaced the spoken word of the prophets. The connection, nevertheless, between the one who proclaims the Word and the one who offers sacrifice continued in the early Christian church, where itinerant apostles and prophets are invited to preside at the Eucharist.

As the Old Testament transitions to the New, John the Baptist arrives on stage as the last and greatest of the prophets (Matt 11:7-14; Luke 7:24-28). His parents, Zechariah and Elizabeth, both belonged to priestly families (Luke 1:5). In John the Jewish belief that Elijah would return before the

---

[4] James A. Mohler, SJ, *The Origin and Evolution of the Priesthood* (Staten Island, NY: Alba House, 1970), 3.

Messiah was fulfilled (Matt 17:13). His mission was to prepare the way for Jesus by baptizing the crowds that came to him at the Jordan River with a baptism of repentance. Jesus himself came from Nazareth in Galilee to be baptized. John testified to him saying, "The one who has the bride is the bridegroom; the best man, who stands and listens for him, rejoices greatly at the bridegroom's voice. So this joy of mine has been made complete. He must increase; I must decrease" (John 3:29-30). Jesus of Nazareth is the long-awaited "messiah" (in Hebrew *māšîah*), the Christ (in Greek *christos*), God's "anointed" one. In the Old Testament this title was reserved principally for kings (1 Sam 16:6; 2 Sam 19:22) but was also applied to prophets (Ps 105:15) and priests (Lev 4:3; Dan 9:25-26). The gospels thus testify that Jesus is "the Christ" anointed as prophet, priest, and king.

Jesus the Good Shepherd: A Royal Priesthood

The gospels clearly proclaim that Jesus is the "son of David" (Matt 22:42; Mark 12:35; Luke 20:41), a descendant of the royal house of Judah, from which the Messiah was to come. Jesus is not a member of the priestly tribe of Levi, and he never applies the title "priest" (*hiereus*) either to himself or to his disciples. However, one should not imply from this fact that Jesus did not view his life and ministry as priestly service. Just as Jesus prohibited the use of the term Messiah in application to himself (Matt 16:20f.; Mark 1:34; 8:30; Luke 4:41; 9:21), because the popular understanding of the title would have been altogether misleading, so too, a comparable situation would have come into play with the title of "priest." Indeed, the priesthood Jesus claims was not like the Jewish priesthood then in place.

The Letter to the Hebrews is the only New Testament work that speaks explicitly of Christ as priest. Written for Jewish Christians who were having second thoughts about their newfound faith, the author wanted to demonstrate that the worship of the old covenant was superseded by the sacrifice of Jesus, and that although Jesus was not a member of the tribe of Levi, his priesthood is vindicated by the application to him of the priesthood of Melchizedek. As Father Jean Galot, SJ, points out, "The Epistle contains a comprehensive doctrine on the priesthood and sacrifice of the Son of God, cast within the cultic framework of the Old Testament, which is itself construed as a prefiguration whose whole reality is to be found in Jesus proclaimed forever a priest of the order of Melchizedek."[5] By

---

[5] Jean Galot, SJ, *Theology of Priesthood* (San Francisco: Ignatius Press, 1985), 31.

comparing the priesthood of Jesus Christ to "the order of Melchizedek," the Letter to the Hebrews wishes to state the fact that it is a royal priesthood constituted by Jesus' divine Sonship. It is "ontological" and not merely functional. The priesthood of Jesus Christ, indeed, far surpasses the Levitical priesthood in reality and scope, just as his messiahship transcends the expectations current among the Jews of his time.

In chapter 7 of the Letter to the Hebrews we find an extended comparison drawn between Jesus and the king-priest Melchizedek, while in Hebrews 8:1–10:18 the author presents us with an elaborate description of Jesus' saving work by referring to the functions of the Aaronic high priest on the Day of Atonement.[6] This New Testament epistle accordingly brings together in a unique way the two major Christological strands of sonship and priesthood (see Heb 5:5-6), which are elements of the ancient royal ideology and a defining component of messianism. According to the Old Testament tradition, Melchizedek is not only a priest but a king (Gen 14:18).

> His name first means righteous king, and he was also "king of Salem," that is, king of peace. Without father, mother, or ancestry, without beginning of days or end of life, thus made to resemble the Son of God, he remains a priest forever. (Heb 7:2b-3)

The royal component of Melchizedek's identity is an all-important interpretative key often passed over in theological treatises on the priestly Christology put forth in this Letter. "Coming as they do, therefore, right at the start of the exposition in Heb 7," D. W. Rooke maintains, "the etymologies of Melchizedek's name set a definite royal tone which is all too easily overlooked in the rush to concentrate on the priestly aspects of the exposition."[7] Righteousness and peace, furthermore, have long been regarded as specific qualities having messianic connotations.

In attempting to explain the nature of Jesus' royal priesthood, the Letter to the Hebrews states, "It is clear that our Lord arose from Judah, and in regard to that tribe Moses said nothing about priests" (Heb 7:14). The word "arose" (*anatellō*) occurs in the Septuagint to denote the appearance of a messianic figure. Jesus being a member of the tribe of Judah satisfies perfectly the messianic criteria that are readily explainable in terms of the ancient sacral kingship.[8] He is a priest by virtue of his identity as king or

---

[6] Rooke, "Jesus as Royal Priest: Reflections on the Interpretation of the Melchizedek Tradition in Heb 7," 82.

[7] Ibid., 86.

[8] Ibid., 90.

Messiah. Jesus, moreover, obtains his priesthood not according to a legal requirement concerning "physical descent but by the power of a life that cannot be destroyed" (Heb 7:16). This is another way of saying that he has been anointed by the power of the Spirit through his Resurrection and remains a priest forever. Lastly, the priesthood of Jesus is granted by an oath ensuring its permanency (Heb 7:20-22) and attesting to the reality that it is the "ontological" priesthood of the monarch, which in itself is qualitatively different from the "functional" priesthood of the Levites, including the high priest.

The author of the Letter to the Hebrews proceeds to describe Jesus' priestly ministry in chapters 8 and 9 in terms of the Levitical high priest. He does not continue his "sacral monarch" theme throughout the priestly analogy but resorts to a mixture of metaphors to depict the many facets of Christ's saving work. Most important, at the same time Jesus is shown functioning as high priest, he is also portrayed as the sacrificial victim (Heb 9:11-14). Jesus as both priest and victim adds a whole new dimension and a qualitative difference to the duties carried out by the earthly priests. Christ's ministrations are definitely efficacious in a way that those of ordinary priests are not (Heb 9:13-14, 24-26; 10:11-14). The Jewish high priest went through numerous ablutions and purifications before entering the Holy of Holies to "see the face of the Lord," but Jesus is purified by his filial obedience and enters the true Holy of Holies by his Resurrection, having offered one sacrifice for sins once and for all (Heb 10:1-18). The redemptive action of Jesus in his irrevocable status of unending self-gift also purifies those in union with him, insofar as they share with him in a priesthood of love and filial obedience. Here we find the true meaning of Christian priesthood and worship "in Spirit and truth" (John 4:23).

The writer of the Letter to the Hebrews finds himself grappling to explain in cultic terms familiar to his audience the true revolution in the meaning of "sanctity," "sacrifice," and "worship" that has transpired with the unfolding of Christ's paschal mystery. Thus, D. W. Rooke writes, "When viewed in this light, the link between chapters 7 and 8–9 becomes clear: all three chapters use the earthly cult as a foil for their descriptions of Jesus' work in terms of a new and better priesthood. . . . [Here] cult is not the norm to which Jesus' ministry is being assimilated, but the element to which it is being contrasted."[9] Indeed, the gospels record that Jesus' attitude toward the comportment of the priests of his day was less than favorable. In the parable of the Good Samaritan, for example, he tells of both a priest and a Levite who "passed by on the opposite side" of the

[9] Ibid., 93.

road without stopping to help the wounded man (Luke 10:31-32). They resort to the legalism of cultic impurity in order to justify their wanton failure to show to a neighbor the love to which he is entitled. The Samaritan, on the other hand, who refuses to be hampered by racial and cultic constraints, exemplifies the compassion, love, and generosity that are to be distinctively characteristic of the new priesthood.

The image of the "shepherd" best embodies for Jesus his own understanding of his ministry. The shepherd image has distinctly "priestly" connotations. He is "the good shepherd" who "lays down his life for the sheep" (John 10:11). At the same time, the shepherd image expands the understanding of priesthood beyond its cultic functions. In the ancient East the shepherd and king motifs are closely allied. As Walter Kasper observes, "Behind both stood the question of sound and healthy order, which gives protection against ruin and chaos, the question of leadership and guidance, security, tranquility and peace."[10] Yahweh is king (Exod 15:18; Ps 145:11ff.; 146:10; etc.) and Yahweh is Israel's shepherd (Ps 23; Gen 48:15; 49:24; etc.). Jesus was reserved in applying the messianic expectations to himself. As Cardinal Kasper further elaborates:

> [T]he Cross destroyed them [i.e., the messianic expectations] completely and made it clear that his rule was of a different order, that of service to the many. So he knows he is sent as a shepherd to seek out the lost sheep (Lk 15:4-7; Mt 18:12-14); he has compassion on the throng that is scattered and without a shepherd (Mk 6:34; Mt 9:36). Consequently he wants to gather together the lost sheep of Israel (Mt 10:6, 15:24). Under the image of shepherd he sees his own death (Mk 14:27f.) as well as the Last Judgment (Mt 25:32). The image of the shepherd, in fact, takes up Jesus' words about discipleship; Jesus goes before those who are his on the way. . . . The fullest treatment of Jesus as the good, that is, true shepherd, is found in the fourth gospel; he gives his life for his sheep, knows his own who know they are safe with him (Jn 10:11-16).[11]

Mark's gospel, moreover, records that the heart of Jesus "was moved with pity" for the vast crowd because "they were like sheep without a shepherd" (6:34). This image is borrowed from Numbers 27:17 where it reflects Moses' anxiety to find a successor lest they be without leadership (see Ezek 34:5).

Important for us to note here is the context in which Mark places Jesus' observation. In the beginning of the passage (Mark 6:30-34), the apostles

---

[10] Walter Kasper, *Jesus the Christ* (Mahwah, NJ: Paulist Press, 1976), 263.
[11] Ibid.

have just returned from their first evangelizing mission. He invites them to get some rest. They get in a boat and head for a deserted place, but the crowd sees them departing and it rushes on ahead of them. When they arrive at the place and Jesus sees the crowd, his heart is moved with pity and "he began to teach them many things" (v. 34). After teaching them at length there is concern about them being hungry, so Jesus tells his disciples,[12] "Give them some food yourselves" (v. 37). Jesus ends up taking and blessing five loaves and two fish and giving them to his disciples to set before the "five thousand men." After all were satisfied, "they picked up twelve wicker baskets full of fragments" (v. 43).

This whole episode presents Jesus as the new Moses, who leads and shepherds his flock in the desert—"a deserted place"—by teaching them and feeding them with the true bread come down from heaven (cf. John 6:48-51). Here he clearly incorporates the apostles in his mission and ministry of shepherding the flock. There are "twelve wicker baskets full of fragments" left over. The Twelve are meant to continue to feed the new Israel from the table of the Word and the table of the Eucharist. As Father Jean Galot, SJ, explains:

> In Christ the shepherd, we find a triple priestly function which corresponds to the three titles which, in the Old Testament perspective, are distinct from each other: prophet, priest, king. This is a sign that Christ intends the mission of the priest to go beyond the sphere of worship which is the specific concern of the priesthood. In the priesthood, he has conjoined the prophetic, the cultic, and the royal functions.[13]

The shepherd image in the Old Testament is also associated with the Servant of God image in Isaiah, who "offers his life in atonement" (Isa 52:10).

The priesthood of the shepherd truly comes to the fore in the Johannine perspective when Jesus asserts, "A good shepherd lays down his life for the sheep" (John 10:11). With these words Jesus recalls the fourth Servant Song of Isaiah, where the Servant "gives his life as an offering for sin" (Isa 53:10). This sacrifice of atonement is priestly in nature and alludes to the high priest, who on the Day of Atonement sprinkles the people with the

---

[12] Mark's gospel often uses "disciples" and "apostles" interchangeably. "The Twelve" form a special inner group of Jesus' disciples and are sometimes referred to as apostles. We shall see below that the term "apostle" is also applied to others elsewhere in the New Testament.

[13] Galot, *Theology of Priesthood*, 45.

blood of the victims. Jesus thus integrates the personal sacrifice of his own life with his mission and ministry of service. He tells the apostles, "For the Son of Man did not come to be served but to serve and to give his life as a ransom for many" (Mark 10:45). In its original sense, ministry means service. In addition, for Jesus, ministry also means life-giving personal sacrifice. Father Galot sums up the concerted significance of these scriptural passages when he writes, "By declaring that he came to serve, Jesus offers himself as a model to all those who would be called upon to exercise the priestly authority after him."[14]

In the Gospel according to John, Jesus further specifies his mission when at the Last Supper he states, "I am the way and the truth and the life" (John 14:6). In the words of Cardinal Kasper, "Jesus Christ through his Spirit is the way (pastor and king), the truth (prophet and teacher) and the life (priest) of the world."[15] This is the same threefold ministry Jesus then entrusted to the apostles, when immediately before his ascension in Matthew's gospel he gives them the great commission:

> All power in heaven and on earth has been given to me. Go, therefore, and make disciples of all nations [*pastor and king*], baptizing them in the name of the Father, and of the Son, and of the holy Spirit [*priest*], teaching them to observe all that I have commanded you [*prophet and teacher*]. And behold, I am with you always, until the end of the age. (Matt 28:18-20)

All four gospel accounts, in fact, conclude with Jesus sending his apostles to accomplish—in, with, and through his enduring presence—what has become known in traditional teaching as his threefold office of prophet, priest, and shepherd. "As the Father has sent me, so I send you" (John 20:21; cf. also John 17:18).

Just as Jesus Christ himself was the way, the truth, and the life, so the apostles must be the same in their turn, like him, with him, and in him. Employing the image of the good shepherd who "lays down his life for the sheep," Jesus has taken the profession of his royal priesthood to a higher level. In effect this image, in the words of Father Galot, has "the advantage of evoking an authority which unfolds in the direction of love. . . . The ministry of the shepherd has a dynamic facet: it entails the effort at gathering a community that will continue to increase in numbers, and will reach out to those who are still outside."[16] It is primarily and

---

[14] Ibid., 44–45.
[15] Kasper, *Jesus the Christ*, 259.
[16] Ibid., 49, 50.

essentially a ministry serving the mission of evangelization, the ultimate goal being that "there will be one flock, one shepherd" (John 10:16).

Apostleship and the Development of Presbyteral Ministry in the New Testament

The call of the apostles is one of the first steps Jesus took after his baptism in the Jordan. "He went up the mountain and summoned those whom he wanted and they came to him. He appointed twelve [whom he also named apostles] that they might be with him and he might send them forth to preach and to have authority to drive out demons" (Mark 3:13-15). Reflecting on this passage, Pope Benedict XVI states:

> In choosing the Twelve, introducing them into a communion of life with himself and involving them in his mission of proclaiming the Kingdom of God in words and works (cf. Mk 6:7-13; Mt 10:5-8; Lk 9:1-6; 6:13), Jesus wants to say that the definitive time has arrived in which to constitute the new People of God, the people of the twelve tribes, which now becomes a universal people, his Church.[17]

The word "apostle" (*apostolos*) means someone who is sent. Jesus "went up the mountain" (a place of divine revelation) and summons the Twelve "that they might be with him" before he sends them forth on mission to preach and cast out demons. They are called in order to be sent. Their vocation is for mission, but before they can go forth to evangelize they need to spend time with Jesus and establish a personal relationship with him. In the words of Pope Benedict XVI, "An apostle is one who is sent, but even before that he is an 'expert' on Jesus."[18] The apostles do not simply impart a message or communicate doctrine, they are sent forth as "witnesses" of the Risen Christ (Luke 24:48; Acts 1:8), inviting their listeners to encounter God's Word in person.

---

[17] Pope Benedict XVI, General Audience, March 15, 2006, in *The Apostles: The Origins of the Church and Their Co-Workers* (Huntington, IN: Our Sunday Visitor, 2007), 11–12. In his *Jesus of Nazareth* (New York: Doubleday, 2007), 171, Benedict XVI further reflects on the words in Mark 3:14, "he appointed [literally: 'made'] twelve." He writes: "The first thing to ponder is the expression 'he made twelve,' which sounds strange to us. In reality, these words of the Evangelist take up the Old Testament terminology for appointment to the priesthood (cf. Kings 12:31; 13:33) and thus characterize apostolic office as priestly ministry."

[18] Ibid., 14.

When first commissioning the Twelve during his public ministry, Jesus gave them the instruction, "Do not go into pagan territory or enter a Samaritan town. Go rather to the lost sheep of the house of Israel" (Matt 10:5b-6). According to the Messianic expectation of Israel, God himself would gather his people through his Chosen One as a shepherd gathers his flock (Ezek 34:22-24). Through this "gathering together" of the people of Israel, the kingdom of God would be proclaimed to all the nations. Such was not to happen before Jesus' Passion, death, and Resurrection, so the Risen Lord then sends his apostles forth to "make disciples of all nations" (Matt 28:19). For this mission, however, Jesus at the Last Supper first prayed for them to the Father: "Consecrate them in the truth. Your word is truth. As you sent me into the world, so I sent them into the world. And I consecrate myself for them, so that they also may be consecrated in truth" (John 17:17-19).

The Word-made-flesh, in the total and obedient surrender of his life in love on the Cross, consecrates himself so that the apostles might likewise be consecrated in the same self-sacrificing and reconciling love for the sake of continuing his mission—the mission of gathering together disciples from all nations into the new Israel, the Church (*ecclesia*). Thus, in the words of Pope Benedict XVI, "it is clear that the entire mission of the Son-made-flesh has a communitarian finality."[19] Apostolic ministry in the New Testament, as a consequence, can only be properly understood in the context of ecclesiology and mission.

Central, moreover, to any understanding of ministry in the postresurrection, apostolic period is the steadfast belief that the Risen Lord continues to be present as the head of his Body, the Church. It is Christ and he alone who continues to shepherd and gather his flock. Jesus assured the Eleven at their great commissioning: "And behold, I am with you always, until the end of the age" (Matt 28:20). While the apostles are delegated to act in his name, they do not exercise authority in his stead. "They bear witness to his guiding presence. They allow his Spirit to work through them for the direction and nurture of the community."[20] They sacramentally proclaim Christ's abiding presence as head and shepherd of his flock.

Just as Christ himself is portrayed as the Apostle of the Father, so those whom he sends as apostles represent what he is himself. "Whoever listens

---

[19] Pope Benedict XVI, *The Apostles*, General Audience of Wednesday, March 15, 2006 (Huntington, IN: Our Sunday Visitor Publishing Division, 2007), 10.

[20] Bernard Cooke, *Ministry to Word and Sacraments: History and Theology* (Philadelphia: Fortress Press, 1976), 48.

to you listens to me. Whoever rejects you rejects me. And whoever rejects me rejects the one who sent me" (Luke 10:16; also Matt 10:40).[21] Saint Paul best sums up the apostles' role when he writes, "Thus should one regard us: as servants of Christ and stewards of the mysteries of God" (1 Cor 4:1). Nowhere in the New Testament does one find a trace of the notion that some designated minister has the function to "make Christ present," for he is never considered to be absent from the gathering of the faithful, from the Church, which is his Body (Matt 18:20).[22]

During his earthly life Jesus sent his disciples to announce the imminent approach of the kingdom of God by words and signs. After the Resurrection they themselves witnessed to the inauguration of the kingdom that had come about through his paschal mystery. Apostolic ministry thus is first and foremost a matter of proclamation; it is a prophetic ministry of proclaiming the gospel, a ministry of the Spirit (*diakonia toū pneúmatos*— 2 Cor 3:8). As Father Gisbert Greshake explains:

> By the apostolic preaching, the self-offering of Jesus for the world is made present; it comes to us 'in the form of the word.' Indeed, it can be said that in Apostolic preaching the Lord himself causes us to come in contact with his sacrifice and in it with himself 'in the form of the word.' . . . Consequently apostolic office can be called 'priestly': not because it has responsibility for cult or because it offers 'sacrifice', but because it testifies to the self-sacrifice of Jesus for us, making this sacrifice present for us as a gift and a task to be performed by us, and because it founds and leads local communities according to this 'programme.'[23]

Saint Paul describes himself as "a minister (*leitourgos*) of Christ Jesus to the Gentiles in performing the priestly service (*hierurgein*) of the gospel of God, so that the offering up of the Gentiles may be acceptable, sanctified by the holy Spirit" (Rom 15:16). Bernard Cooke writes, "Really what the New Testament evidence seems to point to quite conclusively is the view that the Eucharistic breaking of bread is essentially an act of evangelic proclamation."[24] Indeed, St. Paul states, "For as often as you eat this bread

[21] See Joseph Ratzinger, *Principles of Catholic Theology* (San Francisco: Ignatius Press, 1987), 273. Title of German original: *Theologische Prinzipienlehre* (Munich: Erich Wewel Verlag, 1982).

[22] Cooke, *Ministry to Word and Sacraments*, 530.

[23] Gisbert Greshake, *The Meaning of Christian Priesthood* (Dublin: Four Courts Press; Westminister, MD: Christian Classics, 1988), 45. Translation by Fr. Peadar MacSeumais, SJ, of *Priestersein* (Freiburg–Basel–Vienna: Herder, 1982).

[24] Cooke, *Ministry to Word and Sacraments*, 529.

and drink the cup, you proclaim the death of the Lord until he comes" (1 Cor 11:26).

Immediately prior to the passage just cited from First Corinthians, St. Paul had just taken the Christian community of Corinth to task because of their lack of unity and discipline when they gathered for the Lord's Supper (vv. 17-22). He tells them, "For anyone who eats and drinks without discerning the body, eats and drinks judgment on himself" (v. 29). Paul's reference to "discerning the body" here does not refer to the eucharistic species but rather to all the members of the community (see 1 Cor 10:17). If apostolic ministry of its very nature is primarily the proclamation of the gospel, its content is reconciliation both with God and with one another, thereby building up the Body of Christ.

In Second Corinthians, while proclaiming that we have become a "new creation" in Christ through his death and Resurrection, Paul adds, "And all this is from God, who has reconciled us to himself through Christ *and* given us the ministry of reconciliation" (2 Cor 5:18, emphasis added). "Thus at a decisive point, where Paul is describing the central doctrine of the Christian faith, he speaks in the same breath of the ultimate foundation and basic essence of his apostolic office: by the decisive salvific act of reconciliation, God has at the same time and by the same act instituted the ministry of reconciliation."[25] The import of Paul's perspective here must not be overlooked. Ministry or office in the Church has its origin in Christ's paschal mystery and flows from there as the ministry of reconciliation.

Clearly the apostle carries out his ministry as an "ambassador" for Christ. The apostle represents Christ, and this representation is definitely not to be understood in the sense that Christ is absent. Rather, he is a "co-worker" of God (1 Cor 3:9; 1 Thess 3:2) and sacramental sign of Christ himself who continues to be present in his Church. Indeed, such ministry does not replace an immediate relationship with Christ, but actually makes such a relationship possible. Saint Paul, for this reason, primarily sees his work of ministry as introducing others into the life of Christ: "I am again in labor until Christ be formed in you!" (Gal 4:19). And to this end he acts with the authority of Jesus Christ (1 Thess 4:2), who conferred upon the apostles the power to forgive sins (John 20:22-23).

Saint Paul sees his authority as a genuine pastoral power by which he can ask obedience from others (see Phil 2:12; 1 Cor 11:34; 16:1) and even punish disobedience (2 Cor 10:6). He explains that this power (*exousia*)

---

[25] Greshake, *The Meaning of Christian Priesthood*, 34.

has been given him for the sake of building up, not tearing down (2 Cor 10:8). For Paul, moreover, being personally called by Christ is a constitutive element of apostolic ministry (e.g., Gal 1:10-17), and apostleship, as a result, is a specific office that does not belong to all the faithful (1 Cor 12:29). The apostle, finally, can be said to possess a special authority of service (*diakonia*) in two senses. First, he represents and serves Christ, speaking only what Christ gives him to say (Rom 15:18) and rendering an account to him (1 Cor 4:4ff.). Second, he serves the community by not lording it over their faith but by working together with them for their joy (2 Cor 1:24).

By contrast with this developing theology of apostleship, no single pattern of leadership appears to emerge as normative during the first generation for all local churches. Indeed, actual historical details are either scant or nonexistent, and the available sources provide information that is too brief and difficult to interpret. We do know that in the New Testament the title of apostle was extended beyond the Twelve and St. Paul. Indeed, Barnabas (Acts 14:4) and the otherwise unknown Andronicus and Junias (Rom 16:7) are also called "apostles," and Paul includes apostleship among the charismatic offices of the Church (Eph 2:20). Even during Jesus' earthly ministry, Luke records the mission of the seventy-two, which does not differ in power and scope from the mission of the Twelve as he reports it (Luke 9:2-5).

Luke in Acts 6:1-6 recounts the ordination of the Seven, the first ordination to be reported in the life of the early Church. This step was taken to resolve the tension between the Hebrew- and Greek-speaking sections of the Jerusalem church. The Twelve told the community: "It is not right for us to neglect the word of God to serve at table. Brothers, select from among you seven reputable men, filled with the Spirit and wisdom, whom we shall appoint to this task, whereas we shall devote ourselves to prayer and to the ministry of the word" (vv. 2-4). Although they were called to "service" (*diakonia*), Luke does not explicitly refer to the Seven as "deacons." Thus, while this passage has become the classical biblical reference for the institution of the diaconate, another interpretation stretching all the way back to John Chrysostom sees here the actual beginning of the presbyteral ministry. Far from limiting their ministry to charitable relief, one of them, Stephen, was actively engaged in preaching; another, Philip, in evangelizing.

The Seven in Acts are clearly portrayed in the role of presbyteral apostolic assistants. Some scholars view their daily distribution of food to widows as an obvious allusion to the Eucharist. In addition, the term "widow" in the New Testament refers not only to those who are needy but also to women who lived some form of consecrated life. This whole scenario evokes Luke's earlier description of the daily life of the Jerusalem community: "Every day they devoted themselves to meeting together in the temple area and to breaking bread in their homes" (Acts 2:46).[26] In such case, ordained assistants would obviously be needed to help with the daily eucharistic celebrations held in Christian households throughout the city.

Later, when Palestinian Christian Jews, who were scattered by persecution, preach the Gospel in Antioch, many Greeks came to believe. The Jerusalem church then sends Barnabas to organize the community there (Acts 11:20-22). A nucleus of prophet-teachers, which included Saul, gathered around Barnabas. As Mohler writes, "Teaching was an important charism in the early Church, often overlapping apostleship and prophecy. False teachers were common and early documents are constantly warning against them."[27] These prophet-teachers in Antioch with a laying on of hands send Saul and Barnabas to do missionary work elsewhere. The inspiration to do so occurred during a liturgical celebration. These "prophets and teachers" were celebrating liturgy; they played an essential cultic role.

Afterward, as Paul and Barnabas traveled throughout the diaspora, we are told they appointed presbyters to govern the local churches (Acts 14:23). From all that we can piece together from the New Testament evidence, it appears that two forms of ecclesiastical organization developed in the infant Church: "at Jerusalem the Church is governed by a sanhedrin of presbyters under the presidency of James, while in Antioch the Christian community is under a delegated apostle, living temporarily in the community in order to organize it."[28]

In the Pastoral Epistles to Timothy and Titus we see further developments in the role of the Christian presbyters along with a distinction being made between the college of presbyters and its guardian president (*episkopos*). The qualifications for the office of deacon are also given (1 Tim 3:8-13). Furthermore, Timothy and Titus served as regional apostolic vicars of the apostles. As such, their task was twofold. First, they served as custodians or guardians of the truths of divine revelation contained in the apostolic preaching (2 Tim 4:1-5). Second, they organized the apostolic ministry in the local churches by ordaining bishops and deacons, while assuring that the presbyters were fittingly honored (1 Tim 3:1-13; 5:17). They were

[26] Galot, *Theology of Priesthood*, 160–62.
[27] Mohler, *The Origin and Evolution of the Priesthood*, 19.
[28] Ibid., 18.

cautioned to choose such men with care and "not lay hands too readily on anyone" (1 Tim 5:21). By the end of the first century, however, the "bishop" (*episkopos*) is still not clearly distinct from the "presbyter." The threefold hierarchy, which Ignatius of Antioch (d. AD 107) took for granted, is not yet found universally nor is it clearly defined.[29]

An outline for apostolic succession may also be found in the New Testament. In his farewell address to the presbyters of the Church of Ephesus (Acts 20:18-35), St. Paul is "attempting to demonstrate the bond between the apostolic and postapostolic Church by depicting the transfer of pastoral responsibility from apostle to presbyters, who thus become, in practice, the 'successors of the apostles.'"[30] The office of presbyter is an institution of the Holy Spirit, who has appointed them "overseers" (*episkopoi*) of the whole flock (v. 28). The reference to the presbyters being appointed overseers of the flock connotes once again the image of shepherd and shows, as of yet, the lack of a clear distinction between the office of bishop and that of the presbyter. In like manner, 1 Peter 5:1-4 employs the image of shepherd to describe the presbyteral ministry, when the author instructs them, "Do not lord it over those assigned to you, but be examples to the flock" (v. 3). In this passage also the two offices of apostle and presbyter are identified with each other. Thus Ratzinger states, "This, in my opinion, is the strongest linking of the two offices to be found in the New Testament. In practice, it means a transfer of the theology of apostleship to the presbyterate."[31]

What becomes clear in our quest for the biblical foundations of the priestly office in the Church is that we have to begin with the unique and eternal high priesthood of Jesus Christ, who as the Good Shepherd—the true and perfect Pastor—gives his life for his sheep whom he knows by name. His is a royal or "ontological" priesthood. Jesus thus completely redefines the "functional" cultic priesthood as well as the idea of sacrifice by his total self-gift in reconciling Love on the Cross. He is the Good Shepherd and not "a hired hand" (John 10:11-13). After his Resurrection, he continues to be present as the head and Shepherd of his flock, his Church. As Risen Lord, he commissions the apostles, who were with him "beginning from the baptism of John" (Acts 1:22), to go forth in his name and continue his mission and ministry of proclaiming the Gospel and making disciples of all the nations. Thus in the words of the then-Cardinal Joseph Ratzinger, "Apostleship is the immediate measure and starting

---

[29] André Lemaire, *Ministry in the Church* (London: SPCK, 1977), 16.
[30] Ratzinger, *Principles of Catholic Theology*, 278.
[31] Ibid., 279.

point of the office of presbyter. As a continuation of the mission of Jesus Christ, it is, in the first place an office of evangelization. But the ministry of the word, which it thus represents, is to be understood against the background of the incarnate and crucified Word."[32]

The Universal Priesthood of the New Covenant

Jesus applied the title "priest" (*hiereus*) neither to himself nor to his disciples. Indeed, the designation of priest is first applied in the New Testament to the Christian community in 1 Peter 2:5, 9 and Revelation 1:6; 5:10; and 20:6, recalling the promise God had made to the whole Jewish nation: "You shall be to me a kingdom of priests, a holy nation" (Exod 19:6; similarly in Isa 61:6). Certainly this text does not mean that the cultic functions attributed to the priestly tribe of Levi had been transferred to the people. Rather, through the Sinai covenant Israel received "the vocation to establish the right worship of God in the midst of the peoples who do not know him. As the chosen people, Israel has the mission to be the place of true adoration and thus to be at once priesthood and temple for the whole world."[33] Through baptism, which is now seen as the new Sinai, Israel's election passes over to the Church as the new people of God (Rom 15:16). The universal priesthood is understood as strictly collective. It refers to the people as a whole and to the individual only to the extent that he belongs to this people. "Priestly people" is thus a title of honor transferred to the new Israel and does not express a permanent or temporary office of any kind.[34]

The New Testament passages, furthermore, always speak in terms of a "royal" priesthood, accenting its ontological character. It is a participation in Christ's own priesthood, in his self-gift for the life of the world. "Christians are a priestly people because they are the Body of him who is the one high priest; in joining their lives and persons to his sacrifice they are giving to the Father the worship that is due."[35] Therefore, St. Paul writes to the Church at Rome:

[32] Ibid., 281.

[33] Joseph Cardinal Ratzinger, *Called to Communion: Understanding the Church Today* (San Francisco: Ignatius Press, 1996), 125.

[34] Greshake, *The Meaning of Christian Priesthood*, 48.

[35] Cooke, *Ministry to Word and Sacraments*, 530.

> I urge you therefore, brothers, by the mercies of God, to offer your
> bodies as a living sacrifice, holy and pleasing to God, your spiritual
> worship. Do not conform yourself to this age but be transformed by
> the renewal of your mind, that you may discern what is the will of
> God, what is good and pleasing and perfect. (Rom 12:1-2)

Paul here exhorts the Romans to offer their bodies as "a living sacrifice
. . . your spiritual worship [*logike latreia*]." In Greek, *logike latreia* means
worship characterized by the word (*logos*). Ratzinger explains, "We ask
that the Logos, Christ, who *is* the true sacrifice, may 'logify' us, make us
'more consistent with the word', 'more truly rational', so that his sacrifice
may become ours and may be accepted by God as ours. . . . We pray that
his presence might pick us up, so that we become 'one body and one spirit'
with him."[36]

Saint Paul urges us not to offer some external or material sacrifice, as
people once did with the physical sacrifices of old. Rather, he is telling us
that we ourselves must become Eucharist with Christ. This involves an
entire "metamorphosis" or transformation of mind and body "that takes
us beyond this world's scheme of things, beyond sharing in what 'people'
think and say and do, and into the will of God—thus we enter into what
is good and pleasing to God and perfect."[37] Also, in the Johannine gospel
we read of Jesus' encounter with the Samaritan woman at Jacob's well,
where Jesus says, "But the hour is coming, and is now here, when true
worshipers will worship the Father in Spirit and truth; and indeed the
Father seeks such people to worship him" (John 4:23). Galot comments,
"Recent exegetical research shows that the expression 'in spirit and in
truth' evokes on the one hand the Holy Spirit, and on the other the Truth-
in-Person, namely, Christ."[38] Through the Spirit given at baptism each
Christian is immersed into the truth of Christ's self-giving and reconciling
love, his redeeming sacrifice, which itself calls for the surrender of the
self. In this new worship, each one must be engaged and personally responsible for his or her own self-offering.

[36] Joseph Cardinal Ratzinger, *Pilgrim Fellowship of Faith: The Church as Communion*
(San Francisco: Ignatius Press, 2005), 116 (emphasis in the original), where the author
adds: "We find the same word, too, in the Roman Canon, where we ask, immediately
before the Consecration, that our sacrifice may be made *rationabilis*. It is not enough—
indeed, it is quite wrong—to translate this as saying that it should become rational.
We are asking rather that it may become a logos-sacrifice."

[37] Ibid., 117–18.

[38] Galot, *Theology of the Priesthood*, 113.

This universal priesthood of the baptized no more negates the ministerial priesthood of the Church than the common priesthood of Israel did away with the priestly ministrations of the tribe of Levi. Quite the contrary, the priestly office continues the apostolic ministry instituted by Christ in service to the priestly people of God. Indeed, St. Paul states that Christ "gave some as apostles, others as prophets, others as evangelists, others as pastors and teachers, to equip the holy ones for the work of ministry, for building up the body of Christ" (Eph 4:11-12). The ministerial priesthood exists "to equip" the baptized to carry out their priestly mission of evangelization in the world. In the words of Joseph Ratzinger, "The ultimate end of all New Testament liturgy and of all priestly ministry is to make the world as a whole a temple and a sacrificial offering to God. This is to bring about the inclusion of the whole world into the Body of Christ, so that God may be all in all (cf. 1 Cor 15:28)."[39]

---

[39] Ratzinger, *Called to Communion*, 127–28.

Chapter 2

Priestly Ministry in Historical Perspective

Be eager, therefore, to use one Eucharist—for there is one flesh of our
Lord Jesus Christ and one cup for union with his blood, one sanctuary
as there is one bishop, together with the presbytery and the deacons,
my fellow slaves—so that, whatever you do, you do in relation to God.
—Ignatius of Antioch, *To the Philadelphians*, 4[1]

The early apostolic and postapostolic Church lived in the constant awareness that it was the Body of Christ. These first Christians realized that "in Christ"[2] and in his Spirit they shared an intimate communion of life with God and one another (*koinonia*). The outpouring of the Spirit, indeed, constituted the basic religious experience of the early Christian community. The Pentecost event gave birth to a "new creation." In the power of the Holy Spirit the Church was born and a "new humanity" began to take shape (Eph 2:15; Gal 6:15). Christ's paschal mystery had marked the beginning of this whole new reality. Jesus is "the resurrection and the life," and whoever believes in him shall not die (John 11:25). As Risen Lord, Christ is the Last Adam and the Head of a new humanity, which forms his Body. Christ is the true Messiah of the

---

[1] *The Apostolic Fathers*, ed. R. Grant, vol. 4 (New York: Thomas Nelson and Sons, 1964–68), 101.

[2] "In Christ"—with "in the Lord" and "in Him"—occurs 165 times in the Pauline epistles, designating the dynamic, ontological, and eschatological status of the believer, in which Christ and the Christian enjoy as it were a symbiosis, an intimate being together.

"true Israel" (Gal 6:16), the people of the New Covenant. Through faith and baptism "you are all one in Christ Jesus" (Gal 3:28); yet the growing actualization of this communion comes about primarily in the "breaking of the bread" (Acts 2:42). The Church as koinonia is essentially a eucharistic community.

Proclaiming and living Christ's paschal mystery, bearing witness (*martyria*) to the good news of Jesus' Cross and Resurrection constitutes the Church's very life. Saint Luke thus gives us a glimpse of daily life in the primitive Church in Jerusalem:

> They devoted themselves to the teaching of the apostles and to the communal life, to the breaking of the bread and to the prayers. Awe came upon everyone, and many wonders and signs were done through the apostles. All who believed were together and had all things in common; they would sell their property and possessions and divide them among all according to each one's need. Every day they devoted themselves to meeting together in the temple area and to breaking bread in their homes. (Acts 2:42-46)

These first Christians still went every day to the Temple. They did not see themselves as the charter members of a new religion. They thus organized their community along the familiar lines of the Jewish structures of the first century with its ruling elders, itinerant apostles, and a central Sanhedrin. In the first twelve chapters of Acts the ministry and leadership of the apostles with Peter as head appears clearly evident. At the Council of Jerusalem, however, we are told that "the apostles and the presbyters met" (Acts 15:6) with James—identified in Galatians 1:19 as "the brother of the Lord"—who now served as the president of the council and immediate leader of the Jerusalem community.

While there can be no doubt that Jesus called the Twelve to the apostolic ministry, that he personally instituted them as the servant-leaders of the New Israel, and that he commissioned them to go forth in order to teach, baptize, and shepherd his flock, it is also clear that he left no detailed instructions regarding the exact shape the Church was to take. Having provided the essentials, Jesus left the organizational part to the work of the Spirit guiding and building up his Body (1 Cor 12:4-11). Therefore, just as the early Jerusalem Church adopted Jewish structures, so the Church through the centuries would borrow from other governing models. The emperor Constantine's embrace of Christianity greatly influenced the Church's structure and organizational procedures in the fourth century and beyond. The rise of monasticism and the Germanization of the medieval Church in Europe would also leave their impact. In this chapter we shall reflect upon how some of these same influences also shaped the conceptualization and understanding of priestly ministry over the centuries.

The Sub-Apostolic and Pre-Nicene Era
(Second and Third Centuries)

Throughout the pre-Nicene period the life of the Christian community was centered in living Christ's paschal mystery through the communal celebration of the Eucharist and the attainment of martyrdom. Both of these poles pertained to a new way of living in koinonia. As T. L. Westow observes,

> The Christians are a community, live as a community, write to each other as members of a community, are martyred as representatives of a community, pray as a community. The very fact of being constantly subjected to outbreaks of persecution reinforces this sense of community. Even their failures in moral problems of life are principally failures to maintain the "concord and harmony" of the community. The other moral failures are usually grouped in lists, from St. Paul on, with little preference for one sin or another.[3]

Although frequently threatened by persecutions, interior dissensions, and heresies (especially Gnosticism), Christianity during these earliest years more than anything else continued to be a new "Way" (Acts 9:2; 18:25; 19:9, 23; 22:4) of life in which the Risen Lord (*kyrios*) and the Eucharist predominated.

The central importance of the Eucharist for these early Christians can only be adequately grasped when we enter into the eschatological reality that formed their spiritual vision and so captured their imaginations. As John Zizioulas describes:

> The Eucharist was understood in the first centuries as the event that brought together the dispersed people of God "in the same place" (*epi to auto*) not only to celebrate but also to constitute the eschatological messianic community here and now. As such it was the spiritual event par excellence, because it was the eschatological reality manifested and foretasted in history. Baptized persons were led to this community

---

[3] Theo L. Westow, *Variety of Catholic Attitudes* (New York: Herder and Herder, 1963), 22–23.

in order to take their place in it, which involved the privilege of
addressing God as Father—of acquiring the sonship that Christ always
had—and at the same time of addressing the other members of the
church as "brethren" and sharing their eternal destiny. The Eucharist
offered positively what baptism meant negatively: the death of the
old, biological identity was replaced by the birth of a new identity,
which was given in the eucharistic community.[4]

The Eucharist gives eternal life because it is based upon free and undying
relationships, which have their font and source in the eternal filial relationship between the Father and the Son. The Eucharist is the place where all
divisions, both natural and social, "are transcended in the unity of Christ,
in whose kingdom such divisions amounting to death will disappear."[5]

The eschatological vision of the heavenly throne and twenty-four elders
of Revelation 4:2-4, as explained by Gregory Dix, reflected the early Christian liturgy, perhaps at Ephesus where the president sat on his throne
covered with white cloth and faced the people across the eucharistic table
with the twenty-four elders forming a semicircle around him and the
deacons stationed on either side of the throne.[6] Ignatius, in fact, describes
a parallel liturgy in Antioch in AD 115 (*Magn.* 6.1) with the semicircle of
presbyters around the bishop and with the assisting deacons all facing
toward the people. The most notable feature during this period is the
unmistakable emergence of the traditional tripartite ministerial structure
of bishop, presbyter, and deacon.

The apostolic-delegate model of the Pauline Hellenistic communities,
exemplified in the missionary work of Timothy and Titus, gradually
merges with the Jewish Sanhedrin or presbyterate model. The authority
of the apostolic delegate to resolve questions of orthodox doctrine and to
ordain local overseers (*episcopoi*) and deacons is joined with the pastoral
and administrative roles of the proto-presbyter or president of the Jewish
presbyterate model. Although such a tripartite structure is indicated by
the Pastoral Epistles (1 Tim 3:5) and clearly described in the letters of
Ignatius, by the end of the second century it becomes the established
practice throughout the Church.

In the third-century sources, the bishop is described as the high priest
(his liturgical role) and the shepherd (his pastoral role) of the local church.

[4] John D. Zizioulas, "The Early Christian Community" in *Christian Spirituality:
Origins to the Twelfth Century*, ed. Bernard McGinn and John Meyendorff (New York:
Crossroad, 1997), 29.

[5] Ibid., 34.

[6] Gregory Dix, *The Shape of the Liturgy* (Westminster, London: Dacre, 1949), 28.

At the same time there were also itinerant apostles and prophets. The *Didache* bears witness to the eminent position of such visiting leaders, who were considered proper "celebrants" for the Eucharist (*Didache* 10.7). Some of these, however, would eventually espouse Gnostic teachings, or the Montanist heresy. Thus there arose the need for distinguishing the true from the false among both prophets and teachers. Cooke writes that by the third century, "the episcopacy found it necessary to assert its communal faith, grounded in continuity with apostolic teaching, as a criterion that could safeguard the authenticity and integrity of the community's belief."[7] Large numbers of converts were also seeking to join the Church, requiring a careful process of catechumenal preparation and continuing catechesis. The principle, therefore, became established that all instruction regarding the faith, including the giving of homilies, was to be reserved to the clergy and carried out under the bishop's guidance.

As a result of the establishment of apostolic succession, the presbyters' role was realigned. "It now defined itself in terms of a share in the bishop's ministry, just as once upon a time, it had defined itself in terms of its relationship to the apostles themselves. From now on, presbyters would belong to the apostolic succession only through their ordination by bishops who embodied that succession."[8] Nonetheless, it would be an anachronism to see the bishop-presbyter-deacon pattern as three levels of one pastoral office.

In the pre-Nicene church deacons were ordained "not for priesthood, but for the service of the bishop" (*Traditio Apostolica* 8). The deacon was a liturgical assistant of the bishop and was not allowed to act by himself, especially at the Eucharist. Serving directly under the bishop, deacons assisted him by taking charge of property, finances, and the care of the sick. In addition, deacons served as the bishop's eyes and ears by letting him know who was sick; they received the gifts in the liturgy, and if there were not enough presbyters, they held the chalices (*Traditio Apostolica* 23–24).

Presbyters, on the other hand, even though they may have been delegated by the bishop to perform liturgical functions, retained an uncontested autonomy in setting policy for the life of the community. Furthermore, the earliest liturgical sources of this period attest to the belief that ordination— the sacramental laying on of hands so as to consecrate the bishop or presbyter—forges a new bond with Christ and the Holy Spirit that empowers

---

[7] Bernard Cooke, *Ministry to Word and Sacraments: History and Theology* (Philadelphia: Fortress Press, 1976), 63.

[8] Aidan Nichols, *Holy Order: The Apostolic Ministry from the New Testament to the Second Vatican Council* (Lancaster, PA: Veritas Press, 1991), 46.

the ordinand for his designated ministry. The seeds of the doctrine of priestly "character" are already seen here and will play a major part in the theology of Order in the centuries to come.

The rapid growth of the Church across the Mediterranean world during these early centuries also changed the shape of ministry. The delay of the parousia, the Risen Lord's return, meant a growth from but a small-sized movement to a large body, which required changes in structure. House churches with their more familiar liturgies could no longer accommodate the large numbers of Christians. One of the reasons for this rapid expansion was the commonly accepted responsibility of all Christians to evangelize. As Cooke explains, "Christianity remained essentially a missionary community: the gospel had been committed to the entire people, the responsibility of witnessing to it was the task of every Christian—by his words and by his life."[9] The ideal form of witness to the event of Christ's death and Resurrection was, of course, martyrdom. Yet not all Christians were called by circumstances to proclaim the Gospel in this manner, but all knew they were commissioned to evangelize in some form.

Around the year AD 250 in Rome there were about fifty thousand Christians out of a population of approximately one million. Eusebius of Caesarea writes that at the time when Cornelius was Bishop of Rome, the church there was paying a stipend to forty-six presbyters, seven deacons, seven subdeacons, forty-two acolytes, fifty-two exorcists, lectors, and porters, as well as providing daily care for fifteen hundred widows and poor people (see *Hist. Eccl.* VI, 45, 11). The presbyters conducted the daily synaxes, which involved leading the prayers, reading Scriptures, and giving homilies. Such synaxes, which did not include the breaking of bread, were actually inherited from the ancient synagogue services. On the Lord's Day, then, the entire community took part in the Eucharist. "The bishop as president of the urban Eucharist, sent his *fermentum* to be distributed by the deacons to the lesser Eucharists of the smaller church gatherings, at which a presbyter presided, as his representative."[10] Other equally large Christian populations could be found in Carthage, Alexandria, Antioch, and Ephesus.

With increasing numbers of Christians to be attended to, bishops and deacons now found themselves engaged in full-time ministry. Presbyters too were delegated and sent to serve the needs of outlying congregations. In the third century, the expanded house church was still the principal

---

[9] Cooke, *Ministry to Word and Sacraments*, 64.

[10] James Mohler, SJ, *The Origin and Evolution of the Priesthood* (Staten Island, NY: Alba House, 1970), 53.

gathering place of the community, but by the beginning of the fourth century Christians appear to have had public buildings set apart for their use. They adopted not the model of a temple but the plan of the Roman civil assembly hall, the basilica. O'Meara points out, "The basilica offered light, mobility and a focal point for the bishop. The entrance into this large tripartite hall, whose lines drew one forward to the bishop's word, molded the community into laity and ministers."[11] With the growing numbers and the shift from the close-knit house churches to the basilica model, the nature of ministry was changing. The communal gatherings for Eucharist became less personal and familial and more institutionalized. The "de-eschatologizing" of the Church's social existence brought about by the delay in the parousia also indicated the need for more permanent structures.

As a result of this institutionalization, a pattern began to develop of viewing the full-time clergy as "official" Christians in contrast to the rest of the faithful. Presbyters too, in being delegated to direct the increasing number of satellite communities, acted less and less as the corporate counselors of the bishop, who now assumed a greater executive role, assisted by the deacons. The large numbers of faithful also tended to reduce enthusiasm within the community and brought on an unmistakable passivity in regard to doing ministry. "The bishop and his presbyteral vicars not only led ministry, they absorbed it. This new style of leadership in an organized church finds a poignant example in the selection of Calixtus from the upper class of bankers to be bishop of Rome."[12] Historical evidence seems to suggest that the dichotomy between clergy and laity, which would become more apparent in later centuries, already existed in identifiable form at the beginning of the fourth century.

Significant changes in the Church's self-perception also take place along with this growing institutionalization. The imagery employed to convey this self-understanding merits close attention. References to "holy mother church," for instance, reflect a process of personifying the Church and indicate the extent to which the Church is now being looked upon as an entity apart from and beyond the people who make it up. By the fourth century we find that the Church is being viewed as a kind of "moral person" with which the technical abstractions of legal codes can deal. Cooke thus observes:

---

[11] Thomas F. O'Meara, *Theology of Ministry*, rev. ed. (Mahwah, NJ: Paulist Press, 1999), 104.

[12] Ibid., 101.

When one puts together the psychological overtones of an image like that of "mother church" and those attached to the image of shepherd as used in the Scripture for the pastoral office and as then attached to the episcopal-presbyteral-diaconal ministry, one can begin to see the impact this will have on the way the laity will view their own role in the church and their relationship to those in positions of official leadership. The spiritual care that one would expect from a mothering church is what one expects from a shepherding hierarchy. In thinking of the church as "mother" the Christian would think of the church as distinct from himself, as set over against him, and as doing for him precisely what he has come to understand as the task of the episcopacy.[13]

Thus in the realm of imagery and implicit understanding we are here on the verge of identifying the Church with its clerical ministers. They increasingly become the ones solely responsible for evangelization and ministry. This attitude is fostered already in the third century by non-Christian civil authorities who dealt only with the "officialdom" of the Church. These church officers thus tended to be the ones most often singled out for imprisonment or death during times of persecution.

In the third century, moreover, the image of "priest" begins to be applied to the Church's ministers, especially to the bishop. In the Syrian *Didascalia Apostolorum*, the bishops are seen as the high priests of the New Israel. "But the priests and Levites now are the presbyters and deacons, and the orphans and widows. But the Levite and high priest is the bishop" (no. 9). The bishop of the *Didascalia* is a regal, almost divine person. He is the supreme judge of all with the power of binding and loosing. He guards the poor and those in need. "Papa" was a common title given to bishops during this period, expressing the filial reverence of their subjects.[14] In north Africa, Cyprian too in his letters often spoke of the priestly aspect of the Christian ministry (*Ep.* 1.1-2; *Ep.* 43.5; *Ep.* 59.5, 18; *Ep.* 61.3; *Ep.* 67.1; *Ep.* 72.2), indicating a growing sacerdotalism. Tertullian, in addition, provides us with textual evidence that *sacerdos* and *pontifex* were used in African circles as referring to bishops (*De pudicita* 1).

Two historical movements during these early centuries of Christianity chiefly contributed to the transformation of the ministries of bishop and presbyter into a priesthood (*sacerdotium*). First, with *sacerdotes* functioning in the cult of the emperor, as well as in the cults imported from Egypt,

---

[13] Cooke, *Ministry to Word and Sacraments*, 66–67.
[14] Mohler, *The Origin and Evolution of the Priesthood*, 54n1.

there arose a natural desire among Christians to have a priesthood of their own. Even more important were the images and words of the Old Testament, which now tended to have a major impact upon the spiritual lives of a largely Gentile church already two centuries removed from the apostolic community and New Testament writings. As O'Meara observes, "An inspired page no longer struck Christians as a forecast of fulfillment in Christ but as a divine prescription; the Jewish hierarchy of high priest, priest and levite was admired by Clement of Rome, and then assumed as a theology of ministry a century later by Cyprian of Carthage."[15] By the time of the Council of Nicaea in AD 325 the old councils of presbyters with their disciplinary and judiciary powers were dissolving. As the presbyters turned over their authority in such matters to the bishops, they gained in a delegation of the bishop's cultic presidency. Calling presbyters "priests" thereby became fairly common in the East and West as more and more they assumed the role of serving as the normal celebrant of the Eucharist.[16]

The Constantinian Age and the Influence of Monasticism (Fourth and Fifth Centuries)

With the Constantinian embrace of the Church in the fourth century the bishop's sole executive role was further enhanced. Almost immediately, bishops found themselves in the position of part-time civil functionaries. They were given special assignments by the Emperor because of their prominence and acknowledged ability and influence. They presided over episcopal courts that now received full civil recognition; some of these dealt exclusively with ecclesiastical business, others were taken up with matters that would ordinarily be handled by civil courts. The fourth and fifth centuries proved to be the golden age of the episcopacy. During this period the metropolitan sees acquired considerable prominence and the patriarchates emerged. Conciliar canons from Nicaea to Chalcedon determined that under the guidance of the metropolitan, bishops were to be chosen by their fellow bishops of the province with some consultation of the people. Sometimes the Emperor himself selected the candidate. The Synod of Hippo in AD 393 asserted that since the bishop was a family man, his wife and children were to reflect his virtue. Therefore, his whole

---

[15] O'Meara, *Theology of Ministry*, 102.
[16] Nichols, *Holy Order*, 50.

family was to be Catholic. Nonetheless, a trend toward abstinence in marriage and even celibacy was growing during this period, as we shall see when we look at the history and theology of priestly celibacy in chapter 5.

According to *The Apostolic Constitutions* of the late fourth century, the bishop exercises supreme authority in his diocese. He baptizes, blesses, reconciles, ordains, offers, and deprives (AC 8.28). But in case of necessity he can delegate his priestly powers to his presbyters, except that of ordination. Indeed, presbyters are now ordained as helpers of the bishop, much as was previously true of the deacons in Hippolytus' *Apostolic Tradition*, and they are given individual assignments as virtual "mini-bishops" caring for branch communities. Although the bishops of this period still sometimes turn to their presbyteral councils for advice and support in governing, they more frequently meet together in regional synods as a corporate college. With the Church growing in size and the bishop's role becoming more central, and with the ties of bishops with one another becoming more important as they meet in major synods and councils, the notion of a worldwide community or "Great Church" becomes common.[17]

In the midst of this realignment of ecclesiastical structures, the diaconate seems, at first, to jump into the vacuum of authority left in the wake of the dispersion of the presbyters to the rural parishes. Nevertheless, they too were soon assigned by the bishop to assist the presbyters in those same outlying communities. Nichols also suggests that the late fourth-century idea of Orders as graded steps, a *cursus honorum*, contributed to the comparative decline of the diaconate; he explains:

> . . . whereas Cyprian was ordained by jumping—*per saltem*—from layman to the episcopate, Ambrose (c. 339–397), a hundred years later, was elected bishop of Milan while still a catechumen . . . [and] received baptism, confirmation, minor orders, the diaconate, and presbyterate on successive days before receiving the episcopate.[18]

The newer system, the *cursus honorum*, assures that no one will become a bishop who has not first served the Church as a deacon and carried the everyday task of the ministry of the Word and sacraments as a presbyter. The term *ordinatio* was originally used in Rome for appointing civil

---

[17] Certainly the concept of the "Great Church" can be found already in the epistles of St. Paul (e.g., 1 Cor 17:7) and in the letters of St. Ignatius of Antioch. The historical circumstances of the fourth and fifth centuries, however, bring the concept to the fore. In the midst of the Arian controversies, especially, the civil authorities are anxious to promote the peace and unity of the Church throughout the empire.

[18] Nichols, *Holy Order*, 52.

servants to their office. Saint Jerome uses it as a synonym for the Greek *cheirotonia*, the laying on of hands. Those inducted into office in ancient Rome constituted an *ordo*, distinguishing them from the general body of the populace. In the Church it became a proper term for the clergy's special place within the people of God.[19]

The so-called minor orders appeared on the scene in the fourth century as variegated forms of assistance to the deacon. Their number fluctuated. In the East there were often only two—subdeacon and lector; however, in the West there were generally five—subdeacon, acolyte, exorcist, lector, and porter. In the sixth century the Roman church added a rite of admitting new candidates to this entire series of offices, calling it "tonsure." Again, Nichols observes that "in some parts of the Church a distinction arose between two kinds of laying on of hands, one performed at the altar, *cheirotonia*, and the other performed *away* from it, *cheirothesia*, the second being made more freely available to ministers in grades other than those of the classical threefold ministry, and notably to sub-deacons, lectors and deaconesses."[20] As time went on, the ordination ceremonies for bishop, presbyter, and deacon grew richer in symbolism and more complicated. By the Middle Ages, theologians came to lose sight of the centrality of the laying on of hands as the "matter" of Order. Instead, giving the candidate the sacred vessels, the chalice and paten (*porrectio instrumentorum*), was then considered to be the all-important sacramental gesture.

During this proliferation of lesser ministries in the fourth century, deaconesses are mentioned in the East. "Generally from the upper classes, they took over many of the functions of widows, for example, helping in the baptism of women, visiting the sick women of the community."[21] Thus we read in *The Apostolic Constitutions*, "A deaconess does not bless nor perform anything belonging to the order of presbyters or deacons, but only is to keep the doors, and to minister to the presbyters in the baptism of women, on account of decency" (AC 8.28). The Council of Nicaea had stated that deaconesses who had received the laying on of hands were not to be enrolled among the clergy but were considered to be among the laity. As Nichols maintains, such a ceremony was a *cheirothesia*, taking place *away* from the altar. In addition, the Council of Laodicea stated that female elders (*presbytides*) or presidents (*prokathemēnai*) are not to be appointed in the church. Mohler writes, "*Presbytides* may have been older deaconesses who had charge of the younger ones or they may have

---

[19] Ibid.
[20] Ibid., 53–54 with emphasis in original.
[21] Mohler, *The Origin and Evolution of the Priesthood*, 79.

supervised the widows. At any rate, they are not to be ordained in the church, as presbyters and deacons were."[22]

Fourth-century synods and Fathers called for a stricter morality and more careful selection of clergy. As priests of the New Israel they were expected to be superior to their antitypes of old. They were to be clean, pure, and trustworthy. Those who in time of persecution had not proven trustworthy were not to be admitted to the ranks of the clergy. Once ordained, the clergy were expected to continue living their high standard of morality. And according to the Synod of Elvira in the early fourth century, if any of the clergy were found guilty of immorality because of scandal or lewdness, they could not be admitted to communion even at the end of their lives.[23] To ensure maturity, the Synod of Neo-Caesarea directed that presbyters were not to be ordained until thirty years of age, the age at which Christ began his public ministry. Furthermore, because of the experience of backsliding candidates, *clinici* (those converted in the crisis of a serious illness) and recent converts could not be promoted to Orders.

Roman law granted Christian clergy exemption from civil and military service, from subjection to civil courts, and from taxation. They were exempted from paying taxes even if they conducted a business for their own livelihood. The families and servants of clerics were also tax exempt. Many of these same privileges were shared by the Roman civil priests and the Jewish patriarchs, priests, and presbyters. Since there arose an obvious danger of some being attracted to ministry largely because of these tax privileges, *The Theodosian Code* at times set limits on the numbers to be exempted in given cities of the empire. Valentinian III in AD 453 finally had to forbid clerics to engage in trade under penalty of disposition. The Roman government, in addition, tried to encourage the recruitment of clergy from the poorer classes. Moreover, once ordained, it was expected that they not be found visiting widows and potential deaconesses in search of benefices.

By the end of the fourth century sacerdotalism had become the ordinary mode of speaking of the Christian clergy. The disappearance of the pagan mystery cults and priesthood during this period eliminated any danger of confusing Christian ceremonies and terminology with them.[24] An increasing emphasis on ritualism and liturgical gestures now begins to

[22] Ibid., 80.

[23] Ibid., 81 with reference to canon 18.

[24] Sacral terminology was also borrowed from the waning pagan mystery cults, e.g., *hierologia, hierourgia, mystagōgos, pontifex, sacerdos.* See Josef Jungmann, *The Early Liturgy* (South Bend, IN: University of Notre Dame Press, 1959), 158.

overshadow the ministry of the Word, which had originally distinguished earlier Christian clerics from their Jewish and pagan counterparts. Additionally, when the empire became Christian, bishops and priests often became a part of the Roman governmental system. The imperial favor, as well as Constantine's conception of his own role as the Thirteenth Apostle, resulted in the grafting of court customs onto liturgical ceremonies. As P.-M. Gy observes:

> In fact, it seems that from the time of Constantine, bishops, priests and deacons had their place in the strictly hierarchical gradations of Lower-Empire officialdom. They rejoiced in the titles *clarissime, illustre, gloriosissime*, and in the insignia of their rank, among which were the pallium, the stole, the sandals, and probably also the maniple.[25]

Many of the Fathers of the fourth century such as Gregory of Nyssa, John Chrysostom, Ambrose, and Jerome plainly taught the sacerdotal view of the Christian presbyterate.

John Chrysostom in his *On the Priesthood* provided the first theological and systematic treatise on sacerdotal ministry. He sought to show the basic equality of bishops and presbyters as illustrated in the Pastoral Epistles. Hence he preached, "Between presbyters and bishops there was no great difference, both had undertaken the office of teachers and presidents in the church. And what he [St. Paul] said concerning bishops is applicable to presbyters." Bishops are only superior in their power to ordain (*Homily XI on I Timothy 3:1*). Chrysostom underlined the teaching and ruling offices. The priest must excel as a preacher, striving to emulate the eloquence of St. Paul. Furthermore, priests have powers that even angels do not have, for example, binding and loosing, administering the baptism of regeneration, and the eucharistic food (*On the Priesthood* 3.5-6). Gregory of Nyssa in his *On Virginity* recommended that priests abstain from the marriage privileges as in the Old Law, for in the priesthood one is transformed from the human to the angelic. Furthermore, since the priest allies himself with the great High Priest, he is a priest forever even in death (23).[26]

In the West, St. Jerome, referring to the history of the early Church, strongly asserted the dignity of the presbyters. In an analogy with the Old Testament priesthood he compares the bishop, presbyters, and deacons to Aaron, his sons, and the Levites. In fact, there is nothing the bishop

[25] Pierre-Marie Gy, "Notes on the Early Terminology of Christian Priesthood," in *The Sacrament of Holy Orders* (Collegeville, MN: Liturgical Press, 1962), 101.

[26] Mohler, *The Origin and Evolution of the Priesthood*, 83–84.

does that the presbyter cannot do except ordain. This assertion consequently stirred a debate that lasted into the Middle Ages and beyond, wherein theologians refused to recognize the episcopacy as an order distinct from the presbyterate. The debate would only be finally settled by the Second Vatican Council's dogmatic teaching that episcopal consecration confers "the fullness of the sacrament of Orders" (LG 21). Saint Augustine, at the same time, defended the perpetuity of Orders against the Donatists. Therefore, when schismatic priests are received back, they should not be reordained (*Against the Letter of Parmenianus* 2.13, 28). Orders, like baptism, Augustine maintained, have a permanent character.

Saint Augustine also compared ordination to marriage. He argued that although marriage is for the begetting of children, even if this does not happen the bond remains until death. So ordination is performed to gather people, yet if anyone is removed from office because of some fault, he still retains the sacrament once it has been given. While he strongly disapproved of clerical misconduct, Augustine had little patience for those who were hypocritically scandalized by such actions.

> Writing to Felicia (*Letter* 208: 2 & 3), he points out that as Jesus had foretold, there will always be two types of shepherds, namely, the true guardians of the flocks and those who seek the office for their own personal gain. Thus sheep and goats are to be found among the shepherds as well as in their flocks. Some lie in wait for a priest or a nun to fall in order to cluck, "I told you so, they're all like that." Yet when a married woman is found to be an adulteress, they do not accuse their wives or mothers (*Letter* 78:6).[27]

Augustine further maintained that even if a minister does evil, his ministry is still valid because those who receive the Gospel from such ministers are "cleansed and justified . . . by him who gives the increase" (*Answer to the Letters of Petilian* 3, 55, 67). Ordination makes one truly a "minister," that is, a servant of Christ, the Head of the Church. The efficacy of the Church's sacraments thus flows directly from Christ and not in any way from the ordained themselves. To help improve the quality of the clergy, certain bishops from the fourth century on, such as Martin of Tours, Paulinus of Nola, and Augustine, favored the monastic life for their priests living in community with the bishop, which evolved into what eventually came to be called the "canonical life" and the existence of "canons regular."

---

[27] Ibid., 85.

In AD 380, by an imperial decree of Theodosius the Great, the Catholic Church became the official state religion. All citizens necessarily and under pain of legal sanctions became Christians. As a result, monasticism arose as a movement expressing a rejection of conventional worldly values. Louis Bouyer describes this phenomenon:

> It was not by chance that anchoritism, the retreat to the desert, spread so suddenly just as the State made its peace with the Church. There is certainly a very close connection between these two contemporaneous historical facts. When a world in which Christians as such were separated and proscribed was succeeded by a world in which they came to be in honor, but a world whose spirit had hardly changed for all that, the best Christians, by instinct, would freely choose the state of proscription no longer imposed on them by circumstances. In a world which no longer treated them as enemies of the world; they sensed too well that, without this, they would become its slaves.[28]

With the cessation of persecutions and martyrdom, monasticism quickly became the ultimate form of Christian witness.

The origins of monasticism can be traced to ascetics within the Church, living alone or in groups, who appeared in the Near East and northern Africa in the second century. The word *monachos* renders a Syrian technical term meaning "sole," or "single." "The main emphasis was on celibacy; however, at first its principal aim was to attain an inner unity, the opposite of sexual duality, even going so far as a union with 'the only begotten Son' of God."[29] In the late fourth century with everyone suddenly becoming Christian, with catechumenal formation being drastically simplified for want of enough qualified teachers, and with the loss of the familial support and atmosphere experienced in the shift from house churches to large basilica liturgies, a desire to imitate the primitive Church of Acts 2:42-46 led to the rapid development and spread of monastic communities or cenobitism.

We have already seen how Augustine, Martin of Tours, and other bishops of the time encouraged their clergy to live in monastic-like communities. Monasticism, with its roots in a solitary life of prayer and with its emphasis on an individual's growth in virtue, would soon reshape how

[28] Louis Bouyer, *The Spirituality of the New Testament and the Fathers* (New York: Desclée, 1963), 305–6.

[29] Jean Gribomont, "Monasticism and Asceticism: I. Eastern Christianity," in *Christian Spirituality: Origins to the Twelfth Century*, ed. Bernard McGinn and John Meyendorff (New York: Crossroad, 1997), 90.

one envisioned living one's life as a Christian. By the end of the fourth century, as Metropolitan John D. Zizioulas relates, there had developed two types of spirituality:

> [O]n the one hand, the type of spirituality that was based on the eucharistic community and involved the community and its eschatological orientation as the decisive factors of spirituality; and, on the other hand, the type of spirituality that was based on the experience of the individual who struggles against passions and toward the achievement of moral perfection, a spirituality accompanied by a mystical union of the soul or the mind with the Logos of God.[30]

These two types of spirituality are by no means incompatible but in fact complementary. Yet, from this time on the monastic vision would grow to predominate, as the Eucharist-based communal-eschatological vision would struggle to survive. Consequently, there occurred a "shift in the whole context of Christian thinking, perhaps more strongly in the West but by no means exclusively there, a shift from a mystery-incorporation into Christ notion of sanctity to a possession of virtue notion of sanctity."[31] This changing focus is most clearly evident in the *Pastoral Rule* of Pope Gregory the Great (590–604), who wanted to give the secular clergy a counterpart to the monastic Rule of St. Benedict. Here we find a definite shift in the ministry of the Word from instruction about mystery to moral exhortation and admonition. By this time too the separation of the clergy from the laity becomes practically complete. The clergy are seen as the "better Christians" called to a higher life, and a different level of sanctity is expected of them than of ordinary Christians.

Germanization and the Feudal System (Sixth through Eleventh Centuries)

In the year 476 the last Emperor of the West was deposed by the Germanic general Odoacer, and Italy became a barbarian kingdom. The Gothic kings based themselves on the Adriatic coast in the old capital of the Western Empire at Ravenna. The first Germans to convert to Christianity were those who made up the eastern group of Goths, Vandals, and Burgundians. Their initial contact was made in AD 376 with Valens, the Arian

---

[30] Zizioulas, "The Early Christian Community" in McGinn and Meyendorff, *Christian Spirituality*, 41.

[31] Cooke, *Ministry to Word and Sacraments*, 556.

Christian emperor of the Eastern Empire with whom they negotiated to adopt his religion in return for asylum from the Huns. In the West a century later Theodoric, the ferocious successor of Odoacer in Ravenna, decimated the Catholic bishops of northern Italy and replaced them with Arians. It would be the mid-sixth century before the imperial troops recaptured Italy from the Goths.

Rome, repeatedly besieged and plundered, saw its population plummet from 800,000 in AD 400 to 30,000 in AD 546, the year it was captured and sacked by Totila. Despite the accelerating social upheaval of this period, which included not only the Teutonic invasions of Europe and Africa but also the Arian and Monophysite schisms along with the first impact of Islam, the basic elements of episcopal activity remained intact as it had for the past two centuries. The Church survived because its own structure of government and administration, although built on the imperial model, was not considered a threat to the invaders. In the Eastern Empire at this time, Justinian was claiming that the emperor, and not the pope, was God's vicar on earth with the right to make and unmake bishops and to determine the bounds of orthodoxy. Justinian himself defended the Monophysite heresy. The popes, consequently, began a concerted effort to free themselves from the emperor's embrace. As they sought to meet the needs of Italy and the West, the papacy now turned its attention elsewhere.

Gregory the Great (590–604) was the great-grandson of Pope Felix III and a monk when he was elected Bishop of Rome. He rejoiced at the conversion to Catholicism of Recarred, the Visigoth king of Spain, and cultivated friendly relations with the royal family of Gaul. Gregory also began missionary outreach to the world beyond the empire by sending a party of Roman monks led by Augustine to evangelize Anglo-Saxon England. Whereas one of the reasons for the rapid expansion of Christianity in the early centuries appears to have been the commonly held conviction that all Christians are responsible for evangelization, this mission now was officially relegated to a specific group of clergy. Because the vast majority of lay Christians no longer experienced the catechumenate and had little actual formation in the faith, the laity came to be viewed more and more as those who are ministered to by the clergy. Furthermore, the incorporation of the various ministries into minor orders or clerical grades required for ordination to the priesthood only served to foster the separation of the Christian community into those who do ministry professionally and those who are the recipients of such ministry.

Monasticism had been planted among the Celtic peoples of Britain in the fourth century, reportedly influenced by the example of the monk-bishop Martin of Tours. In 429 Pope Celestine sent Germanus of Auxerre to Britain to fight Pelagianism, and St. Patrick, the monk made bishop against his will, succeeded in rapidly converting many leaders of the Irish tribes. Celtic spirituality was characterized by a rigorous asceticism recalling that of the Eastern monks. Indeed, the ascetical and voluntary heroism of the Celtic monks left them susceptible to the ideas of one among them, Pelagius, who propagated his ideas in Britain before traveling to the Continent.[32]

Another Celtic spiritual practice was private penance. The abbot was obliged to direct each monk in his spiritual life and to impose an appropriate penance after the confession of his sins. Little books called "penitentials" were produced, recommending the appropriate penance for every kind of sin. These monks brought this practice to Europe as they sought to evangelize the Germanic tribes. By the twelfth century this private form of penance, having grown in popularity despite strong opposition from official church decrees, replaced the discipline of exomologesis, the canonical form of public penance that traced its origins back to the early patristic era.

Celtic monasticism, consequently, changed how people came to view Christian spirituality and ministry. The preaching of the monks focused on sin and the need for penance. Influenced by the secular legal system with its tariffs (fines) and commutations (substitute penalties) as satisfaction made for crimes, this privatized form of penance led to the human relationship with God being envisioned largely in legal, commercial, and individualistic terms. The Christian life itself essentially became a matter of avoiding sin rather than living the gospel mystery and being formed in Christ. Being "spiritual" now referred to performing individual ascetical practices in order to arrive at the perfection of virtue rather than living in the Holy Spirit and sharing in a koinonia with the Risen Lord and one another, the *Totus Christus* of St. Augustine.

The Pelagian tendency to reduce Christian living to acceptable ethical behavior looked upon leadership within the community primarily in terms of lawgiver or judge. Ordination now served but to grant cultic powers to administer the sacraments. Thus in Scotland and Ireland bishops "were retained simply to provide Holy Order for others, and lived otherwise secluded lives as monks in monasteries, under the authority of abbots who themselves were presbyters. Such abbots, in presbyteral orders, were

[32] Pierre Riché, "Christianity and Cultural Diversity: II. Spirituality in Celtic and Germanic Society," in *Christian Spirituality: Origins to the Twelfth Century*, ed. Bernard McGinn and John Meyendorff (New York: Crossroad, 1997), 165–66.

the actual liturgists, teachers and pastors of the villages of a rural local church."[33]

As the patristic period gives way to the early Middle Ages, the outlying rural baptismal churches in Italy, Gaul, and Spain were merged into a system of large parishes in the seventh and eighth centuries. This parish system found its origins in the Latin countries and in Roman legislation, but it soon came into conflict with the proprietary churches of a Teutonic feudal society. The ancient baptismal churches were directly under the bishop, their ministers were supplied and directed by him, and they held the traditional right to provide Sunday Mass, to burial, to baptism, and weddings.[34]

In the German-speaking lands the "proprietary church system" (*Eigenkirchensystem*) and "proprietary monastery system" (*Eigenklostersystem*) took hold and began to spread. This was a system in which church buildings and property, including the appointment of the pastor or abbot, was in the control of a lay proprietor who profited from the income of the properties. The episcopacy readily saw this as an infringement upon the functioning of church life, and a compromise was worked out under Charlemagne whereby the clergy found themselves in a semi-contractual situation by means of which they were financially remunerated in exchange for their pastoral services. Nevertheless, under this system the clergy tended to become either feudal serfs or feudal lords. Ordinary presbyters were reduced to practical serfdom, becoming part of the lord's entourage of servants. In the later Middle Ages a multiplicity of patterns is found in the parish structure. In rural areas the *Eigenkirchensystem* continued. In other situations churches came into the possession of monasteries, and some churches belonged to families or to pious fraternities.[35]

By the Middle Ages the prevailing vision of the Church, the sacraments, and ordained ministry had been substantially influenced and shaped by historical circumstances both within the Church and in society. Combating heresies within the Christian community always results in a placement of emphasis to what the heretics deny. With Arianism denying Christ's divinity, already in the fourth century one finds a patristic emphasis on the actual presence of God in the Eucharist. Augustine insisted, "No one should eat this flesh if he has not first adored it" (*On the Psalms* 98.9). The Arian form of Christianity accepted by many of the Visigoths in the late

---

[33] Nichols, *Holy Order*, 50.

[34] See Friedrich Kempf, *The Church in the Age of Feudalism (Handbook of Church History)*, vol. 3 (New York: Palm Publishers, 1969), 263.

[35] See Cooke, *Ministry to Word and Sacraments*, 362–64.

fourth century, moreover, was subsequently transmitted to other Germanic peoples. The Gallic bishops and the missionaries evangelizing the Germanic tribes, therefore, also emphasized the divine presence. Bishop Patrick J. Dunn describes how this change in emphasis impacted the celebration of the Roman Mass:

> A ritual confession of sinfulness was added to the introductory rite, and the priests genuflected in adoration after the consecration. The canon was whispered—to protect and honor the mystery. The laity were discouraged from receiving communion too frequently, and certainly not with their hands! The Creed of Nicaea was inserted between the Gospel and the Canon. The priest often prayed with his hands joined in supplication, rather than outstretched in thanksgiving. Because the Mass was seen primarily as a sacrifice the sermon seemed to be increasingly superfluous.[36]

The ministerial priesthood by this time too is not only considered to be like the Old Testament priesthood, but is actually seen as finding its origins in the latter. As a result, the idea of "offering sacrifice" and the power to consecrate the eucharistic elements takes on an increasing centrality in thought about the priestly office. By the eighth century also the laity have been reduced to almost total silence in the celebration of the liturgy. The celebrant has become the high priest offering sacrifice on behalf of the people; he is seen as "the sacred actor performing a mystery rite rather than the prophetic herald of the redeeming gospel of Christ's death and resurrection."[37]

Moreover, starting with the imperial embrace of the Church in the fourth century the communal sense of "church," which dominated the early patristic period, gradually gave way to a more institutional and juridical understanding. Thus Joseph Ratzinger considers the distinction between sacrament (*potestas ordinis*) and jurisdiction (*potestas jurisdictionis*) to be the most crucial development of the Latin West during the Middle Ages, and he describes the historical situation that resulted:

> The Church of the Irish monks had no episcopal authority. Fullness of power for the celebration of the Eucharist was no longer combined with that of administration. The individual church entity that developed according to the legal forms of the Germanic realm led in the

---

[36] Patrick J. Dunn, *Priesthood: A Re-examination of the Roman Catholic Theology of the Presbyterate* (New York: Alba House, 1990), 83.

[37] Ibid., 86.

same direction. The priest became a cult-minister in the retinue of the feudal lord. The Ottonian combination of *imperium* and *sacerdotium*— the employment of the *sacerdotium* in the service of the *imperium*—only seems to point in a different direction: the Church became, as it were, the proprietary Church of the German Empire; as a functionary of the Empire, the bishop was concerned only secondarily with the ecclesial assembly and, of necessity, allowed its concrete functions to be carried out by others. . . . The office, as a legal entity to which certain revenues were due, was bestowed on some important personage, often not even ordained, who relegated the performance of liturgical services to an ill-paid Mass priest. . . . He was not trained to proclaim the word and often restricted himself to the *cultus* alone, which, in practice, lost its real meaning because of this.

From a theological standpoint, the critical effect of this separation of sacrament and jurisdiction seems to have been the resultant isolation of the concept of sacrament. The essential identity of Church and liturgical assembly, of Church and *communio*, was no longer evident. Like any other society, the Church was now, in a certain sense, a juridical instrument, a complex of laws, ordinances, claims. In addition, of course, she had also what was peculiarly her own: the fact that she was the *situs* of cultic acts—of the sacraments. But the Eucharist was just one of these—one liturgical act among others, no longer the encompassing orbit and dynamic center of ecclesial existence per se. . . . The doctrine of the fruits of the Mass gave meaning to the stipend and led to the greatest possible emphasis on the unique fruits of each separate Mass, in which special fruits were granted that would not otherwise exist. The whole seems more like the ideological superstructure of a particular economic situation than like a genuine theological consideration that corrects and transforms human situations. I think we should be honest enough to admit the temptation of mammon in the history of the Church and to recognize to what extent it was a real power that worked to the distortion and corruption of both Church and theology, even to their inmost core. The separation of office as jurisdiction from office as rite was continued for reasons of prestige and financial benefits . . . the Mass became the private possession of the pious (and the impious) by which they hoped to effect a private reconciliation with God.[38]

Other Germanizing influences also contributed to a growing spiritual externalism or positivism during this same period.

[38] Ratzinger, *Principles of Catholic Theology* (San Francisco: Ignatius Press, 1987), 255–56.

A policy of accommodation, practiced by St. Boniface and other early missionaries, began by first "Christianizing" pagan practices, feasts, and sacred places in an attempt to create a receptivity for the Christian world-view. In place of magical incantations the missionaries introduced "Christian incantations" by which the priest blessed the fields, the vineyard, the nuptial bed, the shaving of the first beard, the new well, the soap one used for the bath, etc. Some prayers had power to drive away thunder and tempests. The fact that Germans were also a warrior people influenced their way of living Christianity, in which chivalry, crusade, and hagiography played important roles. In this folk-centered, magico-religious society, the dramatic representational interpretation of Scripture, liturgy, the Passion of Christ, and the lives of the saints also held an eminent place. Additionally, a love of the tangible was evidenced in eucharistic controversies, juridical interests, veneration of relics and tombs of the saints, self-flagellation, and other emotionally laden, private devotions.

The understanding of the role of the ordained minister, furthermore, greatly depends upon how Christians understand the Eucharist. The tendency toward religious externalism here too entered the picture. The disputed opinions of Berengarius of Tours about the Real Presence triggered heated controversy. In popular piety the Eucharist was looked upon as somehow having saving power of a well-nigh magical kind, a power that would work on all who saw "the Sacrament." A frenzy to view as many elevations of the host as possible resulted in the elevation of the consecrated elements becoming the central attraction of the Mass.

Most explanations of the manner in which Christ was "present beneath the appearances of bread and wine" were crassly quantitative and materialistic. "The metaphysical subtlety of Aquinas' theology of Eucharistic change was far beyond the capacity of the age to comprehend; had it been understood it would have been considered heretical or at the very least 'dangerous.'"[39] This then touched upon how the role of the priest was now envisioned; he alone is the "sanctified person" who can stand in the sacred precincts of the altar and change the bread and wine into the Body and Blood of Christ. The celebrant is viewed more and more as the instrumental cause of transubstantiation and less and less as the sacramental leader of a celebrating community. The Mass too is now viewed almost exclusively in terms of Jesus' sacrifice on Calvary. The Canon is no longer seen as the great prayer of benediction over the gifts, as the evangelical proclamation of Christ's paschal mystery; it is no longer envisioned as

---

[39] Cooke, *Ministry to Word and Sacraments*, 117.

the pentecostal moment of transforming the assembly into Body of Christ and of entering into the eschatological communion of saints.

The Middle Ages saw a great proliferation in the number of clergy. Thousands were ordained without much attention given to intellectual and moral credentials. The large number of priests, in fact, caused social and economic problems as well as problems for orderly ecclesiastical life. Many were "Mass-saying" priests attached to benefices and manor houses. As Cooke observes, "Obviously, such utilization of ordained ministers emphasized almost exclusively the 'transubstantiating power' of the priest, although in some instances these men were also on hand to hear confessions. But the notion of ministry of word, of pastoral service to community, was almost totally lacking."[40]

There was also a real division between the educated and influential clergy who worked in the cities and the clergy who served in small towns or rural areas. The latter lived and worked with the common folk, sharing their lifestyle and often ignoring clerical celibacy. These country pastors were usually just as anticlerical as their flocks. By the twelfth century there is an unquestionable shift from viewing the celebrant as the sign of Christ's presence to his making Christ present for the people by transforming the bread and wine. The bishops and priests themselves are now seen as "the church" from whom the laity in turn "receive" salvation.

Pope Gregory VII (1073–86), upon his election to the papacy, had no reservations about exercising the papal claim to immediate jurisdiction over all Christians in his effort to rescue the Church from the scandals of lay investiture and to bring about much needed reform. Of the nineteen popes from Gregory to Innocent III (1198–1216), who himself crystallized many reforms in the conciliar decrees of Lateran IV (1215), eleven of them had been monks or canons regular at the time of their election. The reform popes turned to the monasteries to find men free from the simony, corruption, and unchastity that polluted so many secular clergy and so many of the bishops.[41] Monasticism, therefore, continued to give shape to the Christian life at all levels. The prayer of the secular clergy became the monastic Office, the private recitation of which by the eleventh century became an expected daily practice. Cathedral and rectory had the qualities of a monastic enclosure, the cloister. Even devotional literature written for the laity drew people to the inner life of the soul and urged them to practice monastic detachment and contemplation.[42]

[40] Ibid., 116.
[41] Eamon Duffy, *Saints & Sinners: A History of the Popes* (New Haven & London: Yale University Press, 1997), 103.
[42] See O'Meara, *Theology of Ministry*, 105–9.

The language we use to describe our work and activity is often an accurate indication of how we perceive what we are doing. Under Germanic influences one notices during this period a growing use of military imagery to describe the Christian life. Gregory VII, in particular, was fond of speaking of life as a crusade, a battle against the forces of evil, and of referring to the church on earth as "the church militant." At the same time, the popular understanding of the Christian spiritual life and ministry took a decidedly "objectivistic" turn, which often gave magical and superstitious interpretations to religious happenings. The priest, by virtue of his ordination, was considered to possess certain special powers: the power to change the eucharistic bread and wine into the Body and Blood of Christ; the "power of the keys" to forgive sins by penitential absolution; the power to bless persons, animals, food, and other inanimate things such as "charms" that would help ward off evil. Such common perceptions thus led to interpreting the sacraments as operating almost automatically and requiring little to no active interior participation. In addition, a growing emphasis on jurisdiction also came to the fore with the publication of Gratian's *Decretum* in the twelfth century. The flourishing state of legal studies in Italy, particularly at Bologna and Padua, now provided a predominantly juristic paradigm for viewing the Church and ministry.

The Birth of Religious Orders and Scholasticism (Twelfth through Fifteenth Centuries)

Although the primary focus of monasticism may have been the cultivation of the inner life of prayer and contemplation, the monks also were the great evangelizers and missionaries of the Middle Ages. By the twelfth century, however, a large number of Christians took to the road to preach, imitating Christ's poverty and the mission of the Twelve. They were in many ways the successors of the itinerant apostle-prophets of the early Church. While these preaching movements attempted to reintroduce a public form of apostolic ministry, they frequently proved to be the source of error, disorder, and immorality. What could have resulted in a large unconstrained movement was aptly channeled into society and the Church through two preachers, Francis and Dominic, who formed a new, post-monastic style of religious life.[43] Joseph Ratzinger considers these mendicant orders to be the second great reform movement—with the Gregorian reform being the first—of the Middle Ages. He writes:

---

[43] Ibid., 109.

[T]hese orders struggled to emancipate the Church from the feudal structures and free the gospel from the material structures of the medieval order. In the hunger for the word that had arisen in a Church without the proclamation of the word, Dominic sought to establish the movement of preachers and Francis a simple popular catechesis. From both movements there arose a new type of priestly office, not linked to the episcopacy, but defined essentially by its missionary element, by moving from place to place in the service of the word.[44]

Pope Innocent III strongly encouraged the Franciscan movement and the Dominican friars. They provided competent preachers for "parish missions," preaching zealously for a short period of time, nurturing and correcting the faith of the common people, and then moving on to another location. The thrust of such preaching was not primarily toward understanding but rather toward promoting good behavior and cultivating a genuine personal devotion to Christ and to the saints and angels.

The Dominican friars also were more oriented to the academic life and committed themselves to the intellectual defense of the faith and to the development of theology, giving us Albert the Great and Thomas Aquinas, among others. The Franciscans, for their part, also had Bonaventure and Alexander of Hales. During the twelfth century, the locale for doing theology moved from the monastery to the university. This shift from the cloister to the university lecture hall gave birth to the Scholastic method, which in the process tended to separate theology from spirituality. The predominant thought-form of the time was hierarchical *ordo*. Its philosophical source was the mystical writings of Pseudo-Dionysius, works actually composed by a Neo-Platonist Syrian monk from the sixth century who was thought to be the Dionysius converted by St. Paul on the Athenian Areopagus (Acts 13:33ff.). Thus O'Meara writes, "As a result of his legend, Denys's synthesis of Christian and Platonist forms held a singular position not only in theology but in the entire cultural world of Paris. In mysticism, aesthetics and ecclesiology, in politics and papal theory, the Areopagite's influence was unassailable."[45]

While one can find a number of lengthy systematic works from the Scholastic theologians on *de sacramentis*, none exists on ministry or the priesthood per se. In fact, Gratian's *Decretum* is the source of Peter Lombard's discussion of priesthood, which becomes the springboard for much of the thirteenth and fourteenth centuries' treatment of the topic and gives a

---

[44] Ratzinger, *Principles of Catholic Theology*, 257.
[45] O'Meara, *Theology of Ministry*, 110.

decidedly canonical flavor to the Church's formalized thinking about ministry. And canonical thinking in turn had a tendency to go back to the Levitical legislation of the Old Testament. For Peter Lombard, Order is a sevenfold sacramental reality, and each of the offices has been fulfilled by Jesus Christ in "typical" anticipation of the ministry of the Church. The seventh and final Order in Lombard's catalog is that of *sacerdotes*, which includes both presbyters and bishops, the latter office being the "apex." The differentiation of presbyters and bishops reflects the Seventy and the Twelve sent forth in the gospel accounts during the years of Jesus' public ministry.[46]

Ordination for the Scholastics is primarily a conferral of the power of the keys, the power attached to the *sacerdotium*. For Bonaventure this includes the highest power involved in the eucharistic consecration, which being the sacrifice of Christ is itself the power of reconciliation; he put it succinctly, *ordo est ad sacrificium administrandum*, "Order is for the ministering of sacrifice."[47] For Aquinas the power to confect the Eucharist and the power to absolve sins are grounded in the sacramental character of Order. The word "character," originally meaning a mark or stamp, was borrowed from the Greek Fathers to express in the West what Augustine had called the lasting *signaculum* or "sign-quality," which the sacraments of baptism, confirmation, and Order leave on those who receive them. It entails the permanent consecration of the recipient and resembles grace inasmuch as it is an invisible spiritual reality brought forth and signified by the rite in question. As described by Cooke:

> If one puts the discussion of ordination into the theological context governed, as was that of most medieval theologians, by a theory of ontological modifications, the sacrament was commonly considered to have two effects: the *res et sacramentum* which was the sacramental character of Orders, and the *res* was the grace.[48]

This doctrine of the character conferred by ordination is used by most theologians of the Middle Ages as the key to explaining the efficacy of sacramental actions performed by an unworthy minister.

The constant teaching of medieval theologians and canonists maintained that priests were primarily ordained for eucharistic ministry. Not

[46] Nichols, *Holy Order*, 73–74.

[47] Bonaventure, *In quartum librum Sententiarum*, dist. 24, pars I, a. 2, q. iii.

[48] Cooke, *Ministry to Word and Sacraments*, 580.

that pastoral concerns vanished, but priesthood as a cultic reality gradually took center stage in preference to what in the apostolic and the patristic eras had been the proclamation of the Gospel. Throughout the Middle Ages the level of theological comprehension among the faithful, and even among the greater part of the clergy, was minimal. Given this state of religious understanding, it is surprising that the appreciation of the Eucharist was as profound and authentic as it in fact was. Abuses, nevertheless, were common, such as the undisciplined multiplication of votive Masses celebrated for stipends, the increase of private Masses without a participating congregation, and the "magical" power attributed to Masses said in a certain number or sequence. Quite literally the people assembled on Sunday to "hear Mass," and reception of Communion was generally limited to the fulfillment of one's Easter duty.[49]

A St. Ignatius of Antioch, or any other Christian of the early second century who gathered for the "breaking of bread" in the small familiar house-churches of that day, would hardly have recognized the Christian community assembled to hear its bishop or priest "saying Mass" in any of the great medieval cathedrals of Europe on the eve of the Protestant Reformation. So much had changed over the centuries, beginning with Constantine's embrace of the Church and its rapid growth in numbers, its institutionalization and the clericalization of ministry, the spread of monasticism, the collapse of the Roman Empire, its struggles against heresies like Arianism and Pelagianism, the impact of its evangelizing efforts among the Celtic and Germanic peoples, etc.

Reflecting upon the medieval era, especially with regard to the Eucharist, Cardinal Ratzinger wrote, "The changes in the Middle Ages brought losses, but they also provided a wonderful spiritual deepening. They unfolded the magnitude of the mystery instituted at the Last Supper and enabled it to be experienced with a new fullness."[50] Monasticism, furthermore, fostered the cultivation of the interior life of prayer and promoted a personal devotional attachment to Jesus Christ, his Blessed Mother, and the saints; and the institutionalization of ecclesiastical structures allowed the Church to survive the fall of the Roman Empire and with the help of missionary monks to evangelize and civilize the primitive tribal peoples of northern and western Europe.

---

[49] Ibid., 136.

[50] Joseph Cardinal Ratzinger, *The Spirit of the Liturgy* (San Francisco: Ignatius Press, 2000), 90–91.

The Protestant Reformation, the Council of Trent, and Post-Tridentine Era (Sixteenth through Nineteenth Centuries)

At the beginning of the sixteenth century the Protestant Reformation swept across Christian Europe with remarkable suddenness. A German Augustinian monk, Martin Luther, played a major role as the catalyst of this religious upheaval. A complicated mix of political, cultural, ecclesiastical, and theological forces coalesced. Beginning with the Western Schism (1378–1417), the image of Rome and the papacy as the center of Christian unity was shattered. For a period of several decades the average Christian could no longer look to the papacy as the criterion for orthodoxy or the channel of salvation. A mounting clamor arose for "reformation in head and members," but the real problem was traceable to the decadence of clerical life and behavior. Throughout Europe there arose a widespread and often bitter anticlericalism. This resentment and criticism of the ecclesiastical "establishment" was aimed at both the diocesan clergy and the religious Orders, which also were in extensive need of reform.

During this same time, the humanist movement had spread north from Italy into the university centers of Europe. One of its foremost leaders in northern Europe was the Dutch scholar and theologian Erasmus (1466/ 1469–1536), who dreamed of renewing European life by a sincere return of people to the simple Gospel. Humanism has been described as the "modernism" of its day, representing a wave of new thinking that was a challenge to the established order. It introduced a theological perspective based upon a return to scriptural studies, which sought "to bring people back to the simple teaching of the early church and free them from the confusing subtleties of 'scholasticism.'"[51] Scandalized by the ecclesiastical practices of his day, especially the "selling" of indulgences, and by the overly speculative, abstract nature of Scholastic theology, Luther readily identified with the humanist battle cry of *ad fontes*, "back to the sources." Using "Scripture alone" as the source of theology and church practice, the Reformers rejected many of the essential tenets in the Roman Catholic Church's teaching on the sacraments and the priesthood, not to mention other areas of doctrine.

Interestingly enough, speaking from a purely academic perspective, Diarmaid MacCulloch, a church historian at Oxford, has written, "One conclusion to be drawn from the accumulation of recent research into the Latin Church before the upheaval was that it was not as corrupt and ineffective as Protestants have tended to portray it, and that it generally

---

[51] Cooke, *Ministry to Word and Sacraments*, 141.

satisfied the spiritual needs of late medieval people."[52] Nevertheless, the very nature and extent of the Reformation represents a monumental failure of ministry on both sides, Catholic and Protestant. If ministry within the Church is primarily a ministry of reconciliation, as St. Paul taught in 2 Corinthians 5:19, so that the Church can be a sign and instrument of unity among all the nations, then the separation and violence that erupted in the wake of the Reformation is an indication of a genuine failure of Christian ministry. By the time the first session of the Council of Trent convened in 1545, too much water had already poured over the dam to repair the breech, and the religious division of Europe was an accomplished fact.

Although confronted with serious and radical questioning of its traditional understanding of priesthood and ministry, the Council of Trent did little more than reiterate certain theological viewpoints that had been in existence for centuries. The Council made no attempt to present a comprehensive theological vision of priesthood; rather, it intended simply to restate and reenforce those aspects of Church doctrine that the Protestants had denied. The Council's delimited purpose was to set clear boundaries between acceptable Catholic teaching and unacceptable views. Luther denied that Order considered as a sacrament is founded on Scripture. His own definition of church office was couched solely in terms of preaching, and baptism into the priesthood of all believers was sufficient of itself for providing community preachers and leaders. Thus for him ordination was no more than a rite by which to choose a speaker in the Church. From this follows logically a purely functional interpretation of office.

Trent's *Doctrine of the Sacrament of Holy Orders* (DS 1733–1778) was confined to a rejection of the most important theses in Luther's *Babylonian Captivity*. Ratzinger writes:

> It [the Council's teaching] countered the thesis that the priesthood is just an office of preaching by declaring that it is endowed with the specifically sacramental power of celebrating the Eucharist and of forgiving sins. Luther's functional concept of office was countered by the sacramental concept, in terms of which it was concluded that the conferral of office had also to be sacramental, not political. It is clear from the nature of the text and made even clearer by the Acts of the Council that a complete conciliar doctrine of the priestly office cannot be constructed on the basis of these negations. . . . The Council limited itself deliberately to a rebuttal of Luther's negations in order to prepare the ground for theological discussion.[53]

---

[52] Diarmaid MacCulloch, *The Reformation: A History* (New York: Viking, 2003), xx.
[53] Ratzinger, *Principles of Catholic Theology*, 263.

Luther also rejected the clergy-lay distinction and the notion of a permanent priestly character. He and the other Reformers challenged celibacy and monasticism in an attempt to abolish the class system within the Church and to emphasize their doctrine of justification by faith alone, in which such ascetical works were seen as utterly vain for achieving salvation. Concerning the Lord's Supper he argued for consubstantiation, and dismissed transubstantiation as a Thomistic and Aristotelian fiction. Luther's main purpose, however, was to attack the notion of the Mass as a sacrifice, which through the multiplication of votive and private Masses had turned the divine sacrament into "an article of trade."

The Council of Trent emphatically stressed the "cultic" nature of priesthood in the opening clause of its decree on the sacrament of Order: *"Sacrificium et sacerdotium ita Dei ordinatione coniuncta sunt . . ."* ["Sacrifice and priesthood are thus conjoined by divine ordinance"].[54] It declared that the ordained priest is given the power of "consecrating, offering, and ministering" the Body and Blood of Christ, and it linked to this the power of forgiving and retaining sins. The Council gives no further clarification of the sacrificial role of the ordained minister, but it does maintain that the powers given at ordination come from the sacramental character, which is permanently impressed upon the ordained and that remains a source of effective sacramental action even when he lapses from grace. This priestly character intrinsically distinguishes the priest from the laity; therefore, any notion of the common priesthood of the faithful that denies the essentially hierarchical structure of the Church is to be denied. Galot, moreover, stresses that given the fact Trent did not intend to compile a list of priestly functions nor to offer a doctrinal synthesis on priesthood, "we should not draw from the Council a definition of the priesthood in terms of the sacrificial function."[55]

In addition to its dogmatic pronouncements meant to correct the Reformers' errors, Trent also promulgated Reform Decrees (*Decreta super reformatione*) by which it intended to bring about a positive renewal and that are almost never mentioned or considered. The decree of July 15, 1563, for instance, stated that all those who have the care of souls are commissioned by the words of the Lord "to know their sheep, to offer the holy sacrifice for them, to nourish them by the proclamation of God's word, by the administration of the sacraments and by the example of good works; they are to care, like a father, for the poor and for all needy persons

[54] Promulgated in session 7 (23), July 15, 1563. See *Concilium Tridentinum* 9, 620–22.
[55] Galot, *Theology of the Priesthood*, 130.

and to take upon themselves all the other duties of a shepherd."[56] Furthermore, the decree of November 11, 1563, canon 4 states that "Preaching is the prime duty of the bishop." Consequently, this canon requires the bishop to preach on all Sundays and holy days and daily during Lent and Advent.[57] Ratzinger comments, "Unfortunately, precisely this important part of the accomplishments of Trent has practically disappeared from later theological manuals."[58] It is strikingly clear that the Council of Trent did not limit the ordained priesthood to the cultic or ritual aspect alone but in fact also envisioned it as encompassing the ministry of the Word and the ministry of pastoral care, of building up and shepherding Christ's flock. The Reform Decrees, furthermore, ordered and provided regulations for the erection of seminaries; they even prescribed the theological disciplines to be studied beginning with Sacred Scripture and listed in last place questions of ceremony and ritual.[59]

The Catechism of the Council of Trent, often called the "Roman Catechism" from its Latin title, in its exposition on Holy Orders speaks first and foremost of the prophetic office of the bishop and priest, who are "as it were the interpreters and heralds of God."[60] The Catechism is also clear that all members of the Church are called to holiness, what it terms "the pursuit of piety and innocence," but this in no way diminishes the uniqueness of those who are "initiated into the sacrament of Order" and who have "special duties to discharge, special functions to perform."[61] Robert Bellarmine, the Jesuit ecclesiologist and president of the commission on the Catechism, is probably the most important post-Tridentine theologian of the sacrament of Order. He stressed two points: first, the affirmation that the essential gesture of conferring the sacrament is the laying on of hands; and second, the difference between the episcopate and the presbyterate is itself a sacramental distinction.[62]

During the immediate post-Reformation period theological discourse proved to be quite polemical in purpose and in tone. It concentrated on disproving the theological position of the adversary rather than developing

---

[56] *Conciliorum oecumenicorum decreta*, ed. Josepho Alberigo and others, 3rd ed. (Bologna: Istituto per le Scienze Religiose, 1973), 744, lines 24–28, as cited in Ratzinger, *Principles of Catholic Theology*, 264.

[57] Ibid., *Canon 4* (763).

[58] Ratzinger, *Principles of Catholic Theology*, 265.

[59] *Conciliorum oecumenicorum decreta, Canon 18* (751, lines 6–9); see ibid., 264n45.

[60] *The Catechism of the Council of Trent*, translated into English, with notes, by T. A. Buckley (London, 1852), II.7, 2 (as cited by Nichols, *Holy Order*, 174, fn. 37).

[61] Ibid., II.7, 5.

[62] See Nichols, *Holy Order*, 108.

a positive and constructive reflection on the questions involved. Thus Cooke writes, "Because so much of the anti-Catholic polemic (and, in some instances, persecution) was directed against the Eucharist as 'an act of offering sacrifice' and the use of 'priest' to denominate the ordained minister, Catholic insistence on the cultic identity of the ordained became even more pronounced."[63] Despite the differentiation of theological views in the post-Tridentine centuries, the discussion of priesthood and ministry is quite homogeneous and borrows largely from the writings of Aquinas to expand on the statements of Trent. All teaching on the theology of Holy Orders was but a repetition of the structure and doctrinal elements of his treatment.

Whatever new elements came into the picture came not from theology but from the literature of piety and spirituality, particularly from the seventeenth-century "French School" represented by Pierre de Bérulle, Jean-Jacques Olier, and Vincent de Paul, whose followers were so influential in implementing the Council's call to establish seminaries. The notion of Christ's priesthood implicit in the *Spiritual Exercises* of Ignatius Loyola, furthermore, played a major role in shaping priestly ministry in the post-Tridentine era. In the history of the Western Church three basic styles of living the vowed life have developed over the centuries: the monks, the friars, and the Jesuits. The Society of Jesus set the model and tone for dozens of congregations of men and women that where founded in the three centuries after 1540, many of them missionary in scope bringing the faith to new peoples in non-European lands.

The Jesuits offered a method of prayer and "a replacement of monastic community and spirituality with a modern, professional, ascetic individualism—all at the service of the church."[64] This style of Christian life also influenced many of the laity and the diocesan clergy. Just as the monastic schools had educated many bishops and priests in the Middle Ages, so the Jesuits would assume the training of a good number of future priests throughout the world including popes and bishops. O'Meara speaks of the "Jesuization" of ministry and writes, "We see this influence in the importance of retreats, in the method of prayer based on the *Spiritual Exercises*, in the style of dress and in the rise of private devotions and individual discipline."[65]

The "French School" was a movement determined to develop a spirituality for the diocesan priest that would be as lofty as, and preferably

---

[63] Cooke, *Ministry to Word and Sacraments*, 152.

[64] O'Meara, *Theology of Ministry*, 121.

[65] Ibid.

loftier than, that of the religious. Cardinal Pierre de Bérulle (1575–1629), founder of the Oratory of France, proposed that the ministerial priesthood should be seen above all in relation to the Incarnation. The eternal Word assumed humanity so that there might be a mediator between God and man. Likewise, the priest in a double sense is a continuing mediator between God and man. As described by Nichols: "For, on the one hand, he offers the worship of the faithful to the Father by uniting it with Christ's sacrifice through the Mass. And on the other hand, he acts as God's instrument in the transformation of the world, through evangelising and passing on divine teaching, especially in the direction of souls, and by dispensing the mysteries of Christ's Body and Blood, and administering the other sacraments of the Church."[66] When Vincent de Paul and Jean-Jacques Olier helped to set up the diocesan seminaries in France as called for by the Council of Trent, they took this high doctrine of the priest as a living extension of the ministry of the Word Incarnate as their guiding vision. The priest was thus placed in an exalted, almost mystical position and described as metaphysically equal to or even higher than the angels. His powers to confect the Eucharist and absolve from sin were seen as personal gifts without any source in the Word or community.

After 1848, when the ideas of civil democracy and freedom won the day, the Church looked upon the world, society, and state with distrust. Bishops and priests moved or were moved to the edge of society, "they nourished a theology of the world as sinful, and they turned inward in their theology of the kingdom of God to a spirituality of the soul in prayer."[67] Keeping souls in "the state of grace" became the central task of ministry in an increasingly hostile secular culture. A symbol of this ministerial focus is St. Jean-Marie Vianney, the Curé of Ars, who was beatified in 1905 as a model for diocesan priests. He lived in a rather small rural village, and his preaching and liturgy were admittedly simple and undistinguished. His sanctity, moreover, was found in his personal self-discipline and in his struggle with his own personality and the demonic. In the Curé of Ars the French School produced its most illustrious priestly son. The Church saw him as a beacon for the supernatural in a time of darkness through his long hours of offering forgiveness, spiritual direction, and counsel in the sacrament of penance. As O'Meara observes, "Alone in the confessional he experienced the horizon of the supernatural in life, and he led others to experience, at times dramatically, that power

---

[66] Nichols, *Holy Order*, 112.
[67] O'Meara, *Theology of Ministry*, 125.

at a time when the supernatural was ridiculed as outmoded, replaceable, illusionary."[68]

The first half of the twentieth century witnessed two world wars, the rise of atheistic communist states, and large numbers of people abandoning the practice of the Christian faith, especially in Europe. Three new movements sprang up in response to the new problem of de-Christianization created by growing industrialization and secularization: Catholic Action with its slogan "We shall make our brothers Christian again," the priest-worker movement, and the ecumenical movement. Theologians, at the same time, in seeking to establish common ground for ecumenism, returned to biblical and patristic sources for their discussion of theology, liturgy, and mission.

Catholic theologians at this time described the sacrament of Order as "re-presenting" the unique ministry of Jesus Christ himself. Holy Orders is a visible continuation of the activity of the Word Incarnate, a representation of the threefold office (*munus triplex*) of Christ, which constitutes the main differentiations of his mission as Messiah. Although there can be found hints of such a triplex scheme in the patristic period, its systematic use is a Reformation development. German-speaking Catholic theologians borrowed it from their Lutheran counterparts in the eighteenth century, and John Henry Newman appears to have taken it from Calvin's *Institutes*. Newman applied this threefold analysis both to the Church at large and then quite explicitly to its ministry. Pope Pius XII incorporated it into his two main ecclesiological encyclicals: *Mystici Corporis Christi* of 1943 and *Mediator Dei* of 1947. It was from these encyclicals that it passed into the texts of the Second Vatican Council, to whose theological vision we now turn for a deeper understanding of priestly ministry.[69]

---

[68] Ibid.
[69] Nichols, *Holy Order*, 126–27.

Chapter 3

Consecrated for Mission

By virtue of their consecration, priests are configured to Jesus the good shepherd and are called to imitate and to live out his own pastoral charity.

—Pope John Paul II, *Pastores Dabo Vobis* 22

T he Second Vatican Council from its very inception was conceived as a means and singular opportunity to promote the renewal of the Church through the timely *aggiornamento*, or updating, of her pastoral activities. Unfortunately, there are now some who are all too ready to trivialize the Council's teachings as being just merely "pastoral" and thus by implication not really all that authoritative. It must be recognized, however, that the documents of Vatican II carry the same weight as the teachings and directives of any of the twenty other Ecumenical Councils of the Church. The earlier Councils were called to refute and correct heresies and, therefore, were primarily doctrinal and disciplinary in intent. Vatican II was not convoked in response to any particular heresy. Pope John XXIII, in fact, declared that the task of the Council was not to repeat traditional theology or condemn errors but rather to examine the Church's perennial teaching and to interpret it in contemporary terms.

In the climate of the Cold War between the Western and Soviet blocs and of a growing secularization and de-Christianization of culture and society, witnessed in the definitive decline of the centuries-old reciprocal support between political institutions and the churches, John XXIII believed it was now necessary to specify and distinguish between what belongs to the realm of sacred principles and the perennial gospel, and what changed with the passage of time. . . .We are entering a period that might be called one of universal mission . . . and we need to make our own the admonition of Jesus to recognize the "signs of the times" . . . and to discern amid such great darkness the many indications that give good cause for hope.[1]

The pope formulated the fundamental aim of the Council: to increase Christians' commitment to their faith, "to make more room for charity . . . with clarity of thought and greatness of heart."[2] Giuseppe Alberigo, a historian of Vatican II, summarizes John XXIII's reason and vision for the Council: "The pope wanted a council that would mark the end of an era; a council, that is, that would usher the Church out of the post-Tridentine era, and to a certain extent out of the centuries-old Constantinian phase, into a new phase of witness and proclamation."[3]

According to Archbishop Julian Herranz Casado, President of the Pontifical Council for the Interpretation of Legislative Texts, it is only within the context of Vatican II's consciousness of the need for renewal and evangelization that we can understand the image of the priest intended by the Council with all its theological, spiritual, and disciplinary presuppositions. At a symposium conducted by the Congregation for the Clergy on the thirtieth anniversary of *Presbyterorum Ordinis* he thus stated:

> In effect, in order to return to disclose and sketch today the figure of the priest as understood in Vatican II, it is necessary to reflect on the conciliar theological keys which provide its basis and content. The image of the priest which the Council offers depends strictly upon its fundamental ecclesiological teachings, analogous to the way in which these ecclesiological teachings are found in close relation to its Christological teachings.[4]

[1] *Discorsi Messaggi Colloqui del S. Padre Giovanni XXIII*, 6 vols. (Vatican City: Editrice Vaticana, 1963–67), 1:250, 2:654, 4:868, as cited by Giuseppe Alberigo, *A Brief History of Vatican II*, trans. Matthew Sherry (Maryknoll, NY: Orbis Books, 2006), 2.

[2] *Discorsi Messaggi Colloqui* 1:903 as cited in ibid., 9.

[3] Alberigo, *A Brief History of Vatican II*, 10.

[4] Most Reverend Julian Herranz Casado, "Image of the Priest in the Decree *Presbyterorum Ordinis*: Continuity and Projection Toward the Third Millennium" from the Symposium of the Congregation for the Clergy on the Thirtieth Anniversary of *Presbyterorum Ordinis*, translated from the original Italian by Rev. Christopher J. Schreck and available at the Congregation for Clergy website: http://www.clerus.org/clerus/dati/1998-12/13-6/Herranz_Symposium.rtf.html.

In returning to the doctrinal roots of Vatican II, especially its dogmatic constitutions on the Church (*Lumen Gentium*) and on Divine Revelation (*Dei Verbum*), we begin to see how the Council's teaching on the priesthood finds its source in the Church's mission to evangelize, to proclaim the good news of Christ's self-emptying and reconciling love to the world in word and deed.

The whole Church, consecrated first through baptism, is sent as Christ himself was sent by the Father in the power of the Holy Spirit to continue Jesus' mission and ministry in the world. In his first Holy Thursday Letter to Priests in 1979, Pope John Paul II reflected upon how Vatican II truly deepened the idea of the priesthood by situating it within the office and mission of Jesus Christ himself and within the mission of the whole people of God. He writes:

> If we analyze carefully the conciliar texts, it is obvious that one should speak of a triple dimension of Christ's service and mission, rather than of three different functions. In fact, these functions are closely linked to one another, explain one another, condition one another, and clarify one another. Consequently, it is from this threefold unity that our sharing in Christ's mission and office takes its origin. As Christians, members of the People of God, and subsequently, as priests, sharers in the hierarchical order, we take our origin from the combination of the mission and office of our Teacher, who is Prophet, Priest and King, in order to witness to Him in a special way in the Church and before the world.[5]

This threefold dimension of Christ's mission and office presented in the Vatican II documents moves us beyond the purely "cultic" notion of priesthood. It points as well to the insufficiency of considering in isolation the popular postconciliar image of the priest as "servant-leader."

Within the context of the Church's mission of evangelization the Council declares that "it is the first task of priests as co-workers of the bishops to preach the Gospel to all men" (PO 4). We have seen too in the earliest period of the Church how traveling prophets and teachers had the right to preside at the Eucharist. Defining ordained ministry almost exclusively in terms of preaching became the Protestant option. The Second Vatican Council, however, presents us with the threefold unity of the priestly functions. Perhaps by way of analogy, we might say that just as the tri-unity of Persons in the Holy Trinity has its Source in the Fatherhood of God, so the threefold unity of priestly tasks finds its source in the proclamation

[5] John Paul II, *Letters to My Brother Priests—Holy Thursday (1979–1994)*, 27.

of the Word. Indeed, the life of faith along with all of creation has its beginning in the Word (John 1:1-3). The Word continues to incarnate itself as we likewise give of ourselves to enter ever more deeply into Christ's paschal mystery by means of the sacraments and as we allow this mystery then to transform and rule our lives. Indeed, in Jesus' prayer at the Last Supper before speaking of sending his disciples forth into the world, he prays to the Father, "Consecrate them in the truth. Your word is truth" (John 17:17).

In *Pastores Dabo Vobis* Pope John Paul II reports that the synod Fathers, who met in October 1990 to discuss "The Formation of Priests in the Circumstances of the Present Day," wrote that "The priest's identity, like every Christian identity, has its source in the Blessed Trinity." He then explains that, "It is within the Church's mystery, as a mystery of Trinitarian communion in missionary tension, that every Christian identity is revealed, and likewise the specific identity of the priest and his ministry" (PDV 12). Thus the priesthood can only be rightly understood within the context of Trinitarian communion and of being sent as Christ himself was sent by the Father in the power of the Holy Spirit. The Council's teaching on the priesthood, therefore, both in the Dogmatic Constitution on the Church (LG 28) and in its Decree on the Ministry and Life of Priests (PO 2), begins with the Johannine reference to Jesus as the one "'whom the Father consecrated and sent into the world' (Jn. 10:36)." Consecration is for mission. Hence in this chapter we propose to explore the theological implications of Jesus' being "consecrated" by the Father and what this means for the Christian priesthood, that is, the priesthood of both the baptized and the ordained.

The Christological Context of Consecration

Only in the mystery of the Word made flesh, the mystery of the Incarnation, can we come to a true understanding of Jesus' being consecrated by the Father. "To consecrate" means "to make holy" by setting apart a person or thing for the service of God. At the beginning of his public ministry in the synagogue at Nazareth, Jesus applied the words of the prophet Isaiah to himself: "The Spirit of the Lord is upon me, because he has anointed me to bring glad tidings to the poor" (Luke 4:18). Reflecting upon this passage, Pope John Paul II in *Pastores Dabo Vobis* writes:

> The Spirit is not simply "upon" the Messiah, but he "fills" him, penetrating every part of him and reaching to the very depths of all that

he is and does. Indeed, the Spirit is the principle of the "consecration" and "mission" of the Messiah. . . . Through the Spirit, Jesus belongs totally and exclusively to God and shares in the infinite holiness of God, who calls him, chooses him and sends him forth. (PDV 19)

Patristic theology maintained that the "consecration" of Jesus as high priest took place in the hypostatic union. Indeed, Proclus of Constantinople taught that "God" became "priest" in the temple of the Blessed Virgin (*"O templum, in quo Deus sacerdos effectus est"*).[6] Galot, therefore, states, "For Christ, 'being consecrated' and 'being sent into the world' are the two aspects of the one journey which is the Incarnation, two facets indissolubly linked one to the other."[7]

When in the Creed we profess our faith in "Jesus Christ," God's anointed one, it is important for us to realize that "Christ" is not a proper name but a title, the definition of what this Jesus is. Therefore, Ratzinger states, "with Jesus it is not possible to distinguish office and person. . . . The person *is* the office; the office *is* the person. The two are no longer separable."[8] As a result, there can be no private area reserved for an "I" that remains in the background and at some time or other is "off duty." Thus he adds, "[Jesus] has identified himself so closely with his word that 'I' and word are indistinguishable: he *is* word. In the same way . . . he performs *himself* and gives *himself*; his work is the giving of himself."[9] Furthermore, as the Word-made-flesh sent by the Father, Jesus is consecrated in his relationship of oneness with the Father through the power of the Holy Spirit (see Luke 4:18) in everything he says and does.

In the Gospel according to John, Jesus is referred to as the Word and the Son. Both titles denote a being in relationship. "Word" cannot exist alone by itself; it always comes "from someone else" and is addressed "to someone else."[10] Likewise, for John, "Son" means being from another. In no uncertain terms, Jesus Christ reveals that "God is love" (1 John 4:16); He is the very act of relating or pure relatedness. God is not the lone independent *Esse subsistens* (supreme being) of the philosophers but is rather revealed in Jesus Christ as *Relatio subsistens* (pure relatedness). Saint

---

[6] PG LXV, 683 B cited by Aloys Grillmeier, "Dogmatic Constitution on the Church," Commentary on Chapter III, Article 28, in *Commentary on the Documents of Vatican II*, ed. Herbert Vorgrimler, vol. 1, 220 (New York: Herder and Herder, 1969).

[7] Jean Galot, SJ, *Theology of Priesthood* (San Francisco: Ignatius Press, 1985), 204.

[8] Joseph Cardinal Ratzinger, *Introduction to Christianity* (San Francisco: Ignatius Press, 1990, 2004), 203 with emphasis in the original.

[9] Ibid., 203–4 with emphasis in original.

[10] Ibid., 189.

Augustine thus wrote, "In God there are no accidents, only substance and relation."[11] The "three Persons" in God are constituted as persons by their relationships to one another. In the Trinity relationship is primary; their relationships give each of the Three their identity as Person.

Yet, we need to understand that relation is at the same time pure unity. Again in the words of Joseph Ratzinger:

> Thus in Christianity the profession of faith in the oneness of God is just as radical as in any other monotheistic religion; indeed, only in Christianity does it reach its full stature. But it is the nature of Christian existence to receive and live life as relatedness and, thus, to enter into that unity which is the ground of all reality and sustains it. This will perhaps make it clear how the doctrine of the Trinity, when properly understood, can become the reference point of theology that anchors all other lines of Christian thought.[12]

Perhaps now we can better comprehend why Pope John Paul II maintained that "the specific identity of the priest and his ministry" like that of every Christian identity is revealed "within the Church's mystery, as a mystery of Trinitarian communion in missionary tension . . ."[13] (PDV 12). In a Christian theological context "mission" is a theology of "being as relation" (as is understood from the two divine missions within the Holy Trinity) and of relation itself then as a mode of unity or communion. Jesus said to his disciples, "As the Father has sent me, so I send you" (John 20:21; also 13:20; 17:18). Christian existence as mission is, in Jesus' words here, "expounded as being 'from' and 'for', as relatedness and hence as unity."[14] In other words, Jesus is sent "from" the Father "for" the purpose of calling and sending his disciples so that they in turn might gather all the nations into his Body, the Church, in order that they may be one in him.

Jesus in his human nature, according to patristic theology, was consecrated as high priest by his hypostatic union, his Incarnation. Nonetheless, it is only on the Cross, in his paschal mystery, that the Incarnation reaches its completion, when he fully consecrates himself in the truth of God's

---

[11] See *De Trinitate* 5, 5, 6 (PL 42:913f.).

[12] Ratzinger, *Introduction to Christianity*, 188. The author writes earlier on page 147: "*The philosophical God is essentially self-centered*, thought simply contemplating itself. The God of faith is basically defined by the category of relationship. He is creative fullness encompassing the whole." (Emphasis in original).

[13] Here the word translated from the original Latin into English as "tension" means not stress but more accurately an "inner dynamic thrust."

[14] Ratzinger, *Introduction to Christianity*, 189.

self-emptying (*kenosis*) and reconciling or "in-gathering" love (*agapē*). Therefore, in John's gospel at the Last Supper Jesus prays to the Father, "Consecrate them in the truth. Your word is truth. As you sent me into the world, so I sent them into the world. And I consecrate myself for them, so that they also may be consecrated in truth" (John 17:17-19). The disciples are consecrated in the truth of Jesus Christ's self-giving and reconciling love, which he fully reveals on the Cross. In the gospels it is very clear that truth is not, in the first place, a doctrine or a teaching or a written law, but a person, Jesus Christ himself, who is "the way and the truth and the life" (John 14:6).

While it is indeed all important for us to realize the sacrificial aspect of what Jesus said and did at the Last Supper, it is at the same time truly unfortunate that popular devotions to the Cross often imagine a God who demands human sacrifice, namely, the sacrifice of his own Son to satisfy his unrelenting righteousness. Ratzinger contends, "This picture is as false as it is widespread." He then adds that "in the Bible the Cross . . . is the expression of the radical nature of the love that gives itself completely . . . the expression of a life that is completely being for others."[15] That is why the formula of consecration at the Eucharist invokes Jesus' words over the bread and wine at the Last Supper: "This is my body, which will be given *for* you" and "This cup is the new covenant in my blood, which will be shed *for* you" (Luke 22:19-20 with emphasis added). Here what Ratzinger has called the principle of the "for" takes center stage.[16] Rather than *giving up* his life as the price for our salvation, the true sacrificial meaning of the Cross is Jesus' *giving* himself to his friends so that they may live.[17]

In its Christological context "consecration" means being incorporated into Jesus Christ by sharing in his paschal mystery; it means entering into a covenantal relationship of love, the new covenant in his blood sealed by the Spirit. In Sacred Scripture "covenant" is a ritual agreement, a relational bond of fidelity and love (*hesed* in Hebrew), which may be violated but can never be broken. The marriage bond itself is seen as such a covenant. For this reason the spousal image of Christ as the Bridegroom is often found in the New Testament to portray this enduring intimate relationship. Bernard Cooke writes, "Paul, in Ephesians, is not speaking, then,

---

[15] Ibid., 282.

[16] Ibid., 251–54.

[17] Bernard Cooke, *Ministry to Word and Sacraments: History and Theology* (Philadelphia: Fortress Press, 1976), 637.

in metaphor when he describes Jesus' death and resurrection as a marital giving of self."[18] He further explains:

> In thus giving life and sonship by giving himself, the risen Christ sacramentalizes the Father's own life-giving love and so bears witness to the Father. Christ's transforming gift of self to others is his worship service of his Father; the heavenly nuptials of the Lamb, the risen Christ's self-giving to men and women, constitute the heavenly liturgy.
>
> Jesus' priestly act of sacrifice, precisely because it is constituted by his dynamic relationship to others, is formative of community. This is by no means an incidental by-product. . . . Divine-human community is the goal that finalizes the Incarnation itself, the mission of Jesus, and therefore his priesthood.[19]

God the Father "consecrated and sent" Jesus as high priest of the new and eternal covenant in order to reconcile the world to himself (see 2 Cor 5:19) and to make his Body the Church, in St. Cyprian's words, "a people brought into unity from the unity of the Father, the Son, and the Holy Spirit."[20] Accordingly, Pope Benedict XVI, in speaking of the sacramental "mysticism" of the Eucharist, writes in his first encyclical *Deus Caritas Est*: "I cannot possess Christ just for myself; I can belong to him only in union with all those who have become, or who will become, his own. Communion draws me out of myself towards him, and thus also towards unity with all Christians" (DCE 14).

The Royal Priesthood of Believers

All Christians are consecrated and made sharers in Christ's priesthood through the sacraments of baptism and confirmation. The Second Vatican Council's Dogmatic Constitution on the Church teaches that "the baptized, by regeneration and the anointing of the Holy Spirit are consecrated to be a spiritual house and a holy priesthood"; and it clarifies that "though they differ essentially and not only in degree, the common priesthood of the faithful and the ministerial priesthood or hierarchical priesthood are none the less ordered to one another; each in its own proper way shares

---

[18] Ibid., 638.
[19] Ibid.
[20] *De Orat. Dom.* 23: PL 4, 553 as cited in *Lumen Gentium* 4.

in the one priesthood of Christ" (LG 10). Accordingly, *Presbyterorum Ordinis*, immediately after recalling Jesus' consecration and mission from the Father, states that Jesus "makes his whole Mystical Body sharer in the anointing of the Spirit," and it adds that "all the faithful are made a holy and kingly priesthood, they offer spiritual sacrifices to God through Jesus Christ, and they proclaim the virtues of him who has called them out of darkness into his admirable light" (PO 2). In this way the decree sets the stage for its teaching on the ministerial priesthood, which is conferred by its own particular sacrament and gives "the sacred power of Order."

While St. Thomas Aquinas recognized the common priesthood of all the baptized,[21] he saw it as being passive or receptive in nature as compared to the ordained priesthood, which was active in its orientation. The latter for him "is the power of *giving* rather than simply *receiving* sacraments."[22] Vatican II, however, moves beyond St. Thomas's concept of the common priesthood by seeing it too as having an active orientation. *Lumen Gentium* teaches that "the faithful who by Baptism are incorporated into Christ . . . in their own way share the priestly, prophetic and kingly office of Christ, and to the best of their ability carry on the mission of the whole Christian people in the Church and in the world" (LG 31). In succeeding paragraphs the document summarizes the ways in which the laity participate in Jesus Christ's threefold office of priest (LG 34), prophet (LG 35), and king (LG 36). Earlier it defined the special vocation of the laity as "to seek the kingdom of God by engaging in temporal affairs and directing them to God's will" (LG 31).

All the faithful share in Christ's royal priesthood by seeking first the kingdom of God and directing temporal affairs in accord with God's will. In the biblical perspective, as we have already seen in chapter 1, such a royal priesthood is ontological in nature and not merely functional. Accordingly, Pope John Paul II wrote in *Pastores Dabo Vobis* that "the new priestly people which is the church not only has its authentic image in Christ, but also receives from him a real ontological share in his one eternal priesthood, to which she must conform every aspect of her life" (PDV 13). Through the sacraments of baptism and confirmation the Christian becomes one with Jesus Christ in his mission to establish the kingdom of his Father. This transformation of the person "in Christ" constitutes a consecration of the most ultimate sort, so that the Christian can say with St. Paul, "yet I live, no longer I, but Christ lives in me" (Gal 2:20).

---

[21] See *Summa Theologiae* 3, q. 63, aa. 3–6.
[22] Cooke, *Ministry to Word and Sacraments*, 592 with footnote reference to ibid., a. 6.

Lumen Gentium in its fifth chapter outlines the call of the whole Church to holiness, emphasizing that the fullness of Christian life is the vocation of all the baptized and not just of priests and consecrated religious. The Council thus corrected a centuries-long misconception when it declared that Christ "loved the Church as his Bride, giving himself up for her so as to sanctify her (cf. Eph. 5:25-26). . . . Therefore all in the Church, whether they belong to the hierarchy or are cared for by it, are called to holiness, according to the apostle's saying: 'For this is the will of God, your sanctification' (1 Th. 4:3; cf. Eph. 1:4)" (LG 39). The Council proceeded then to define holiness as the "perfection of love" and recommended the practice of the evangelical counsels, which have traditionally been "undertaken by many Christians whether privately or in a form or state sanctioned by the Church . . . [as] a striking witness and example of that holiness" (LG 39).

Saint Paul in like manner invited Christians "to offer [their] bodies as a living sacrifice, holy and pleasing to God, your spiritual worship (*logike latreia*)" (Rom 12:1). Origen gave a remarkable commentary on this passage when he wrote:

> All those who have received the anointing have become priests. Each one carries his sacrifice within himself, and he himself puts the fire on the altar, so that he becomes an endless sacrifice. If I renounce everything I own, if I carry my cross and follow Christ, I have made an offering on God's altar. If I deliver my body . . . and pursue the glory of martyrdom, I have offered a sacrifice on God's altar, and I become the priest of my own sacrifice.[23]

Pope John Paul II reflects on this same scriptural passage from St. Paul when he writes in his apostolic exhortation *Christifideles Laici*:

> The lay faithful are sharers in the *priestly mission*, for which Jesus offered himself on the cross and continues to be offered in the celebration of the Eucharist for the glory of God and the salvation of humanity. Incorporated in Jesus Christ, the baptized are united to him and to his sacrifice in the offering they make of themselves and their daily activities. (CL 14)[24]

---

[23] *In Leviticum, homilia IX*, 9, PG 12:522-523, as cited in Paul Evdokimov, *Woman and the Salvation of the World*, trans. Anthony P. Gytheil (Crestwood, NY: St. Vladimir's Seminary Press, 1994), 109.

[24] *Christifideles Laici* 14.5 with emphasis in original and reference to Rom 12:1-2.

He further states that "The participation of the lay faithful in the threefold mission of Christ as Priest, Prophet, and King finds its source in the anointing of Baptism, its further development in Confirmation and its realization and dynamic sustenance in the Holy Eucharist" (CL 14).

The Meaning of the Sacramental Priestly Character

The Council of Trent taught, "in three sacraments, namely, baptism, confirmation, and order, there is . . . imprinted on the soul a character, that is, a certain spiritual and indelible mark, by reason of which they cannot be repeated" (DS 1609).[25] This teaching on the sacramental "character" of Holy Orders has implicit biblical foundations, is referred to by the early Church Fathers, and is explicitly put forward by St. Augustine in his clarification of the Church's theology of the sacraments, especially in his response to the Donatist heresy. Galot writes, "In his considerations, Augustine strongly emphasizes the parallel between baptism and ordination: both the 'sacrament of baptism' and the 'sacrament of the administration of baptism' are consecrations. The difference that some seek to posit between the value of the baptismal character and of the priestly character is manifestly contrary to the doctrine of Augustine."[26] Furthermore, Augustine argued that since the baptized or the ordained person has the "sacrament," injury would be done "to the sacrament" if baptism and ordination were repeated. This unrepeatability results from the character; it is not, however, its foundation.[27]

Martin Luther held that a priest who never preaches the Word of God has stopped functioning and thereby ceases to be a priest. The idea of an indelible character for him was a human invention lacking scriptural basis. Luther did not consider ordination to be a sacrament but simply an ecclesiastical ceremony, something like the blessing of vessels for Holy Communion.[28] In the period immediately after the Second Vatican Council some Catholic authors, in an endeavor to advance ecumenical relations, began to question the Council of Trent's intention in its teaching on the permanence of priestly ordination. They proposed that Trent did not mean

---

[25] Session 7, *Decree Concerning the Sacraments in General*, canon 7.

[26] Galot, *Theology of the Priesthood*, 199.

[27] See ibid., 200.

[28] See Aidan Nichols, *Holy Order: The Apostolic Ministry from the New Testament to the Second Vatican Council* (Lancaster, PA: Veritas Press, 1991), 91.

to impose a definition of faith but was merely stating the common teaching presented by contemporary Scholastic theologians.[29] As a result they concurred with the Reformation hermeneutics that ordination imparts only a "functional specialization" within the baptismal mission of all Christians. Priestly ministry thus should be considered simply a profession like that of a physician, lawyer, engineer, or plumber. If we are to speak of a sacramental character, in their perspective it simply denotes a capacity to exercise a function within the Christian community and lacks any ontological value.

From the conciliar debates that disclose the intention of the Council of Trent, it is evident that the Fathers meant to condemn the denial of the sacramental character in the case of baptism, confirmation, and Order as heretical.[30] The Middle Ages had known a variety of opinions on the nature of sacramental character, but the Council, wanting to avoid theological speculation, did not endorse any particular Scholastic opinion. Indeed, St. Thomas Aquinas's theory, which limits sacramental character to cultic empowerment and which had won such great prominence before and after the Council, was never officially sanctioned by the conciliar Fathers. Trent in fact restricted itself to the basic affirmation of a spiritual and indelible mark without intending to determine more precisely the nature of this mark.

The Second Vatican Council clearly reaffirmed the Church's traditional teaching when it stated that through the sacrament of Holy Orders "priests by the anointing of the Holy Spirit are signed with a special character [*speciali charactere signantur*] and so are configured to Christ the priest in such a way that they are able to act in the person of Christ the head [*in persona Christi capitis*]" (PO 2). Vatican II deliberately chose not to use the term "another Christ" (*alter Christus*) in referring to the priest, but rather selected the phrase "in the person of Christ" (*in persona Christi*). In a very real sense every Christian by baptism can be understood to be *alter Christus*. Pope John Paul II points this out explicitly when in *Christifideles Laici* he

[29] See, for example, Edward Schillebeeckx, OP, *Ministry: Leadership in the Community of Jesus Christ* (New York: Crossroad, 1981), 149n13; Hervé-Marie Legrand, OP, "The Presidency of the Eucharist according to Ancient Tradition," *Worship* 53 (1979): 431; André Lemaire, *Ministry in the Church* (London: SPCK, 1977), 118.

[30] See Galot, *Theology of Priesthood*, 127, and 127n12 for further explanation. It should also be noted that amid the controversy swirling among some theological circles immediately after Vatican II questioning the nature of the Church's teaching on sacramental character, the 1971 Synod of Bishops in its document *Ultimis Temporibus: The Ministerial Priesthood and Justice in the World* explicitly affirmed that "this is a doctrine of faith" (UT, I, 5).

cites the words of St. Augustine speaking to the baptized: "Let us rejoice and give thanks: we have not only become Christians, but Christ himself . . . Stand in awe and rejoice: we have become Christ!" (CL 17; cited again in *Veritatis Splendor* 21).

By choosing to use the phrase *in persona Christi capitis* the Council Fathers wished to recognize that while every Christian becomes a member of the Body of Christ through baptism and confirmation, the priest sacramentally represents Christ the head. This constitutes a genuine doctrinal development in the Church's thinking on this matter.[31] Galot thus explains, "For the sake of precision, note that the priestly character is not added to the other two. It deepens the mark already there by imprinting upon the self the project of a priestly life that is to come to fruition with the help of graces conferred during the exercise of the ministry. It impresses upon the being of the baptized person an orientation which commits the whole self to the mission of the priest."[32] He further adds, "What distinguishes the priestly character from the character impressed by baptism and confirmation is that a man's being is conformed to Christ the Shepherd. The image of the good shepherd is impressed on the soul of the ordained person as a principle and basic blueprint of the ministry to be carried out."[33] This pastoral power, which configures the priest to Christ the Shepherd, can only be legitimately exercised in love and service. Exercised in any other way, it would no longer be exercised in the name of Christ.

Historically, what the Church came to call a permanent sacramental character has its roots in the New Testament. Saint Paul writes to Timothy reminding him "to stir into flame the gift of God that you have through the imposition of my hands" (2 Tim 1:6; also 1 Tim 4:14). The transforming gift of the Spirit that Timothy received at his ordination is without doubt seen by Paul to be a perduring reality. Earlier Paul, alluding to Christian initiation, spoke of those who have been marked with a seal (2 Cor 1:22; Eph 1:13; 4:30). For the baptized this mark (*sphragis*) signifies that they belong to God. It is a distinguishing mark, which on the day of judgment gives them access to eternal salvation. Christ is the first to carry a character, a seal, or a *sphragis*. In the Bread of Life Discourse in John's gospel, Jesus tells the crowd to work for "the food that endures for eternal life, which the Son of Man will give you. For on him the Father, God, has set his seal" (John 6:27). Only in Hebrews 1:3 might we find the actual word

---

[31] See David L. Toups, *Reclaiming Our Priestly Character* (Omaha, NE: IPF Publications, 2008), 69n115.

[32] Galot, *Theology of Priesthood*, 201.

[33] Ibid., 207.

"character," where it is employed in reference to God's relationship to a son, "who is the refulgence of his glory, the very imprint [*charaktēr*] of his being."

The Church Fathers speak of a spiritual *sphragis*, an invisible reality, by which God recognizes those who have become his very own. Patristic writings in the fourth century refer to it as being indestructible. Cyril of Alexandria talks of baptism producing the "ineffaceable '*sphragis*' of the Holy Spirit." John Chrysostom invokes the example of the material *sphragis* branded on a soldier, which remains even should he become a deserter.[34] The mark then is seen as something different than sanctifying grace. Gregory of Nyssa went so far as to compare the "transformation" brought about in the soul of a priest to what takes place in the eucharistic species at the moment of consecration.[35] "But when Augustine wishes to designate directly and in non-metaphorical language the seal thus imprinted, he prefers the term 'sacrament.' He means thereby the permanent element that lasts unimpaired even in the wicked and cannot be lost, not even by people who sever themselves from the unity of the Church."[36]

At the end of the twelfth century, theology set out to develop in a systematic way the notion of character. Saint Thomas Aquinas maintained that in the priestly character the sacramental character attains its highest expression, because even in baptism and confirmation the character is by its very essence a conformity to the priesthood of Christ. For him, sacramental character of its very nature is ordered to divine worship in this life and the next; it is a *deputatio ad cultum divinum* to receive (in the case of the baptized) or to act (in the case of the ordained) in the sacramental life of the Church.[37] Galot adds, "The priestly character is character in the highest degree, in its most complete realization, the most intense participation in the priesthood of Christ."[38] The Council of Trent, as already mentioned above, did not endorse this Thomistic viewpoint per se.

Vatican II in a true doctrinal development took a different approach than Aquinas and the Scholastics. First of all, Cardinal Dulles observes:

---

[34] See Jean Galot, SJ, *La nature du caractère sacramental: étude de théologie médiévale* (Paris-Louvain: Desclée de Brouwer, 1958), 35.

[35] J.-M. Garrigues, J.-J. Le Guillous, and A. Riou, "Le caractère sacerdotale dans la tradition des pères grecs," *Nouvelle revue théologique* 93 (1971): 809.

[36] Galot, *Theology of Priesthood*, 199.

[37] See ST III, q. 63, a. 1.

[38] Galot, *Theology of Priesthood*, 201.

The council refuses to attribute a higher grade or degree to the ministerial, as though the common priesthood ranked lower than it on the same scale. Instead, it situates the two kinds of priesthood in different categories, like oranges and apples. The ministerial priesthood involves a public representational function rather than a personal giftedness. If anything, the common priesthood is more exalted, for the ministers are ordained for the sake of service toward the whole people of God.[39]

Secondly, the sacramental character of the ministerial priesthood configures one to Jesus Christ as "head" of his Body, the Church. This is a further specification of the character imprinted by baptism and confirmation, which "differ essentially and not only in degree" (LG 10). The different essence of the ministerial priesthood is that it exists in order to serve the common priesthood of all the faithful. As Pope John Paul II would later write in *Pastores Dabo Vobis*, "Jesus Christ is the head of the church, his body. He is the 'head' in the new and unique sense of being a 'servant.' . . . Jesus' service attains its fullest expression in his death on the cross, that is, in his total gift of self in humility and love" (PDV 21).

Explaining the Second Vatican Council's perspective on the nature of the sacramental priestly character, the then-Cardinal Joseph Ratzinger stated: "What we may see as being new, by contrast with Trent, is the marked insistence on interrelations in the Church and on the communal journey of the whole Church, in the context of which this classic vision is set."[40] He then develops St. Augustine's image of the priest as *servus Dei* or *servus Christi*, which has its source in the hymn to Christ found in Philippians 2:5-11: Christ, the Son who is equal to God, took on the form of a servant and became a servant for us. Ratzinger adds:

What is important for our question is that the concept of *servant* refers to a relationship. Someone is a servant in relation to someone else. If the priest is defined as being a servant of Jesus Christ, this means that his life is substantially determined in terms of a relationship: being oriented towards his Lord as servant constitutes the essence of his office, which thus extends to his very being. . . . Belonging to the Lord who became a servant is belonging for the sake of those who are his. . . . If "character" is thus the expression of a fellowship of service,

[39] Avery Dulles, SJ, *The Priestly Office: A Theological Reflection* (New York/Mahwah, NJ: Paulist Press, 1997), 11.
[40] Joseph Cardinal Ratzinger, "The Ministry and Life of Priests," *Pilgrim Fellowship of Faith* (San Francisco: Ignatius Press, 2005), 157.

then, on the one hand, it shows how ultimately the Lord himself is always acting and how, on the other hand, in the visible Church he nonetheless acts through men.[41]

Furthermore, when priesthood is thus viewed within this Christological and ecclesial context, we also must recognize its essential Trinitarian character, since "the Son is in his nature coming from the Father and going toward him. He shares himself in the Holy Spirit, who is Love—and therefore giving—in person."[42]

If baptism marks a person's transformation or adoption as a child of God and incorporation into the Body of Christ, then ordination marks a baptized man's configuration to Christ as head and shepherd of the Church through his incorporation into the presbyteral order, which is the continuing sacramental enfleshment of the one priesthood of Jesus Christ. Both sacraments mark a new creation, a new belonging to God "in Christ." In his Chrism Mass homily on Holy Thursday 2007, Pope Benedict XVI stated, "With regard to what happens in Baptism, St. Paul explicitly uses the image of clothing . . . we put on Christ, he gives us his garments and these are not something external. It means that we enter into an existential communion with him, that his being and our being merge, penetrate one another." He then adds, "This theology of Baptism returns in a new way and with a new insistence in priestly Ordination. . . . *In persona Christi*: at the moment of priestly Ordination, the Church has also made this reality of 'new clothes' visible and comprehensible to us externally through being clothed in liturgical vestments. In this external gesture she wants to make the interior event visible to us, as well as our task which stems from it: putting on Christ; giving ourselves to him as he gave himself to us."[43]

The permanent sacramental mark imprinted on the soul by baptism/confirmation and ordination designate a new existential relationship, a belonging to a new corporate reality (the Body of Christ/the Church and the one priesthood of Jesus Christ/the priestly Order, respectively) by a spiritual bond that can never be broken. Thus Pope John Paul II wrote, "The ordained ministry has a radical 'communitarian form' and can only be carried out as 'a collective work'" (PDV 17). The priestly sacramental mark constitutes a covenantal relationship, a covenant of friendship based

[41] Ibid., 162–63.

[42] Ibid., 165.

[43] Benedict XVI, Chrism Mass Homily on April 5, 2007; text available on Vatican web site: http://www.vatican.va/holy_father/benedict_xvi/homilies/2007/documents/hf_ben-xvi_hom_20070405_messa-crismale_en.html.

on Christ's irrevocable call and promise, which he made within the context of the Last Supper: "I have called you friends, because I have told you everything I have heard from my Father. It was not you who chose me, but I who chose you and appointed you to go and bear fruit that will remain, so that whatever you ask the Father in my name he may give you. This I command you: love one another" (John 15:15b-17).

In his 2006 Chrism Mass homily Pope Benedict XVI stated, "I no longer call you servants but friends: in these words one could actually perceive the institution of the priesthood. The Lord makes us his friends; he entrusts everything to us; he entrusts himself to us, so that we can speak . . . *in persona Christi capitis*." Expanding upon this fundamental relational dynamic of priestly ministry, he adds, "Being friends with Jesus is par excellence always friendship with his followers. We can be friends of Jesus only in communion with the whole Christ, with the Head and with the Body; in the vigorous vine of the Church to which the Lord gives life." That Pope Benedict XVI clearly meant to describe the nature of the permanent sacramental mark of priesthood here is evident, when he continued, "The core of the priesthood is being friends of Jesus Christ. Only in this way can we truly speak *in persona Christi*, even if our inner remoteness from Christ cannot jeopardize the validity of the Sacrament."[44]

While the Council of Trent did not subscribe to any particular theological interpretation when it defended the existence of the sacramental character, Vatican II—as well as Pope John Paul II and Pope Benedict XVI afterward—have expounded upon its essentially relational nature. When one ceases to treat it in theological isolation but rather places sacramental character within its proper Trinitarian, Christological, and ecclesial context, it is seen as irrevocably marking or sealing one's "belonging to" and "existing for" other persons, divine and human. We might better understand how this is so when we consider, first of all, the reality of the sacramental character as described by Jean Galot, SJ:

> We are dealing with a real mark which perdures in the soul. It is not a "thing," which is the reason why the charge of "reification" [for example, by Schillebeeckx] is pointless. A thing is something separate, whereas a mark is impressed on the soul, is for this very reason inseparable from it, and together with it constitutes one reality. And yet, although it is not a "thing," the character is real. It is a mark that

[44] Benedict XVI, Chrism Mass Homily on April 13, 2006; text available on Vatican web site: http://www.vatican.va/holy_father/benedict_xvi/homilies/2006/documents/hf_ben-xvi_hom_20060413_messa-crismale_en.html.

has been really effected and brings about a genuine change in the personal self.[45]

Secondly, describing eternal life and the soul, Ratzinger has written:

Immortality does not inhere in a human being but rests on a relation, on a *relationship*, with what is eternal, what makes eternity meaningful. This abidingness, which gives life and can fulfil it, is truth. It is also love. Man can therefore live forever, because he is able to have a relationship with that which gives the eternal. "The soul" is our term for that in us which offers a foothold for this relation. Soul is nothing other than man's capacity for relatedness with truth, with eternal love.[46]

In this theological context we can see how sacramental character marks or seals one in a new transformative and eternal relationship with truth and love—the Trinitarian missions of the Word and Spirit. It is an unbreakable bond constituted by divine initiative as an irrevocable call or vocation. Trying to describe this spiritual reality, the Roman Catholic tradition over the centuries has employed the term "character." Jesus himself in referring to this reality preferred to speak in terms of covenant and friendship and often employed spousal imagery.

Writing from an Eastern Orthodox perspective, Alexander Schmemann also focuses on the essential relational nature of priesthood when he states that "the sacrament of ordination is, in a sense, identical with the sacrament of matrimony."[47] He proceeds to explain, "It is not 'priesthood' that the priest receives in his ordination, but the gift of Christ's love, that love which made Christ the only priest. . . . The priest is indeed married to the Church . . . it is this marriage of the priest with the Church that makes him really *priest*, the true minister of that Love which alone transforms the world and reveals the Church as the immaculate bride of Christ."[48] Metropolitan John Zizioulas also, writing from the context of the Greek patristic tradition, states, "If ordination is understood as constitutive of the community and if the community being the koinonia of the Spirit is by its nature a *relational entity*, ministry *as a whole* can be describable as a

---

[45] Ibid., 197–98.

[46] Joseph Ratzinger, *Eschatology: Death and Eternal Life*, trans. Michael Waldstein (Washington, DC: Catholic University of America Press, 1988), 259 (italics in original).

[47] Alexander Schmemann, *For the Life of the World: Sacraments and Orthodoxy* (Crestwood, NY: St. Vladimir's Seminary Press, 1973), 94 with emphasis in original.

[48] Ibid.

complexity of relationships within the Church and in its relation to the world."[49]

Zizioulas, moreover, considers problematic the Scholastic theology of ministry and ordination, which tends to approach both realities "as *autonomous* subjects: they are treated quite apart from Christology or Trinitarian theology."[50] And for him employing the term "relationship" to describe the nature of ministry in no way treats *relatio* as simply an abstract or logical term, but rather comprehends it as having a "deeply ontological and soteriological meaning."[51] Zizioulas, moreover, points to concrete evidence of the fundamental relational nature of priesthood found in the ancient tradition common to both the East and the West, which held that all ordinations must take place within the eucharistic assembly, as is clearly stated in the *Apostolic Tradition* of Hippolytus. In addition, the canonical provisions of the early Church against "absolute ordinations," such as canon 6 of Chalcedon, demonstrate that ordinations must be related to a concrete community.[52] The longstanding practice of the Church assigning "titular bishops" to a no longer existing see has deep ecclesiological implications: "it becomes clear that a bishop is not *first* ordained as a bishop of the universal Church and *then* 'assigned' to a place within it, but he is a bishop of the universal Church only in and by becoming a bishop of a concrete community."[53]

Ordination, consequently, can rightly be seen as placing the office bearer in a twofold representative relationship. *In persona Christi* the priest represents the head of the Church, and *in persona ecclesiae* he represents the Body of Christ, the Church, built up and filled by the Holy Spirit. Care needs to be taken, however, when we use the notion of "representation" since it is a term more commonly understood as meaning the mere substitution of one person for another. Thus Cardinal Dulles writes, "In theology, however, the idea of representation is not juridical but organic. The priest is configured to Christ in order that Christ may act in him as an instrument."[54] Archbishop Daniel Pilarczyk at the 1990 Synod of Bishops linked this twofold representation to the indelible sacramental character when he wrote: "The priest [i.e., presbyter] is a member of the Christian

---

[49] John D. Zizioulas, *Being as Communion: Studies in Personhood and Church* (Crestwood, NY: St. Vladimir's Seminary Press, 1985), 220 with emphasis in original.

[50] Ibid., 209.

[51] Ibid., 220.

[52] Ibid., 212–13.

[53] Ibid., 239n92 with emphasis in original.

[54] Dulles, *The Priestly Office*, 14.

faithful who has been permanently configured by Christ through holy orders to serve the Church, in collaboration with the local bishop, as representative and agent of Christ, the head of the Church, and therefore as representative and agent of the Church community before God and the world."[55]

Because the priest by his ordination becomes sacramentally one with Christ as head and shepherd of the Church, he is Christ's representative. It is apparent that Jesus clearly intended this when he instructed the apostles: "Whoever receives you receives me, and whoever receives me receives the one who sent me" (Matt 10:40). Saint Paul demonstrates this same understanding of his apostolic ministry when he writes, "So we are ambassadors for Christ, as if God were appealing through us. We implore you on behalf of Christ, be reconciled to God" (2 Cor 5:20).

Yet at the same time it is in accord with the oldest tradition of the Church that "the priest is not only an instrument of the risen Lord but also an organ of the community: because the word he proclaims is the faith of the Church."[56] As Gisbert Greshake further explains, "The sacraments which the priest celebrates are not only the sacraments of Christ but also celebrations of the community which are only valid if the office-bearer has the intention 'of doing what the *Church* does.' And up to the high Middle Ages it was taken for granted that the entire priestly Church offers the eucharistic sacrifice through the priest—not that the priest alone celebrates the Eucharist for the community in virtue of a commission from Christ."[57]

Configuration to Christ: The Vocation to Holiness

When addressing the priest's "specific" vocation to holiness, Pope John Paul II in *Pastores Dabo Vobis* recalls the celebrated words of St. Augustine: "For you I am a bishop, with you I am a Christian. The former title speaks of a task undertaken, the latter of grace; the former betokens danger, the latter salvation" (PDV 20).[58] The pope accordingly begins his treatment of priestly holiness by describing first the common baptismal vocation of all the faithful. Referring to Jesus' citing the prophet Isaiah in Luke 4:18, John Paul II continues, "This same 'Spirit of the Lord' is 'upon' the entire

---

[55] Daniel Pilarczyk, "Defining the Priesthood," *Origins* 20 (October 18, 1990): 297–300, at 299 as cited in ibid.

[56] Gisbert Greshake, *The Meaning of Christian Priesthood* (Dublin: Four Courts Press; Westminister, MD: Christian Classics, 1988), 77.

[57] Ibid., with emphasis in original.

[58] With footnote reference to St. Augustine, *Sermo* 340, 1: PL 38:1483.

People of God, which becomes established as a people 'consecrated' to God and 'sent' by God to announce the Gospel of salvation." He then adds, "the apostle Paul reminds us that a Christian life is a 'spiritual life,' that is, a life enlivened and led by the Spirit toward holiness or the perfection of charity" (PDV 19).

The priest's vocation to holiness has its foundational source in his baptismal vocation. Pope John Paul II then lists those aspects that constitute the "specific quality" of the priest's spiritual life:

> These are elements connected with the priest's "consecration," which configures him to Christ the head and shepherd of the Church, with the "mission" or ministry peculiar to the priest; which equips and obliges him to be a "living instrument of Christ the eternal priest" and to act "in the name and in the person of Christ himself" and with his entire "life," called to manifest and witness in a fundamental way the "radicalism of the Gospel." (PDV 20)[59]

While the Second Vatican Council teaches that all Christians through their baptismal vocation are called to embrace the radicalism of the Gospel by practicing the evangelical counsels according to their own state in life, and thereby "tend to the perfection of love" (LG 39), priests, in addition, are called still more specifically to the perfection of "pastoral charity" (PO 14).

The priest's configuration to Christ as head and shepherd finds its concrete manifestation in his continual practice of pastoral charity. Pope John Paul II thus explains:

> The essential content of this pastoral charity is the gift of self, the total gift of self to the Church, following the example of Christ. "Pastoral charity is the virtue by which we imitate Christ in his self-giving and service. It is not just what we do, but our gift of self, which manifests Christ's love for his flock. Pastoral charity determines our way of thinking and acting, our way of relating to people. It makes special demands on us." (PDV 23)

In the total gift of himself to the Church through his growth in pastoral charity, the priest bears witness to and strengthens his "consecration," and thus becomes "the living image of Jesus Christ, the spouse of the Church" (PDV 22).

---

[59] With footnote reference to 1990 Synod of Bishops "Proposition 8."

Vatican II, furthermore, teaches that "pastoral charity is derived chiefly from the eucharistic sacrifice which is the center and source of the entire life of the priest" (PO 14). The rite of ordination, accordingly, gives the priest the invitation and admonition: "Live the mystery that has been placed in your hands!" Through their practice of pastoral charity priests thereby come to live Christ's "Paschal Mystery in such a way that they will know how to initiate into it the people committed to their charge" (OT 8). It is, therefore, very clear that an intimate bond exists between the priest's spiritual life and the exercise of his ministry. Consecration is for mission, and only by faithfully carrying out that mission is the priest perfected in holiness.

In the priest's spiritual life, prayer and ministry are intimately connected; they are, as it were, two sides of one coin. Indeed, the Second Vatican Council, when speaking of the spiritual formation of future priests, states, "The exercises of piety which are commended by the venerable practice of the Church should be strongly encouraged, but care must be taken that spiritual formation does not consist in these alone, nor develop religious sentiment, merely" (OT 8). The Council thus explains that seminarians should learn to live according to the standard of the Gospel and be firmly established in faith, hope, and charity, while allowing these to lead them to a spirit of prayer, the cultivation of other virtues, and to a zeal for the Church's mission of evangelization. Pope Benedict XVI, in his prepared text for the priests and deacons in Freising, stated that "generous self-giving to others is impossible without discipline and constant recovery of true faith-filled interiority. The effectiveness of pastoral action depends, ultimately, upon prayer; otherwise, service becomes empty activism."[60]

The gospels tell us that Martha and Mary are sisters (Luke 10:38-42). In the spiritual life sisters symbolize side-by-side realities that are meant to be together. Pastoral activity and prayer, in the same vein, may rightly be called "sisters"; they are interconnected realities that are meant to be together. Mary chose "the better part," namely, communion with God in and through Jesus Christ, which is "the one thing necessary" for effective discipleship and ministry. Pope John Paul II affirms this same underlying spiritual dynamic when he writes in *Pastores Dabo Vobis*, "Thanks to the insightful teaching of the Second Vatican Council, we can grasp the conditions and demands, the manifestations and fruits of the intimate bond

---

[60] Benedict XVI, "It Is All About Being With Christ," Pope's Prepared Text for Clergy of Freising (Date: 2006-09-14), Vatican translation of the address Benedict XVI prepared, but did not deliver, posted at Zenit.org.

between the priest's spiritual life and the exercise of his threefold ministry of word, sacrament and pastoral charity" (PDV 26).

The priest, first of all, as minister of the word of God must "abide" in the Word, Pope John Paul II explains, "such that his words and his choices and attitudes may become ever more a reflection, a proclamation and a witness to the Gospel" (PDV 26). Careful and prayerful preparation for the ministry of proclaiming the Word, as well as the actual ministry of preaching and teaching itself, can cause the word of God to abide ever more deeply in the minister's own heart. When the priest personally enters into the celebration of the sacraments, especially the Eucharist, by actually praying the words—by making them his own prayer and not just "saying" them—he grows in oneness with Christ who is acting through him, and the people readily recognize it. John Paul II thus states, "It is above all in the celebration of the sacraments and in the celebration of the Liturgy of the Hours that the priest is called to live and witness to the deep unity between the exercise of his ministry and his spiritual life" (PDV 26).

Finally, as the priest strives to encourage and lead the ecclesial community with "the authority of Jesus Christ as head" which "coincides then with his service, with his gift, with his total, humble and loving dedication on behalf of the Church" (PDV 21), he in turn grows more and more in those qualities and virtues that configure him to Christ, the Good Shepherd: "qualities and virtues such as faithfulness, integrity, consistency, wisdom, a welcoming spirit, friendliness, goodness of heart, decisive firmness in essentials, freedom from overly subjective viewpoints, personal disinterestedness, patience, an enthusiasm for daily tasks, confidence in the value of the hidden workings of grace as manifested in the simple and the poor (cf. Ti. 1:7-8)." Pope John Paul II prefaces this list of pastoral qualities by stating, "This ministry demands of the priest an intense spiritual life" (PDV 26). Consequently, serving God's people in a Christ-like way both flows from and at the same time nourishes the priest's communion with Christ. The spirituality of the diocesan priest is in reality found amid the interaction between priest and people.

The Eucharist is the central act of Christian worship. *Pastores Dabo Vobis* accordingly states, "The high point of Christian prayer is the Eucharist, which in its turn is to be seen as the 'summit and source' of the sacraments and the Liturgy of the Hours" (PDV 48). Through the liturgy we are inserted in a living way into the paschal mystery of Jesus Christ. The Eucharist is indeed the central act of worship and the central act of priestly ministry, but it can never be rightly separated from the rest of ministry to which the priest is called. Most of all, we must never look upon eucharistic spirituality as a private matter between Jesus and me, as Ratzinger explains:

The Eucharist is never an event involving just two, a dialogue between Christ and me. *Eucharistic Communion* is aimed at a complete reshaping of my own life. *It breaks up man's entire self and becomes a new "we." Communion with Christ is necessarily also communication with all who belong to him: therein I myself become a part of the new bread that he is creating by the resubstantiation of the whole of earthly reality.*[61]

As Pope Benedict XVI, he later writes in his encyclical *Deus Caritas Est* that "sacramental 'mysticism' is social in character, for in sacramental communion I become one with the Lord, like all other communicants. . . . I cannot possess Christ just for myself; I can belong to him only in union with all those who have become, or who will become, his own" (DCE 14).

The sacraments, including the Eucharist, are not an end in themselves but a means to a spiritual end, namely, the fullness of Christ, the Final Adam. By incorporating us ever more fully into his paschal mystery, Christ unites us with himself, as though one person. The Eucharist through the power of the Spirit of the Risen Christ is but "the foretaste and promise of the paschal feast of heaven."[62] Christ, the Risen Lord, as head and shepherd of the Church, continues to build up his Body by nourishing it at the table of his Word and sacrament through the ministry of those men ordained to serve—in the words of St. Augustine—in an *amoris officium*. In his own reflection upon this Augustinian phrase, Pope John Paul II writes:

This objective reality itself serves as both the basis and requirement for a corresponding ethos, which can be none other than a life of love, as St. Augustine himself points out: *Sit amoris officium pascere dominicum gregem.* This ethos, and as a result the spiritual life, is none other than embracing consciously and freely—that is to say in one's mind and heart, in one's decisions and actions—the "truth" of the priestly ministry as an *amoris officium.*" (PDV 24)[63]

The priest's configuration to Christ, like that of every baptized Christian, fully manifests itself, moreover, in the depth of his commitment to live the radicalism of the Gospel. "A particularly significant expression of the radicalism of the Gospel is seen in the different 'evangelical counsels' which Jesus proposes in the Sermon on the Mount (cf. Mt. 5–7), and among them the intimately related counsels of obedience, chastity and poverty"

---

[61] Ratzinger, *Pilgrim Fellowship of Faith*, 78 with emphasis in original.
[62] Eucharistic Preface VI (P34) for Sundays in Ordinary Time.
[63] See St. Augustine, *In Iohannis Evangelium Tractatus* 123, 5: CCL 36, 678.

(PDV 27). Before assuming the form of a threefold vow in the twelfth century and being given canonical status for consecrated religious and members of secular institutes, the evangelical counsels in the early Church called Christ's followers beyond the minimum of observing commandments to the fullness of life and love in Christ Jesus.

The counsels show us how to respond in love to the Good News of God's unsurpassing love.[64] They make evident the essence of apostolic life, the koinonia or "mutual sharing" (Acts 2:42-44; Heb 13:16), which was a definitive mark of the early Church. They show us how to live Christ, who "emptied himself, taking the form of a slave . . . becoming obedient to death" (Phil 2:7-8) and who for our sakes "became poor although he was rich" (2 Cor 8:9). To some, furthermore, is given the gift of "the Father (cf. Mt. 19:11; 1 Cor. 7:7) to devote themselves to God alone more easily with undivided heart (cf. 1 Cor. 7:32-34) in virginity or celibacy" (LG 42). In fact, Christ himself is the only evangelical counsel who shows us how to love God more than self and to "live in love" (Eph 5:2).

The Second Vatican Council in speaking of the universal vocation of all the baptized to a holiness of life tells us that the Church's holiness finds expression in "this practice of the counsels prompted by the Holy Spirit, undertaken by many Christians whether privately or in a form or state sanctioned by the Church" (LG 39). As a commitment to love, the evangelical counsels hold forth a new way of life for every Christian. Rather than suggesting an "otherworldly" spirituality, "they are symbols of the whole church's call to sexual and material restraint and obedience to the Gospel. . . . Poverty, chastity, and obedience are the flip side of the coin of money, sex, and power, the three principal means by which we try to force the world to center upon ourselves."[65] They provide us with the ability to see the world and to live in it with the attitude of Jesus Christ, making us his followers not only in name but in fact. Although diocesan priests do not take vows of poverty, chastity, and obedience like consecrated religious, they at ordination do make the promises of lifelong celibacy and of obedience to their bishop.

The gospel records Jesus saying, "I do not seek my own will but the will of the one who sent me" (John 5:30; also 4:34 and 6:38). Pope John Paul II points out that obedience in the spiritual life of the priest takes on special characteristics: it is apostolic, lived without servility, has a community dimension, and is pastoral in character. First of all, it is *apostolic* in nature;

[64] See CCC 1973–74.
[65] Hunter Brown, "Counsels for the Baptized," *Commonweal* CXIV, no. 17 (October 9, 1987): 559–60.

it recognizes, loves, and serves the Church in her hierarchical structure. Secondly, when properly motivated and *lived without servility*, the obedience of the priest allows him to exercise the authority entrusted to him "free from authoritarianism or demagoguery" (PDV 28). Indeed, the Second Vatican Council in its Decree on the Training of Priests emphasized that "students must clearly understand that it is not their lot in life to lord it over others and enjoy honors, but to devote themselves completely to the service of God and the pastoral ministry" (OT 9). Thirdly, obedience has a *"community" dimension*; it is part of the unity of the presbyterate, and as such, is not "too bound up in one's own preferences or points of view" nor prone to "jealousy, envy and rivalry" (PDV 28). Priestly obedience, furthermore, is "pastoral" in character. Hence the priest lives "in an atmosphere of constant readiness to allow oneself to be taken up, as it were 'consumed,' by the needs and demands of the flock. These last ought to be truly reasonable and at times they need to be evaluated and tested to see how genuine they are" (PDV 28).

Evangelical poverty for the diocesan priest means being one with Christ who said of himself, "Foxes have dens and birds of the sky have nests, but the Son of Man has nowhere to rest his head" (Luke 9:58). Reflecting upon this gospel passage in relation to the priest's spiritual life, Pope John Paul II stated:

> These words show a complete detachment from all earthly comforts. However, one should not conclude that Jesus lived in destitution. Other Gospel passages state that he received and accepted invitations to the homes of rich people, he had women who helped support him in his financial needs, and he was able to give alms to the poor. Nevertheless, there is no doubt about the spirit and life of poverty that distinguished him.[66]

Evangelical poverty helps the priest cultivate the right attitude to material goods, for it is "certainly not a matter of despising or rejecting material goods but of a loving and responsible use of these goods . . ." (PDV 30). We could even say, it is not just a matter of the things we own, but of the things that own us. We can become possessed by and obsessed with many things—things we devote most of our time to, whether actually doing

[66] John Paul II, "Priests: Following Christ as Model of Priestly Poverty and Detachment," General Audience of Wednesday, July 21, 1993, in *Priesthood in the Third Millennium* (Princeton, NJ: Scepter Publishers; Chicago: Midwest Theological Forum, 1994), 86–93, at 91.

them or constantly dreaming about them, including any number of self-indulgent pleasures, such as travel, food, sex, personal luxuries, surfing the internet, TV, pet ideas, hobbies, and the like.

Evangelical poverty, moreover, requires of priests "a total 'honesty' in the administration of the goods of the community, which he will never treat as if they were his own property . . ." It will help him also, "to stand beside the underprivileged, to practice solidarity with their efforts to create a more just society . . . and to promote a preferential option for the poor" (PDV 30). The prophetic witness of priestly poverty, most of all, cannot be overlooked. "A truly poor priest is indeed a specific sign of separation from, disavowal of and non-submission to the tyranny of a contemporary world which puts all its trust in money and material security."[67] In the same way, the diocesan priest's promise and witness of lifelong celibacy has a prophetic value in today's world. By it the priest is configured to Jesus Christ the head and spouse of the Church. In the words, once again, of John Paul II, "The Church, as the spouse of Jesus Christ, wishes to be loved by the priest in the total and exclusive manner in which Jesus Christ her head and spouse loved her" (PDV 29). The history and theology of priestly celibacy will be addressed more fully in a later chapter of this work.

At his ordination the priest, like Christ himself, is consecrated for mission. Indeed, during the Rite of Ordination of Priests the bishop amid a series of questions asks the elect: "Do you resolve to be united more closely every day to Christ the High Priest, who offered himself for us to the Father as a pure sacrifice, and with him consecrate yourselves to God for the salvation of all?" The elect then responds: "I do, with the help of God." We can hear in the extended ritual dialogue the reverberating echo across the centuries of the Risen Lord's threefold questioning of Peter when they had finished breakfast on the shore of the Sea of Tiberias: "Jesus said to Simon Peter, 'Simon, son of John, do you love me more than these?' He said to him, 'Yes, Lord, you know that I love you.' He said to him, 'Feed my lambs . . . Tend my sheep . . . Feed my sheep.'" (John 21:15-17).

---

[67] 1990 Synod of Bishops, Proposition 10 as quoted in PDV 30.

Chapter 4

Sent to Build Up the Body of Christ

The ultimate end of all New Testament liturgy and of all priestly ministry is to make the world as a whole a temple and a sacrificial offering to God. This is to bring about the inclusion of the whole world into the Body of Christ, so that God may be all in all (cf. 1 Cor 15:28).
—Joseph Cardinal Ratzinger (Pope Benedict XVI)[1]

Tracing our steps backward to the origin of priestly ministry, we find that all the aspects of that ministry are summed up by Jesus and brought into unity in the image of the shepherd (or *pastor* in Latin). Jesus defines himself as a shepherd, and as such the threefold dimensions of his mission—preaching, worship, and leadership—become manifest. In the Good Shepherd discourse found in chapter 10 of John's gospel we read first that "the sheep follow him, because they recognize his voice" (John 10:4). Jesus then speaks of the true worship he will offer by sacrificing himself in order to impart to us a share in God's own life when he says, "I am the good shepherd, and I know mine and mine know me, just as the Father knows me and I know the Father; and I will lay down my life for the sheep" (John 10:14-15). Finally, referring to his leadership role, Jesus adds, "I have other sheep that do not belong to this fold. These also I must lead, and they will hear my voice, and there will be one flock, one shepherd" (John 10:16). It is this shepherding role

---

[1] Joseph Cardinal Ratzinger, *Called to Communion: Understanding the Church Today* (San Francisco: Ignatius Press, 1996), 127–28.

that the Risen Lord then entrusts to the apostles—and to the bishops and priests who will continue their apostolic ministry—when he tells Peter on the shore of Tiberias: "Feed my sheep" (John 21:15-17).

This image that Jesus used to describe his own mission clearly shaped the understanding that the apostles had of their mission and ministry. It also governed the early Church's vision of its raison d'être. By the time of the Council of Trent, however, the image of the priest had become almost exclusively cultic; indeed, the dogmatic texts of Trent virtually limited the role of the priest to saying Mass and absolving sins. We saw above in chapter 2 how the Reform Decrees of the Council clearly presented a more comprehensive picture, yet in the popular imagination the priest's cultic role continued to hold center stage for centuries. The Second Vatican Council, in a return to the earliest Christian sources, was determined to free the ministerial priesthood from being too narrowly identified with cult. Clearly, this was a deliberate decision of the Council Fathers as is evident in their changing the title of the proposed Decree on the Priesthood. It began as *De Clericis* (Concerning the Clergy), was changed to *De Sacerdotibus* (Concerning Priests), and finally ended up as *De Presbyterorum Ministero et Vita* (Concerning the Ministry and Life of Presbyters). The word "presbyter" (elder) comes from the New Testament and the vocabulary of the early Church.[2]

The English translations of the Vatican II documents unfortunately conceal the theological precision the Council Fathers were striving to attain. Bishop Patrick J. Dunn thus writes:

> As a general rule the conciliar texts try to follow the Scriptures and to restrict the word "priest" (*sacerdos*) to Jesus himself and to the "common priesthood" of the baptized; and then talking about the ordained they use the word "*presbyteros.*" But the English translation uncritically translates both "*sacerdos*" and "*presbyteros*" as "priest." By way of illustration, the word "priest-priestly-priesthood" occurs 14 times in the English version of paragraph 2 of *Presbyterorum Ordinis*; on 10 of these occasions the Latin original has used the word "*presbyteros*"; "*sacerdos*" is used only 4 times—twice referring to Jesus, once to all the baptized, and only once with reference to the ordained priesthood.[3]

---

[2] See Herbert Vorgrimler, ed., "Decree on the Ministry and Life of Priests," Commentary on the Decree, *Commentary on the Documents of Vatican II*, vol. 4, 210 (London: Burns & Oates; New York: Herder and Herder, 1969).

[3] Patrick J. Dunn, *Priesthood: A Re-examination of the Roman Catholic Theology of the Presbyterate* (New York: Alba House, 1990), 110.

The New Testament word "presbyter" commends itself among other things to its collegial and fraternal nature, which is expressed in the concept of presbytery or presbyterium.[4] From ancient times both bishops and presbyters have been seen as sharing in Christ's own priesthood and thus constituting together a *sacerdotium*. Vatican II's Dogmatic Constitution on the Church, accordingly, teaches that priests are "associated with them [i.e., bishops] by reason of their sacerdotal dignity; and in virtue of the sacrament of Orders, after the image of Christ, the supreme and eternal priest (Heb. 5:1-10; 7:24; 9:11-28), they are consecrated in order to preach the Gospel and shepherd the faithful as well as to celebrate divine worship as true priests of the New Testament" (LG 28).

The Second Vatican Council embraces the threefold offices of teaching, sanctifying, and leading in order to describe the nature of the Church's ministry as handed down from the apostles. It is appropriate to note, however, that these so-called offices can be distinguished only partially and are in no way meant to be exhaustive. Indeed, they often overlap. "For example, one might hand over the teaching office to the pastoral office; likewise there is a reciprocity between the teaching and the priestly office: the word of preaching has a sacramental character and the sacramental action becomes efficacious only in and through the word."[5] It is precisely in this coordination of word and sacrament that we find the basic theological structure of Christ's own redemptive activity in the Church.

Saint Paul explains, furthermore, that the purpose of the different gifts and ministries the Lord gives to his Church is "to equip the holy ones for the work of ministry, for building up the body of Christ" (Eph 4:12); likewise, in 2 Corinthians he refers to his apostolic "authority, which the Lord gave for building you up and not for tearing you down" (2 Cor 10:8 and 13:10). Beyond any doubt, seen from its apostolic perspective the sole purpose of ministry is to build up the Body of Christ, the Church. Therefore, a correct perception of the priest's identity today, as Pope John Paul II maintained, is found in Vatican II's teaching on the Church as mystery, community, and mission: "She is *mystery* because the very life and love of the Father, Son and Holy Spirit are the gift gratuitously offered to all those who are born of water and the Spirit (cf. *Jn* 3:5) and called to relive

---

[4] See *Lumen Gentium* 28: "The priests, prudent cooperators of the episcopal college and its support and mouthpiece, called to the service of the People of God, constitute, together with their bishop, a unique sacerdotal college (*presbyterium*)."

[5] Friedrich Wulf, "Decree on the Ministry and Life of Priests," Commentary on the Decree, Articles 1–6, *Commentary on the Documents of Vatican II*, ed. Herbert Vorgrimler, vol. 4, 217 (New York: Herder and Herder, 1969).

the very *communion* of God and to manifest it and communicate it in history [mission] . . ." (CL 8; PDV 12).[6]

Priesthood within the Context of the Church's Mission of Evangelization

The Church exists to evangelize, to proclaim the Good News of the Word-made-flesh. The Second Vatican Council teaches: "The Church on earth is by its very nature missionary since, according to the plan of the Father, it has its origin in the mission of the Son and the Holy Spirit. This plan flows from 'fountain-like love,' the love of God the Father" (AG 2). Thus Pope Paul VI maintains in *Evangelii Nuntiandi* that "evangelizing is in fact the grace and vocation proper to the Church, her deepest identity. She exists in order to evangelize" (EN 14); and he adds, "Having been born consequently out of being sent, the Church in her turn is sent by Jesus. . . . She prolongs and continues Him. And it is above all His mission and His condition of being an evangelizer that she is called upon to continue" (EN 15).

Only when we realize that God gathers us together in communion and fellowship as members of Christ's Body (koinonia) for the purpose of mission, of bearing witness to his hidden plan (see Col 1:26), only then are we really and truly Church. Vatican II thus describes the Church " 'as the universal sacrament of salvation,' at once manifesting and actualizing the mystery of God's love for men" (GS 45). The marks of the early Church "gathered together" in Acts 2:42—teaching, fellowship, breaking bread, and prayer—served to make the disciples "witnesses" of the Risen Lord (see Luke 24:48 and Acts 1:8). The communion of life and fellowship, which the early Christians shared with the Risen Christ and with one another, manifested the continual unfolding and incarnation of God's love revealed by Jesus on the Cross. "Everything is not contained in the command 'go' and teach. There is also the prayer that 'they may be one *as*' the Father and the Son are one '*so that* the world may believe' (*Jn. 17:21-23*)."[7]

John's gospel does not conclude, as do the Synoptics, with the great missionary mandate to go and teach all nations. Instead, it tells us that the world will believe in Jesus' mission if it sees that we are one in him,

---

[6] Emphasis and brackets in original.

[7] L. Legrand, J. Pathrapankal, and M. Vellanickal, *Good News and Witness: The New Testament Understanding of Evangelization* (Bangalore: Theological Publications in India, 1973), vi, with emphasis in original.

as he is one with the Father. The evangelist clearly wishes to point out that the community of life we share with the Father and the Son becomes evangelization. Perhaps now we can better understand why St. Paul taught that ministry (or "office") in the Church has its origin in Christ's paschal mystery and flows therefrom as the ministry of reconciliation (see 2 Cor 5:18). Jesus came to proclaim the Good News of repentance for the forgiveness of sins, and he entrusted this same mission to his Church (see Luke 24:47). The Good News is the message that in Christ we are being reconciled for he, indeed, has nailed our enmity to the Cross.

"To evangelize and be evangelized" might also be appropriately phrased as "to reconcile and be reconciled." Nine years after the publication of *Evangelii Nuntiandi*, Pope John Paul II intimated this when in his own apostolic exhortation *Reconciliatio et Paenitentia* he stated:

> In intimate connection with Christ's mission, one can therefore sum up the church's mission, rich and complex as it is, as being her central task of reconciling people: with God, with themselves, with neighbor, with the whole of creation; and this in a permanent manner, since, as I said on another occasion, "the Church is also by her nature always reconciling." (RP 8)

Each member of the Church through baptism is incorporated into Christ, and because of baptism has a share in his evangelizing mission (AG 35; LG 33). According to our responsibilities, whether ordained or non-ordained, or consecrated religious, and according to our gifts and talents, we must bring Christ's reconciliation and peace to bear upon every relationship and aspect of our lives.

Warning against formulating any partial or fragmentary definition of evangelization (see EN 17) Paul VI offers a one-sentence description of this mission. "The Church evangelizes," he says, "when she seeks to convert, solely through the power of the message she proclaims, both the personal and collective consciences of people, the activities in which they engage, and the lives and concrete milieu which are theirs" (EN 18). The purpose of evangelization, he adds, is not just to reach out to "ever wider geographic areas," but to bring about "this interior change" affecting the human race's "criteria of judgment, determining values, points of interest, lines of thought, sources of inspiration and models of life, which are in contrast with the Word of God and the plan of salvation" (EN 19). Every task and every ministry within the Church serves the continuation of Jesus' mission and ministry among us. All ministries, whether in the area of missionary extension or pastoral care, whether in outreach to the un-churched and inactive Catholic, whether in the areas of family life, catechesis, preaching, international life, peace, justice, and liberation—all ministries converge to serve the one "primary and essential mission" of evangelization (see EN 29, 42, 44, 45).

Pope John Paul II throughout all the years of his papacy continued to develop Paul VI's focus on evangelization. In *Christifideles Laici* he writes, "The entire mission of the Church, then, is concentrated and manifested in *evangelization*" (CL 33). The goal of mission, he emphasizes, is communion. He explains, "*communion represents both the source and the fruit of mission: communion gives rise to mission and mission is accomplished in communion*" (CL 32). Such communion characteristically exhibits the fruits of the Church's threefold priestly office. "Through evangelization the Church is built up into a *community of faith*: more precisely, into a community that *confesses* the faith in full adherence to the Word of God which is *celebrated* in the Sacraments and *lived* in charity, the principle of Christian moral existence" (CL 33).[8]

A favorite theme of John Paul II was "re-evangelization" or "the new evangelization." He referred almost constantly to the need of countering the spread of secularism and atheism, as well as the growing indifference to religion in nations and cultures where Christianity formerly flourished. Again in *Christifideles Laici* he writes, "*Humanity is loved by God!* This very simple yet profound proclamation is owed to humanity by the Church. . . . This re-evangelization is directed not only to individual persons but also to entire portions of populations in the variety of their situations, surroundings and cultures" (CL 34). Then a decade later, in *Ecclesia in America*, he stressed, "everyone should keep in mind that the vital core of the new evangelization must be a clear and unequivocal proclamation of the person of Jesus Christ . . . and the Kingdom which he has gained for us by his Paschal Mystery" (EIA 66). "The Church," the pope continued, "must make the crucified and risen Christ the center of her pastoral concern and her evangelizing activity" (EIA 67). And borrowing a phrase from Paul VI, he pointed out that one of the most important fruits of the new evangelization is "building a world enlivened by the law of love, a *civilization of love*."[9]

The whole Church is incorporated into the Risen Christ through baptism—that is, through literally being "immersed"—into his paschal mystery, the mystery of his self-giving, reconciling love enfleshed and revealed

---

[8] Emphasis in original.

[9] John Paul II, General Audience, December 15, 1999; text available at Vatican web site: http://www.vatican.va/holy_father/john_paul_ii/audiences/1999/documents/hf_jp-ii_aud_15121999_en.html.

on the Cross. This is "the mystery of faith" proclaimed at every Mass. It is the revelation of the God who is Love, as Jesus takes his life in his hands, gives thanks to the Father, and pours it out that others too might have Life. "No one has greater love than this, to lay down one's life for one's friends" (John 15:13). "In him, with him, and through him," we share a communion of truth and love as we pour out our lives in self-giving service to God and neighbor. In him we become one Bread, one Body, enlivened by the eternal law of Love, building a "civilization of love." This is the meaning of the universal priesthood of all the baptized. This is what it means to evangelize, and this is why we are Christians in the first place.

In *Pastores Dabo Vobis* we read that Jesus established the apostolic ministry "for the sake of this universal priesthood" (PDV 14). Pope John Paul II there explains that, "The ministry of the priest is entirely on behalf of the Church; it aims at promoting the exercise of the common priesthood of the entire People of God . . ." (PDV 16). Thus, as stated earlier in this work, one can aptly describe the charism of the diocesan priest as being the spirituality and mission of the laity. The Second Vatican Council taught, and Pope John Paul II never tired of reiterating the conciliar teaching, that "the mission of Christ—Priest, Prophet-Teacher, King—continues in the Church. Everyone, the whole People of God, shares in this threefold mission" (CL 14). By nurturing the spirituality and mission of the lay faithful in these three areas the priest himself fulfills his own ministry and grows in holiness.

The Priest as Prophet-Teacher

The Second Vatican Council states that "it is the first task of priests as co-workers of the bishops to preach the Gospel [*primum officium evangelium evangelizandi*] to all men" (PO 4). Preaching is rightly put first because salvation begins with the revelation of God's Word, as we read in the opening verse of the Gospel according to John, "In the beginning was the Word" (John 1:1). The Letter to the Hebrews—the only New Testament work to use the term "priest" and then only in reference to Christ—also begins, "In times past, God spoke in partial and various ways to our ancestors through the prophets; in these last days, he spoke to us through a son" (Heb 1:1-2). Additionally, at the beginning of his public ministry, Jesus describes his own mission by mentioning first his being anointed to proclaim good news (Luke 4:18), and in the course of his ministry we are told that he had pity on the vast crowd "for they were like sheep without a shepherd; and he began to teach them many things" (Mark 6:34). The celebration of the Eucharist, and indeed of all the sacraments, begins with a Liturgy of the Word.

Pastores Dabo Vobis maintains, "The priest is first of all a minister of the word of God. He is consecrated and sent forth to proclaim the good news of the kingdom to all, calling every person to the obedience of faith and leading believers to an ever increasing knowledge of and communion in the mystery of God, as revealed and communicated to us in Christ" (PDV 26). The Church of the patristic era distinguished three forms of the ministry of the Word: preaching (*kerygma*), religious instruction (*catechesis*), and doctrinal teaching (*didache*). In the early Church, when there were yet no Christian schools, no systematic catechetical instructions for children, and no organized missionary outreach, the liturgy itself substituted for all these and nourished the life of love and koinonia (fellowship) the first generations of Christians experienced in union with the Risen Christ. In the proclamation of the Word, in the *kerygma*, Christ is not only proclaimed, but he is also made present in the proclamation, as Jesus himself said: "Whoever listens to you listens to me" (Luke 10:16).[10]

What does proclaiming the Gospel (*evangelium evangelizandi*) actually mean? Jesus himself points to the preaching of the kingdom of God as the reason why he came (Luke 4:43). In Jesus, the kingdom is the power of God's Spirit of Love erupting in time and transforming our world. It is the revelation of what God is working to bring about in our lives, of God's plan for the human race. In practical terms, it is what would occur if everyone faithfully kept the two Great Commandments. To preach the kingdom of God is to call everyone to conversion (*metanoia*). It is a call to reconciliation, inviting all men and women to a new relationship among themselves and with God in Jesus Christ.

Indeed, as Jesus' preaching continues it becomes clearer "that the 'Kingdom' and his own person belong together, that the Kingdom is coming in his own person."[11] In the early postresurrection period the evangelists did not hesitate to identify Jesus with both the Good News and the kingdom (Mark 8:35; 10:29). In St. Paul's letters we find that the content of his

---

[10] David Bohr, *Evangelization in America: Proclamation, Way of Life, and the Catholic Church in the United States* (New York: Paulist Press, 1977), 49–50: "The kerygma is thus a charismatic, dynamic and life-giving power summoning its hearers to confident faith and constituting the Church as the fellowship of those who hear and follow the Word of God. . . . In the liturgy of the early Church it could be said that Christ was 'kerygmatically present.'"

[11] Joseph Cardinal Ratzinger, *Pilgrim Fellowship of Faith: Understanding the Church Today* (San Francisco: Ignatius Press, 1996), 159.

message is no longer the kingdom of God, but "the gospel of Christ" (1 Thess 3:2; Gal 1:7) that is "the power of God for the salvation of everyone who believes" (Rom 1:16). In addition, St. Paul describes "the word of God" as "the mystery hidden from ages and from generations past. But now it has been manifested to his holy ones . . . it is Christ in you, the hope for glory" (Col 1:26-27). For St. Paul, Jesus Christ is at one and the same time the Gospel, its message, and its content.

God's plan of salvation, his kingdom or reign, is *fully* revealed in the paschal mystery of Jesus Christ—in his dying, rising, returning to the Father, and sending of the Spirit. This paschal event is, in fact, the heart of the Good News. All four gospel accounts lead up to it. It is the gospel Paul received and handed on (see 1 Cor 15:3-5). It is the mystery into which we are baptized (see Rom 6:3-4), and we remember it, celebrate it, and are ritually united to it at every Eucharist. Indeed, in the paschal mystery Word and sacrament become indivisible. Furthermore, sharing in Christ's dying and rising we are given new life (Rom 6:4) and we dare hope to become like him, he who is "the last Adam a life-giving spirit" (1 Cor 15:45). By appropriating Christ's paschal mystery in our own lives, by putting on the mind and attitude of Christ (Phil 2:5), we indeed truly become "a new *creation*."

Jesus Christ is the Logos; he is the Word-made-flesh. The ministry of the Word, therefore, is really a matter, not of words, but of *the* Word. At the center of Christian faith stands, not a book, nor a doctrine, nor a law, but a person—Jesus Christ. To proclaim the Gospel, to preach the Word, the priest therefore must first "abide" in the Word and "become a perfect disciple of the Lord" (PDV 26). Ratzinger thus writes, "The ministry of the Word requires of the priest a sharing in the kenosis of Christ, dissolving oneself and submerging oneself in Christ. The requirement that he speak, not of his own volition, but as bringing someone else's message does not of course mean any lack of personal involvement—quite the opposite: it means losing oneself in Christ so as to accept the path of his Paschal Mystery, thus leading to true self-discovery and to fellowship with him who is the Word of God in person."[12]

The word of God in the Old Testament (in Hebrew *dabar*) possesses both dynamic and noetic aspects. On the one hand, it creates the world and sets history in motion, and on the other hand, it makes known God's will, his salvific plan.[13] It conveys both knowledge and power. The priest's

---

[12] Ibid., 161.

[13] See Rene Latourelle, SJ, *Theology of Revelation* (New York: Alba House, 1966), 30.

personal relationship to God's Word of truth and love, to the Son and the Holy Spirit, therefore, must inform his ministry of the Word. Proclaiming the Good News can only rightly proceed from the depths of the priest's own interior life. As Father Robert Schwartz has written, "By the very nature of the presbyteral mission, the spirituality of the priest is contemplative. The priest must study, contemplate and internalize God's word until it becomes the very fabric of his being. The priest must reek with the word and be a living sign of its meaning and power."[14] Bishop Fulton J. Sheen in the same vein wrote, "Preaching is not the act of giving a sermon; it is the art of making a preacher. The preacher then becomes the sermon. . . . The absence of an inner spiritual life makes sermonizing dull, stale, flat and unprofitable."[15]

Preparing to celebrate the Liturgy of the Word, which constitutes an integral part of the rite of each sacrament, the priest also needs to develop a knowledge of its linguistic and exegetical aspects. Thus Pope John Paul II maintains, "In particular, continuing theological study is necessary if the priest is to faithfully carry out the ministry of the word, proclaiming it clearly and without ambiguity, distinguishing it from mere human opinions, no matter how renowned and widespread these might be" (PDV 72). Such continuing theological study is best done in a contemplative manner. Deacon James Keating in speaking of the intellectual journey of the seminarian thus perceptively asks, "Can we not consider contemplative theology to be an extension of the Liturgy of the Word, as we consider Eucharistic adoration to be an extension of the Liturgy of the Eucharist?"[16] In similar fashion, the priest might envision his continuing study and prayerful reflection in preparation to preach or teach as an extension of the Liturgy of the Word. This prayerful preparation, as well as his actual preaching and teaching, can serve to nourish the priest's own spiritual life, drawing him into ever closer communion with the Word-made-flesh.

---

[14] Robert M. Schwartz, "Servant of the Servants of God: A Pastor's Spirituality," in *The Spirituality of the Diocesan Priest*, ed. Donald B. Cozzens (Collegeville, MN: Liturgical Press, 1997), 5.

[15] Fulton J. Sheen, *The Priest Is Not His Own* (New York: McGraw-Hill, 1963), 126.

[16] Rev. Mr. James Keating, "How Can Catholic Spirituality Be More at the Heart of Priestly Formation?" in *Interiority for Mission: Spiritual Formation for Priests of the New Evangelization* (Fourth Annual Symposium on the Spirituality and Identity of the Diocesan Priest, held at St. John Vianney Theological Seminary, Denver, CO—March 3–6, 2005), ed. Edward G. Mathews Jr. (Omaha, NE: Institute for Priestly Formation, 2005), 21.

Saint Augustine in meditating upon the role of John the Baptist in the New Testament often had recourse to the image of "voice"—"*vox Christi*" (see *Serm.* 288; 293:3; *Serm.* Dolbeau 3; etc.) and "*vox Verbi*" (see *Serm.* 46:30-32)—to describe the nature of priestly service. Indeed, in the figure of John the Baptist he saw a prefiguration of the role of the priest, as Joseph Ratzinger explains:

> Ultimately, the task of the priest is simply to be a voice for the word: "He must increase, but I must decrease"—the voice has no other purpose than to pass on the word; it then once more effaces itself. On this basis the stature and humbleness of priestly service are both equally clear: the priest is, like John the Baptist, purely a forerunner, a servant of the Word. It is not he who matters, but the other. Yet he is, with his entire existence, *vox*; it is his mission to be a voice for the Word, and thus, precisely in his being radically referred to, dependent upon, someone else, he takes a share in the stature and mission of the Baptist and in the mission of the Logos himself.[17]

The priest or deacon, who as minister of the Word places himself center stage, taking delight in hearing himself talk and in winning the adulation of the crowd, serves not Christ but his own ego. Indeed, the same can be said of the minister who when preaching presents theological positions that run contrary to authentic Church teaching. Consequently, Pope John Paul II states, "in order that he himself may possess and give to the faithful the guarantee that he is transmitting the Gospel in its fullness, the priest is called to develop a special sensitivity, love and docility to the living tradition of the Church and to her magisterium. These are not foreign to the word, but serve its proper interpretation and preserve its authentic meaning" (PDV 26).

Giving the homily at Mass, as well as breaking open the word of God during other sacramental celebrations, constitutes a major part of the ministry of the Word for most diocesan priests. Pope Benedict XVI thus maintains in his post-synodal apostolic exhortation *Sacramentum Caritatis*:

> The homily is "part of the liturgical action," and is meant to foster a deeper understanding of the word of God, so that it can bear fruit in the lives of the faithful. . . . The catechetical and paraenetic aim of the homily should not be forgotten. During the course of the liturgical year it is appropriate to offer the faithful, prudently and on the basis

---

[17] Ratzinger, *Pilgrim Fellowship of Faith*, 164.

of the three-year lectionary, "thematic" homilies treating the great themes of the Christian faith, on the basis of what has been authoritatively proposed by the Magisterium in the four "pillars" of the *Catechism of the Catholic Church* and the recent *Compendium*, namely: the profession of faith, the celebration of the Christian mystery, life in Christ and Christian prayer. (SCar 46)

The homily, however, is by no means the only way the priest carries out the ministry of the Word. Pastors also have the responsibility of providing suitable catechetical instruction for everyone in their parish; for this task they are encouraged to engage the assistance of qualified lay and religious educators. Aidan Nichols, OP, as a result, sees the prophetic office of the presbyter having three components: evangelizing the unconverted, teaching sound doctrine in faith and morals to the converted, and forming others to be apostolic.[18]

Consequently, the priest's prophetic ministry encompasses the proclamation of the Word in all its dimensions, as Cardinal Avery Dulles, SJ, elaborates:

> Evangelization, broadly defined, includes the proclamation of the gospel to those who are afar and the nurturing of believers in the faith, so that they may more effectively understand and practice it. . . . It is not enough to evangelize those who come into our buildings; as bearers of the gospel, we must move into the neighborhoods and workplaces to evangelize. . . . Evangelization should be a dimension of every parish organization, including those dedicated to religious education, liturgy, youth, social justice, and the like. An evangelizing parish will have a vigorous program for keeping in contact with inactive and alienated parishioners and for making unchurched persons feel welcome.[19]

In personally reaching out to the inactive and unchurched and by helping to form the laity to do the same, the priest himself continues his active engagement in the ministry of the Word.

Forming the laity for their apostolate in the world, furthermore, necessarily includes instructing them in the social doctrine of the Church. As the Vatican's *Compendium* states:

---

[18] Aidan Nichols, *Holy Order: The Apostolic Ministry from the New Testament to the Second Vatican Council* (Lancaster, PA: Veritas Press, 1991), 142.

[19] Avery Dulles, SJ, *The Priestly Office: A Theological Reflection* (New York/Mahwah, NJ: Paulist Press, 1997), 53–54.

The Church's social doctrine is an integral part of her evangelizing ministry.
Nothing that concerns the community of men and women—situations
and problems regarding justice, freedom, development, relations
between peoples, peace—is foreign to evangelization, and evangelization would be incomplete if it did not take into account the mutual
demands continually made by the Gospel and by the concrete, personal and social life of man" (no. 66). "Through suitable formation
programmes, the priest should make known the social teaching of the
Church and foster in the members of his community an awareness of
their right and duty to be active subjects of this doctrine. . . . He
should animate pastoral action in the social field, giving particular
attention to the formation and spiritual accompaniment of lay Christians engaged in social and political life" (no. 539).[20]

Some priests, also, may be assigned to full-time ministry of the Word
through their involvement in catechetical formation or in teaching, retreat
work, seminary formation, and even theological research as talent recommends and pastoral need requires.

The Priest as Sanctifier

While *Presbyterorum Ordinis* teaches that the first task of priests is to
preach the Gospel (PO 4), it likewise states that priests fulfill their "principal function" in celebrating the Eucharist (PO 12). At first glance, the
two statements may appear to contradict one another, but in reality they
do not. Some, indeed, have seen in these apparently contrasting statements
the carryover of a conflict between those Council Fathers who wanted to
retain a strictly cultic notion of the priesthood and those who wanted to
advance a more evangelical view of the ordained minister as primarily a
preacher of the Word. The 1971 Synod of Bishops, however, maintained,
"The ministry of the Word, if rightly understood, leads to the sacraments
and to the Christian life, as it is practiced in the visible community of the
Church and in the world. . . . Unity between evangelization and sacramental life is always proper to the ministerial priesthood and must be
carefully kept in mind by every priest."[21]

[20] Pontifical Council for Justice and Peace, *Compendium of the Social Doctrine of the
Church* (Città del Vaticano: Libreria Editrice Vaticana, 2004), with emphasis in original
English edition.
[21] Synod of Bishops, *Ultimis temporibus*, November 30, 1971, in *Vatican Council II:
More Post Conciliar Documents*, ed. Austin Flannery, OP, vol. 2, 682–83 (Northport, NY:
Costello Publishing Co., 1982).

Divine revelation, God's self-communication, begins with the Word and reaches its fulfillment in the paschal mystery of the Word-made-flesh. In Christian worship we become one with the Word, with Christ's Pasch, in his "passing over" from death to life, to the unity of God and man. As the Council Fathers explain:

> For in the most blessed Eucharist is contained the whole spiritual good of the Church, namely Christ himself our Pasch and the living bread which gives life to men through his flesh—that flesh which is given life and gives life through the Holy Spirit. Thus men are invited and led to offer themselves, their works and all creation with Christ. For this reason the Eucharist appears as the source and the summit of all preaching of the Gospel . . . (PO 5)

Saint Augustine, indeed, maintained that the sacraments are both "visible words" and "audible symbols."

The center of the liturgical action is the eucharistic prayer, which the Church Fathers called the *oratio*. The word *oratio* originally meant, not "prayer" (which in Latin is *prex*), but a solemn public speech. Ratzinger explains:

> What the Fathers are saying was this: The sacrificial animals and all those things you had and have, and which ultimately satisfy no one, are now abolished. In their place has come the sacrifice of the Word. We are a spiritual religion, in which in truth a Word-based worship takes place. Goats and cattle are no longer slaughtered. Instead, the Word, summing up our existence, is addressed to God and identified with *the* Word, the Word of God, who draws us into true worship.[22]

In the Eucharist the words of Jesus to the Samaritan woman at Jacob's well are fulfilled: "But the hour is coming, and is now here, when true worshipers will worship the Father in Spirit and truth; and indeed the Father seeks such people to worship him" (John 4:23).

By bringing into focus once again the New Testament teaching on the universal priesthood of all the baptized, the Second Vatican Council also recaptured the understanding, taken for granted up to the Middle Ages, that the entire priestly Church offers the eucharistic sacrifice through the priest. It is not the priest alone who celebrates the Mass on the laity's

[22] Joseph Cardinal Ratzinger, *The Spirit of the Liturgy* (San Francisco: Ignatius Press, 2000), 172.

behalf. Thus the priest celebrant serves as the president of the eucharistic assembly as he leads all the faithful present to make their own priestly self-offering with Christ in the *logike latreia* described by St. Paul (Rom 12:1). *Presbyterorum Ordinis* clearly intends to emphasize this very point when it states, "Therefore the eucharistic celebration is the center of the assembly of the faithful over which the priest presides. Hence priests teach the faithful to offer the divine victim to God the Father in the sacrifice of the Mass and with the victim to make an offering of their whole life" (PO 5).

The Letter to the Hebrews quotes Jesus as saying, "'Sacrifices and offerings, holocausts and sin offerings, you neither desired nor delighted in.' These are offered according to the law. Then he says, 'Behold, I come to do your will.' He takes away the first to establish the second. By this 'will,' we have been consecrated through the offering of the body of Jesus Christ once for all" (Heb 10:8-10). Jesus in this way is both priest and victim. Likewise, when we give of ourselves to do God's will, we exercise our baptismal priesthood and are one with Christ in his paschal sacrifice. We do God's will when we keep Jesus' new commandment: "love one another. As I have loved you, so you also should love one another" (John 13:34). Pope Benedict XVI in his first encyclical *Deus Caritas Est* writes, "The ancient world had dimly perceived that man's real food—what truly nourishes him as man—is ultimately the *Logos*, eternal wisdom: this same *Logos* now truly becomes food for us—as love. The Eucharist draws us into Jesus' act of self-oblation. More than just statically receiving the incarnate *Logos*, we enter into the very dynamic of his self-giving" (DCE 13). He accordingly points out that only by contemplating Jesus' pierced side (John 19:37) can we find where "our definition of love must begin. In this contemplation the Christian discovers the path along which his life and love must move" (DCE 12).

The ministerial priesthood is at the service of the baptismal priesthood. The priest sanctifies (that is, "makes holy") God's people when he increases the depth of their love, their relationships, their communion with Jesus Christ and one another. This is why priesthood is essentially a ministry of reconciliation (2 Cor 5:18). Holiness, the Second Vatican Council teaches, "is expressed in many ways by the individuals who, each in his own state of life, tend to the perfection of love, thus helping others grow in holiness . . ." (LG 39). This communion of love finds its "source and summit" in the Eucharist. Scripture and the Church Fathers have recourse to marital imagery to describe this marvelous communion. Jesus thus frequently referred to himself as the Bridegroom, and as Joseph Ratzinger has observed:

> Paul compares what happens in Holy Communion with the physical union between man and woman. To help understand the Eucharist, he refers us to the words of the creation story: "The two [= man and wife] shall become one" (Gen 2:24). And he adds: "He who is united to the Lord becomes one spirit [that is, shares a single new existence in the Holy Spirit] with him" (1 Cor 6:17).[23]

Participating in Holy Communion is comparable on the spiritual level to the conjugal love of a man and a woman on the physical level. The Eucharist is an act of giving and receiving love.

Through baptism we first enter into an irrevocable covenant of love with Jesus Christ, much as a husband and wife do when they exchange their vows in marriage. The couple, then, continue to give themselves to each other, to celebrate and grow in love through their conjugal embrace, which opens itself to new life and to building a family of love. Comparably, the Eucharist is the "daily Bread" that nourishes our koinonia, our communion of love, with God and one another; it is the spiritual conjugal embrace that continues to unite Bridegroom and Bride, Christ and his Church, building up God's family. Once again in the words of Ratzinger, "To be in communion with Christ is by its very nature to be in communion with one another as well. No longer are we alongside one another, each for himself; rather, everyone else who goes to communion is for me, so to speak, 'bone of my bone and flesh of my flesh' (cf. Gen 2:23)."[24]

The Eucharist, therefore, is never a private devotion for personal sanctification only. It is *leiturgia*, literally the "work of the people." In the eucharistic prayer we name the pope and the diocesan bishop reminding us of the worldwide and local community of the Church. As Kevin Irwin notes, "Belonging to a particular diocese and parish reflects our belonging to the church everywhere and at any time. The notion of a diocese and parish based on 'territory' is meant to foster relationships with those near whom we live and socialize."[25] Indeed, the English word "parish" comes from the Greek *paroikos*, which means "dwelling beside or near." Likewise, the words "diocese" and "diocesan" come from the Greek *dioikein*, which means "to keep house" or "to manage a household." They are unmistakably familial and communal terms.

---

[23] Joseph Cardinal Ratzinger, *God Is Near Us: The Eucharist, the Heart of Life*, ed. Stephan Otto Horn and Vinzenz Pfnür (San Francisco: Ignatius Press, 2003), 77.

[24] Ibid., 117.

[25] Kevin W. Irwin, *Models of the Eucharist* (Mahwah, NJ: Paulist Press, 2005), 72.

Conveying a proper understanding of the essential communal nature of the Eucharist presents no little difficulty in today's highly individualistic society. As Irwin observes:

> Through and in the liturgy we are always challenged to be less self-concerned and ever more self-transcendent. We are always challenged to be concerned with "the whole church." This kind of focus—on the other and on the self only in relation to others—offers a challenge to us Americans. Specifically, it has to do with the relationship between freedoms for the individual as highly prized "American" values and the demands of belonging to a church whose very identity is bound up with that which is corporate, communal, and concerned with the common good. At its essence, the Eucharist can be counter-cultural, since it is about prayer in common leading to concern about the good of each other and all others.[26]

Furthermore, it is significant to note that in the writings of the Church Fathers the *corpus verum* (true or real body) of Christ was the Church, and the Eucharist itself was referred to as the *corpus mysticum*, or the "mystical body" of Christ. However, as a result of the medieval controversies that shifted the focus from the sacramental enactment of Christ's paschal mystery to the eucharistic species themselves, the term *verum corpus* began to be applied to the consecrated species, and the Church then came to be referred to as the "mystical body."[27] In the process, unfortunately, the integral connection between the Eucharist and ecclesiology was for all practical purposes lost.

In addition, Pope Benedict XVI reminds us that, "every eucharistic celebration sacramentally accomplishes the eschatological gathering of the People of God. For us, the eucharistic banquet is a real foretaste of the final banquet foretold by the prophets (cf. *Is* 25:6-9) and described in the New Testament as 'the marriage-feast of the Lamb' (*Rev* 19:7-9), to be celebrated in the joy of the communion of saints" (SCar 31). John Zizioulas explains, "The eucharist is the moment in the Church's life where the anticipation of the *eschata* takes place. The *anamnesis* of Christ is realized not as a mere re-enactment of a past event but as an *anamnesis of the future*, as an eschatological event. In the eucharist the Church becomes a reflection of the eschatological community of Christ, the Messiah, an image of

---

[26] Ibid., 71.

[27] See ibid., 77–78, with reference to Paul McPartlan, "The Eucharist as the Basis of Ecclesiology," *Antiphon* 6, no. 2 (2001).

the Trinitarian life of God."[28] The ancient liturgies of John Chrysostom and Basil, for instance, speak of *anamnesis* or "remembering" in the Eucharist not only in reference to the past events of salvation history but also to the Second Coming. This *remembering of the future* is an essential aspect of the Eucharist that is all too frequently forgotten.

Eucharistic communion, as well, necessarily implies mission. In *Christifideles Laici* Pope John Paul II reflects upon the dignity and mission of the laity within the context of Jesus' imagery of the Vine and the Branches (John 15:1-17). Here our communion with Christ, our being engrafted to the vine, carries the clear expectation of bearing fruit: "Whoever remains in me and I in him will bear much fruit" (v. 5a). The Holy Father adds, "Bearing fruit is an essential demand of life in Christ and life in the Church. The person who does not bear fruit does not remain in communion . . ." (CL 32). In addition, the English word "Mass" comes from the Latin closing words of the Eucharistic Rite: "*Ite, missa est.*" As Pope Benedict XVI explains, "These words help us to grasp the relationship between the Mass just celebrated and the mission of Christians in the world. In antiquity, *missa* simply meant 'dismissal.' However in Christian usage it gradually took on a deeper meaning. The word 'dismissal' has come to imply a 'mission.' These few words succinctly express the missionary nature of the Church" (SCar 51). Therefore, the Christian faithful at the end of Mass are "missioned" to bring the love of Christ, which they have just celebrated and received, into the world. In the truth of Christ's love, they are sent forth to transform the world into a "civilization of love."

Leading the faithful in the celebration of the Eucharist, the priest is the sacramental sign of Christ as head, shepherd, and spouse of the Church. He sanctifies Christ's Bride in truth and love. Serving the spirituality and mission of the laity in this way, he leads them to come to an ever deeper understanding of their baptismal vocation and priesthood, of their consecration and being sent. Archbishop Fulton J. Sheen keenly observed:

> The lesson is clear. We are Eucharistic priests. Watch a priest read Mass and you can tell how he treats souls in the confessional, how he ministers to the sick and the poor, whether or not he is interested in making converts, whether he is more consumed with pleasing the Lord Bishop than the Lord God, how effective he is in instilling patience and resignation in those who suffer, whether he is an administrator

---

[28] John D. Zizioulas, *Being as Communion: Studies in Personhood and Church* (Crestwood, NY: St. Vladimir's Seminary Press, 1985), 254.

or a shepherd, whether he loves the rich, or the rich and the poor, and whether he gives only money-sermons or Christ-words.[29]

The priest, furthermore, sanctifies and builds up the Body of Christ through the celebration of other sacraments as well—baptism, penance, marriage, and anointing of the sick—and by being an example and teacher of prayer. Pope John Paul II highlighted this point in *Pastores Dabo Vobis*: "One aspect of the priest's mission, and certainly by no means a secondary aspect, is that he is to be a 'teacher of prayer.'" He adds, "A necessary training in prayer in a context of noise and agitation like that of our society is an education in the deep human meaning and religious value of silence as the spiritual atmosphere vital for perceiving God's presence and for allowing oneself to be won over by it" (PDV 47).

Eucharistic adoration of its very nature can teach us silent prayer. In addition, "[t]he act of adoration outside Mass prolongs and intensifies all that takes place during the liturgical celebration itself. Indeed, 'only in adoration can a profound and genuine reception mature. And it is precisely this personal encounter with the Lord that then strengthens the social mission contained in the Eucharist, which seeks to break down not only the walls that separate the Lord and ourselves, but also and especially the walls that separate us from one another'" (SCar 66). In addition, *lectio divina* and contemplation of the Mysteries of the Rosary also serve to unite and consecrate us to Christ, and the Liturgy of the Hours sanctifies our day as we remain focused on doing God's will in work and leisure. In teaching such prayer, and encouraging other forms of appropriate devotional prayer, the diocesan priest helps form his parishioners in Christ; he nurtures their spirituality and consecrates them for mission. Pope John Paul II expresses the fundamental hope and vision in his apostolic letter *Novo Millennio Ineunte* that

> our Christian communities must become genuine *"schools" of prayer*, where the meeting with Christ is expressed not just in imploring help but also in thanksgiving, praise, adoration, contemplation, listening and ardent devotion, until the heart truly "falls in love." Intense prayer, yes, but it does not distract us from our commitment to history: by opening our heart to the love of God it also opens it to the love of our brothers and sisters, and makes us capable of shaping history according to God's plan. (NMI 33)

---

[29] Sheen, *The Priest Is Not His Own*, 226.

The Priest as Shepherd-King

When he is brought before Pilate, Jesus acknowledges that he is a king, but adds that his kingship is not of this world. The title of "king" is then affixed to the Cross. This latter fact in itself justifies referring to the priest as a shepherd-king. In Christ's self-sacrifice of love on the Cross, he turned the image of kingship on its head. He is the Good Shepherd who lays down his life for his friends (John 10:11; 15:13). His kingly power is wholly religious in nature and integral to his own priesthood. It expresses the power to lead, a power that is his because he is a shepherd. Through the sacrament of Holy Orders, the priest is configured to Christ, head and shepherd of the Church. He becomes a sacramental sign of Christ leading his flock as he continues to carry out the Risen Lord's command to the Eleven: "Go, therefore, and make disciples of all nations" (Matt 28:19a).

In Jesus' time, shepherds were held in low esteem; city-dwellers tended to look upon them with contempt. Galot suggests that Jesus employs this image because he "intends to stress the humility which ought to characterize authority in the Church, a humility which translates into service and sacrifice."[30] Pope John Paul II accented this very point when he stated, "Those who in virtue of priestly ordination, receive the mission of *shepherds* are called to present anew in their lives and witness to in their actions the heroic love of the *Good Shepherd*. . . . Above all this love is humble. . . . As a result the mission of shepherd cannot be carried out with a superior or authoritarian attitude, which would irritate the faithful and perhaps drive them from the fold."[31]

The shepherd's task, according to Jesus, is to lead his flock (John 10:3). He knows them and calls them by name. He goes in search of the ones who stray (Luke 15:4). Building up and tending to the Christian community, the Body of Christ, requires of the priest the ability to relate well and to cooperate with others. As *Pastores Dabo Vobis* states, "This is truly fundamental for a person who is called to be responsible for a community and to be a 'man of communion.'" It further elaborates:

> In order that his ministry may be humanly as credible and acceptable as possible, it is important that the priest should mold his human personality in such a way that it becomes a bridge and not an obstacle for others in their meeting with Jesus Christ the Redeemer of humanity. It is necessary that, following the example of Jesus who "knew

---

[30] Jean Galot, SJ, *Theology of Priesthood* (San Francisco: Ignatius Press, 1985), 49.

[31] Pope John Paul II, *Priesthood in the Third Millennium*, General Audience of Wednesday, July 7, 1993 (New York: Scepter Publishers, 1994), 76 with emphasis in original.

what was in humanity" (Jn. 2:25; cf. 8:3-11), the priest should be able to know the depths of the human heart, to perceive difficulties and problems, to make meeting and dialogue easy, to create trust and cooperation, to express serene and objective judgments. (PDV 43)

Father Jean Galot, SJ, aptly characterizes the level of capacity for relationships needed by the priest when he writes that, "As shepherd, he claims not the quality of a father, but rather of a brother . . . the shepherd is one who sustains a brotherly relation to the people entrusted to his care."[32]

In addition to the human capacity of being able to relate to others one-on-one, Pope John Paul II also pointed out:

The presbyter is responsible for the organic functioning of the community. To fulfill this task the bishop gives him a necessary share in his authority. It is his responsibility to ensure that the various services, indispensable for the good of all, are carried out harmoniously; to find appropriate assistance for the liturgy, catechesis and spiritual support for married couples; to foster the development of various spiritual and apostolic associations or 'movements' in harmony and cooperation; to organize charitable aid for the needy, the sick and immigrants.[33]

To carry out this responsibility successfully the pastor needs to collaborate with others and to coordinate their efforts.

Vatican II's Dogmatic Constitution on the Church teaches, "The pastors, indeed, should recognize and promote the dignity and responsibility of the laity in the Church. They should willingly use their prudent advice and confidently assign duties to them in the service of the Church, leaving them freedom and scope for acting. Indeed, they should give them the courage to undertake works on their own initiative." The Council Fathers then add that, "Many benefits for the Church are to be expected from this familiar relationship between the laity and the pastors" (LG 37). Indeed, such familiar (that is, "family-like") cooperation serves to reflect in the parish the inner life of God, who is a communion of love, who is Trinity. Father Robert Schwartz, therefore, fittingly asks: "If grace is a share in God's life, and God is Trinity, can we be anything other than collaborative if we are being faithful to grace?"[34]

---

[32] Galot, *Theology of Priesthood*, 50. See also *Lumen Gentium* 32.

[33] Pope John Paul II, *Priesthood in the Third Millennium*, 46–47.

[34] Schwartz, "Servant of the Servants of God: A Pastor's Spirituality," 18.

This koinonia of love, this cooperation and collaborative spirit, are further elaborated upon by Pope John Paul II in *Novo Millennio Ineunte* as he reflects upon the pastoral needs of the twenty-first century:

> Communion must be cultivated and extended day by day and at every level in the structures of each Church's life. There, relations between Bishops, priests and deacons, between Pastors and the entire People of God, between clergy and Religious, between associations and ecclesial movements must all be clearly characterized by communion. To this end, the structures of participation envisaged by Canon Law, such as *the Council of Priests and the Pastoral Council,* must be ever more highly valued. These of course are not governed by the rules of parliamentary democracy, because they are consultative rather than deliberative; yet this does not mean that they are less meaningful and relevant. The theology and spirituality of communion encourage a fruitful dialogue between Pastors and faithful: on the one hand uniting them *a priori* in all that is essential, and on the other leading them to pondered agreement in matters open to discussion. (NMI 45)

At the same time, as we plan and labor to build up this communion of love, John Paul II counsels us:

> If in the planning that awaits us we commit ourselves more confidently to a pastoral activity that gives personal and communal prayer its proper place, we shall be observing an essential principle of the Christian view of life: *the primacy of grace.* There is a temptation which perennially besets every spiritual journey and pastoral work: that of thinking that the results depend on our ability to act and to plan. God of course asks us really to cooperate with his grace, and therefore invites us to invest all our resources of intelligence and energy in serving the cause of the Kingdom. But it is fatal to forget that "without Christ we can do nothing" (cf. *Jn* 15:5).
>
> It is prayer which roots us in this truth. It constantly reminds us of the primacy of Christ and, in union with him, the primacy of the interior life and of holiness. When this principle is not respected, is it any wonder that pastoral plans come to nothing and leave us with a disheartening sense of frustration? We then share the experience of the disciples in the Gospel story of the miraculous catch of fish: "We have toiled all night and caught nothing" (*Lk* 5:5). (NMI 38)

Building up the Body of Christ can only happen when we bring the fruit of our prayerful appropriation of Jesus' paschal mystery to bear upon overcoming the sundering effects of sin in all its aspects. This is primarily a ministry of reconciliation through which our relationships to God, to one another, to our selves, and to all creation are healed and restored. As such it constitutes the goal of the Church's essential mission of evangelization. It is for this evangelizing mission that we are consecrated in Word and sacrament. As Deacon James Keating has commented, "The priest is supposed to *lead his bride somewhere*, and that *somewhere* is not simply the conventionalities of present culture. . . . Ultimately, this *somewhere* is a *someone*. . . . Here is where the pastor must lead his people: participation in the paschal mystery."[35] He furthermore concludes that, "As a priest sacrifices his life in service to the conversion of his people, who receive their joy from such conversion, so a priest lives fully in joy when the laity symbolically give him their sacrificed lives in the work of building both the domestic church and a civilization of love."[36]

In describing himself as the Good Shepherd, Jesus also stated: "I have other sheep that do not belong to this fold. These also I must lead, and they will hear my voice, and there will be one flock, one shepherd" (John 10:16). Cardinal Avery Dulles, SJ, opines that the one dimension of the doctrine of the priesthood not sufficiently emphasized by Vatican II is the ecumenical, despite the Council's thrust toward ecumenism. He writes: "From many books and articles on the subject, even since Vatican II, one gets the impression that the priest is a strictly denominational functionary, responsible only for the internal life of a single communion or a single parish."[37] He recommends that priests take a proactive role in advancing ecumenism by joining ministerial associations and councils of churches that are open to Protestants, Anglicans, and Orthodox.

Indeed, Pope John Paul II in his encyclical *Ut Unum Sint* teaches that, "it is absolutely clear that ecumenism, the movement promoting Christian unity, *is not just some sort of "appendix"* which is added to the Church's traditional activity. Rather, ecumenism is an organic part of her life and work, and consequently must pervade all that she is and does . . ." (UUS 20).[38] Priests, as shepherds, need to demonstrate to the faithful and encourage them to participate in the many opportunities that already exist for ecumenical cooperation. The pope himself elaborates: "With increasing frequency Christians are working together to defend human dignity, to promote peace, to apply the Gospel to social life, to bring the Christian

---

[35] Keating, "How Can Catholic Spirituality Be More at the Heart of Priestly Formation?" 15–16.

[36] Ibid., 19.

[37] Dulles, *The Priestly Office*, 56.

[38] Emphasis in original.

spirit to the world of science and of the arts. They find themselves ever more united in striving to meet the sufferings and the needs of our time: hunger, natural disasters and social injustice" (UUS 74). This working for reconciliation among Christians is thus also an integral part of the Church's mission of evangelization (cf. UUS 98).

The priestly image of Jesus as the Good Shepherd embodies his self-giving, reconciling love, which is God's redeeming love (cf. John 3:16-17). Those whom the Lord calls to share in his unique ministerial priesthood are by their consecration and configuration to Christ, head and shepherd, expected to make their whole lives a manifestation of "pastoral charity." Hence every attempt to lord it over others, all authoritarianism, all forms of clericalism are objectively grave sins against pastoral charity when they kill or wholly conceal God's love, which Jesus the Good Shepherd has come to reveal and pour forth into our lives.

In Jesus Christ we are given, in the words of Father Jean Galot, SJ, the "new visage of the sacred."[39] This new understanding of the sacred, he maintains, is manifested in four ways. First of all, in the person of the Risen Christ the sacred shifts from things to persons, and participation in the sacred no longer happens "through mere bodily contact with physical things, but through interpersonal relations."[40] Secondly, the sacred is dynamic in nature; it unfolds in the power of the Holy Spirit. Thirdly, the new sacred does not seek to rescue one from the profane but to bring about the most fundamental sacralization of it. "Finally, the sacred as it appears concretely in Jesus does not arouse fear. . . . On the contrary, it manifests the effusion of God's love and seeks to bring God and mankind closer to each other."[41]

The Mission or Apostolate of the Laity

Pope John Paul II frequently emphasized the teaching of Vatican II's Dogmatic Constitution on the Church that "the ministerial priesthood . . . essentially has the royal priesthood of all the faithful as its aim and is ordered to it" (CL 22).[42] The Council also affirmed that there remains a "true equality between all [the lay faithful, pastors and other Church ministers] with regard to the dignity and to the activity which is common

---

[39] Galot, *Theology of the Priesthood*, 40.

[40] Ibid.

[41] Ibid.

[42] With footnote reference to *Lumen Gentium* 10.

to all the faithful in the building up of the Body of Christ" (LG 32). This conciliar teaching stood in compelling contrast to the then-formulations of the Church's canon law, which prior to the 1983 Code defined the laity negatively as those not ordained. Consequently, in his apostolic exhortation *Christifideles Laici* of 1988, John Paul II constantly appeals to authoritative conciliar texts in order to call the whole Church to a deeper understanding of the lay vocation, of the laity's dignity and mission. In his memoir on the fiftieth anniversary of his priestly ordination, *Gift and Mystery*, he stated that he "rejoiced" over Vatican II's teaching on the laity: "what the Council was teaching corresponded to the convictions which had guided my activity ever since the first years of my priestly ministry."[43]

Both *Lumen Gentium* and *Christifideles Laici* again and again refer to the "secular character" of the lay vocation. Pope John Paul II structures the latter document around the Johannine image of the vine and the branches (John 15:1-5) and the Synoptic image of the laborers in the vineyard (Matt 20:1-6). Indeed, the vineyard is for him the world with its economic, social, political, and cultural affairs; it is "the field in which the faithful are called to fulfill their mission" (CL 3). More than living in the world, John Paul II believes that lay Christians also have a mission to the world, the world that is so loved by God (cf. John 3:16) and is "destined to glorify God the Father in Christ" (CL 15). As branches on the vine that is Christ, the lay faithful share a mystical communion with Christ and with one another, and thus have, in the words of Vatican II, "the exalted vocation" and "obligation to bring forth fruit in charity for the life of the world" (OT 16). This secular vocation of the laity "has the purpose of making everyone know and live the 'new' communion that the Son of God made man introduced into the history of the world" (CL 32).[44]

The *Compendium of the Social Doctrine of the Church* by the Pontifical Council for Justice and Peace elaborates further upon the laity's spirituality and mission. It states:

> *The lay faithful are called to cultivate an authentic lay spirituality by which they are reborn as new men and women, both sanctified and sanctifiers, immersed in the mystery of God and inserted in society.* Such a spirituality will build up the world according to Jesus' Spirit. It will make people capable of looking beyond history, without separating themselves from it, of cultivating a passionate love for God without looking away

---

[43] Pope John Paul II, *Gift and Mystery: On the Fiftieth Anniversary of My Priestly Ordination* (New York: Doubleday, 1996), 70.

[44] See also CCC 898–900.

from their brothers and sisters, whom they are able to see as the Lord sees them and love as the Lord loves them. This spirituality precludes both an *intimist spiritualism* and a *social activism*, expressing itself instead in a life-giving synthesis that bestows unity, meaning, and hope on an existence that for so many different reasons is contradictory and fragmented. Prompted by such a spirituality, the lay faithful are able to contribute "to the sanctification of the world, as from within like a leaven, by fulfilling their own particular duties. Thus, especially by the witness of their own life . . . they must manifest Christ to others" (no. 545).[45]

The diocesan priest, therefore, needs not only to know well the things of God—Scripture, theology, prayer—but he must also know human realities well and understand how the two come together in his own spiritual life and in the lives of the people he is sent to serve.

Saint Francis de Sales in his still acclaimed *Introduction to the Devout Life*, first published in 1613 and well renowned for its discussion on how to live a holy life in the secular world, maintained that the spiritual life—which he referred to as "devotion"—must be practiced in different ways and adapted to the strength, occupation, and duties of each particular person. He accordingly asks

> whether it is proper for a bishop to want to lead a solitary life like a Carthusian; or for married people to be no more concerned than a Capuchin about increasing their income; or for a working man to spend his whole day in church like a religious; or on the other hand for a religious to be constantly exposed like a bishop to all the events and circumstances that bear on the needs of our neighbor. Is not this sort of devotion ridiculous, unorganized and intolerable?[46]

A spirituality that is "purely contemplative, monastic and religious," St. Francis held, simply cannot be practiced in such situations. The diocesan priest, therefore, needs to be knowledgeable of the various types of spiritualities and devotions that can support the members of the laity in their secular vocations and in their mission to the world. Thus Robert Schwartz insists that, "While not assigned a role in economics, politics, the arts, or even family life by ordination, the effective pastor studies and

---

[45] With footnote reference to CL 59. Emphasis in original.

[46] Francis de Sales, *Introduction to the Devout Life*, Pars 1, cap. 3; translation taken from Office of Readings for the feast of the saint, January 24, in *The Liturgy of the Hours*, vol. 3 (New York: Catholic Book Publishing Co., 1975), 1318.

contemplates all that touches the lives of those he serves. The parish priest who is out of touch with the daily realities of the laity is of no earthly good to them. This is tragic indeed, since the laity must find and serve God in the midst of these realities, not in some other world."[47]

Primarily, it is through the sacraments of baptism, confirmation, and the Eucharist that the identity, spirituality, and mission of the lay faithful are born and nourished. In the Eucharist especially the faithful are nourished by the gift of Jesus Christ's self-sacrificing and reconciling love for the salvation of the world. Thus as the *Compendium of the Social Doctrine of the Church* so aptly summarizes, "*Lay Catholics are disciples of Christ starting with the sacraments, that is, by virtue of what God has wrought in them, marking them with the very image of his Son Jesus Christ.* It is from this divine gift of grace, and not from human concession, that is born the threefold *'munus' (gift and duty)* that characterizes the lay person as *prophet, priest, and king*, according to his secular nature" (no. 541).[48] By the sacraments all the faithful are consecrated for the Church's mission of evangelization, and through their threefold *munus* they embrace this mission and continue to build "the civilization of love."

For their part the lay faithful participate in Christ's *prophetic mission* when "the power of the Gospel . . . shine[s] out in daily family and social life" (LG 35). In their married and family life, the Council Fathers state, "they must be witnesses of faith and love of Christ to one another and to their children," and "even when occupied by temporal affairs, the laity can, and must, do valuable work for the evangelization of the world" (LG 35). John Paul II further affirms that "the lay faithful are given the ability and responsibility to accept the gospel in faith and to proclaim it in word and deed, without hesitating to courageously identify and denounce evil" (CL 14).

The laity also share in Christ's *priestly mission* when they unite themselves to him and to his sacrifice in the offering they make of themselves and their daily activities. Thus Vatican II teaches that, "all their works, prayers and apostolic undertakings, family and married life, daily work, relaxation of mind and body, if they are accomplished in the Spirit—indeed even the hardships of life if patiently borne—all these become spiritual sacrifices acceptable to God through Jesus Christ" (LG 34). Then at the Eucharist under the sacramental leadership of the ordained priesthood, the laity unite themselves to Christ's self-sacrifice as the priest of their own lives.

---

[47] Schwartz, "Servant of the Servants of God: A Pastor's Spirituality," 6.
[48] Emphasis in original.

The lay faithful, moreover, participate in Christ's *royal mission*, according to Vatican II's Dogmatic Constitution on the Church, when by serving others in Jesus' name they spread his kingdom: "the kingdom of truth and life, the kingdom of holiness and grace, the kingdom of justice, love and peace. In this kingdom creation itself will be delivered from the slavery of corruption into the freedom of the glory of the sons of God (cf. Rom. 8:21). . . . Therefore, by their competence in secular disciplines and by their activity, interiorly raised up by grace, let them work earnestly in order that created goods through human labor, technical skill and civil culture may serve the utility of all men according to the plan of the creator and the light of his word" (LG 36). This apostolate requires first of all, as the Council Fathers teach, that the laity "by self-abnegation of a holy life, overcome the reign of sin in themselves (cf. Rom. 6:12)."

In the Trinitarian, Christological, and ecclesiological perspective of the Second Vatican Council, the whole Church is called to holiness and mission. Pope John Paul II reconfirms the Council's theological vision when he writes in *Christifideles Laici*: "We come to a full sense of the dignity of the lay faithful if we consider *the prime and fundamental vocation* that the Father assigns to each of them in Jesus Christ through the Holy Spirit: the vocation to holiness, that is, the perfection of charity" (CL 16).[49] Furthermore, he suggests that the gospel images of salt, light, and leaven are particularly significant and truly applicable to all Jesus' disciples "because they speak not only of the deep involvement and the full participation of the lay faithful in the affairs of the earth, the world and the human community, but also and above all, they tell of the radical newness and unique character of an involvement and participation which has as its purpose the spreading of the Gospel that brings salvation" (CL 15).

After maintaining that the "primary and immediate task" of the laity is to bring the Gospel to bear on the affairs of the world, Pope Paul VI in *Evangelii Nuntiandi* additionally affirms that "the laity can also feel themselves called, or be called, to work with their pastors in the service of the ecclesial community for its growth and life, by exercising a great variety of ministries according to the grace and charisms which the Lord is pleased to give them" (EN 73). Among these ministries Paul VI names catechists, directors of prayer and chant, as well as other ministers of the Word, those involved in charitable works, heads of small communities, and persons in charge of apostolic movements (cf. EN 73). Especially in the wake of the liturgical renewal promoted by Vatican II, the laity have come forward to fulfill the many tasks not requiring an ordained minister. John Paul II,

---

[49] Emphasis in original.

to that end, observes that "there is a natural transition from an effective involvement of the lay faithful in the liturgical action to that of announcing the word of God and pastoral care" (CL 23). He further mentions, however, that the 1987 Synod Assembly expressed concern about "the too-indiscriminate use of the word 'ministry' . . . [and of] the tendency towards a 'clericalization' of the lay faithful . . ." (CL 23).

A decade later in 1999, in *Ecclesia in America*, John Paul II explains that there are two areas in which the laypeople live their vocation: the first is "the secular world, which they are called to shape according to God's will"; the second area "can be called 'intraecclesial'." In this latter area they "contribute their talents and charisms 'to the building of the ecclesial community as delegates of the word, catechists, visitors to the sick and the imprisoned, group leaders, etc.'" (EIA 44).[50] The pope advises, "There is a need to promote positive cooperation by properly trained lay men and women in different activities within the church, while avoiding any confusion with the ordained ministries and the activities proper to the sacrament of Orders . . ." (EIA 44). Finally, on this point, he states that, "while the intraecclesial apostolate of lay people needs to be promoted, care must be taken to ensure that it goes hand in hand with the activity proper to the laity, in which their place cannot be taken by priests: the area of temporal realities" (EIA 44).

The diocesan priest exists as servant of lay holiness and mission. In the parish (*paroikos*) he "dwells beside" the members of Christ's Body as a witness to the fundamental presence of God's loving care. There, he continues Christ's threefold mission as priest, prophet, and king by faithfully serving God's people entrusted to his care and forming them "in Christ," in his paschal mystery. With St. Paul he should be able to say, "it was I who fathered you in Christ Jesus, by the gospel" (1 Cor 4:15 NJB). The priest, in carrying out his ministry, is the primary collaborator with the bishop and assists him in the work of teaching, sanctifying, and guiding the community of the faithful. As the USCCB's *Co-Workers in the Vineyard of the Lord* states:

> In union with the bishop, whom he makes present in the local community, the priest sacramentally represents Christ, the Head of the Church, and so serves to guide the Body of Christ in its mission of salvation and transformation of the world:
>
>> Inasmuch as he represents Christ the head, shepherd and spouse of the Church, the priest is placed not only *in the*

[50] With footnote reference to Synodal Proposition 56.

Church but also *in the forefront of the Church.* The ordained priesthood, along with the word of God and the sacraments which it serves, belongs to the constitutive elements of the Church. The ministry of the priest is entirely on behalf of the Church; it aims at promoting the exercise of the common priesthood of the entire people of God.[51]

---

[51] USCCB Committee on the Laity, *Co-Workers in the Vineyard of the Lord* (Washington, DC: USCCB, 2005), 23, with indented quotation from PDV 16; emphasis in original.

Chapter 5

The Spousal Meaning of Celibacy

The celibate priest can more fittingly represent Christ in his nuptial relationship to the church, which . . . is displayed in every celebration of the Eucharist.

—Cardinal Avery Dulles, SJ[1]

Through the gift of chaste celibacy the priest is identified more closely with Jesus Christ, the Eternal High Priest, who continues to pour himself out in love for the Church, his Bride. Celibacy unites the priest more fully with Christ's consecration and mission. It makes him one with Christ as head, shepherd, and spouse of the Church. The Second Vatican Council teaches that celibacy is "based on the mystery of Christ and his mission," and it further explains that "by means of celibacy, then, priests profess before men their willingness to be dedicated with undivided loyalty to the task entrusted to them, namely that of espousing the faithful to one husband and presenting them as a chaste virgin to Christ. They recall the mystical marriage, established by God and destined to be fully revealed in the future, by which the Church holds Christ as her only spouse" (PO 16).

Vatican II also states that, "While recommending ecclesiastical celibacy this sacred Council does not by any means aim at changing that contrary discipline which is lawfully practiced in the Eastern Churches" (PO 16).

---

[1] Avery Dulles, SJ, *The Priestly Office: A Theological Reflection* (New York/Mahwah, NJ, Paulist Press, 1997), 70.

The Council Fathers, however, see a true harmony between the priesthood and celibacy. "By preserving virginity or celibacy for the sake of the kingdom of heaven priests are consecrated in a new and excellent way to Christ. They more readily cling to him with undivided heart and . . . are less encumbered in the service of his kingdom . . . " (PO 16). The Council acknowledges that celibacy is not "demanded of the priesthood by its nature," but it is indeed recommended by Christ and serves as a "sign of pastoral charity." Furthermore, celibacy makes the priest "a living sign of that world to come . . . a world in which the children of the resurrection shall neither marry nor be given in marriage" (PO 16).

In his encyclical letter on priestly celibacy *Sacerdotalis Caelibatus* in 1967, Pope Paul VI, in addition to elaborating upon the theological vision of celibacy presented by the Second Vatican Council, addresses some of the contemporary objections raised against celibacy, provides a brief history of the differing traditions in the East and the West, confirms the law in the Western Church, and presents further theological and pastoral reasons for it. The primary reason he gives is Christological; he accordingly writes, "Christ, the only Son of the Father, by the power of the Incarnation itself was made mediator between heaven and earth, between the Father and the human race. Wholly in accord with this mission, Christ remained throughout his whole life in a state of celibacy, which signified his total dedication to the service of God and men" (SCael 21). By living a celibate life the priest more perfectly imitates Christ and becomes a more authentic sign, or sacrament, of Christ's eternal priesthood and of the "love which Christ has shown us so sublimely" (SCael 24).

Many reasons have been put forward in opposition to priestly celibacy. Most are totally pragmatic, such as there would be more vocations, many priests are unfaithful to their promise of celibacy, others have left to marry and would return to active ministry if allowed to do so. In addition, celibacy sets the priest apart from the people he is sent to serve, making it difficult for him to understand their domestic problems. Then there is the area of ecumenism: Orthodox and Protestant clergy are allowed to marry. Psychological reasons are also given: it violates the freedom of those called to the priesthood but who do not believe they are meant to be celibate; it is unnatural and prevents mature psychosexual development as demonstrated by recent scandals, especially the sexual abuse of minors; and it tends to promote a homosexual culture, as well as a self-centered "bachelorhood" mentality. Still others challenge what they see as the theological tradition the Church has used to support celibacy: they point out that the New Testament does not demand celibacy and that the Church Fathers justify it mainly by arguments based upon an overly pessimistic view of the body and sexuality, as well as upon predominantly Old Testament notions of ritual purity.

This chapter hopes to touch on many of these objections as it offers some historical, theological, and human reflections upon the gift-call of lifelong priestly celibacy. Father Jean Galot, SJ, has observed, "Today's crisis has the advantage of alerting us to the need for a new theological effort. . . . Too many priests have lived their celibacy far too instinctively. Or celibacy has been observed as if it were just a law requiring that life be chaste. . . . In the future, the significance and motivations of celibacy must be made to stand out more clearly, both in the doctrinal reflection on the priesthood, and in the preparation of seminarians for the priestly way of life."[2] The chapter will conclude then with a brief look at the separate, but not unrelated, question of the admission of women to the ministerial priesthood.

The Evolution of the Evangelical Ideal of Celibacy for the Sake of the Kingdom

In the gospels celibacy for the sake of the kingdom of heaven is a gift that Jesus Christ gave to the Church (cf. Matt 19:12). It is not something he required of his disciples and is not a charism belonging essentially or exclusively to the priesthood. Jesus first commends celibacy to his disciples within the context of his teaching on the indissolubility of marriage. For him "not to marry" is a gift of the Father given "only those to whom [it] is granted" (Matt 19:11). Jesus' words here defied Jewish tradition, which looked upon marriage and raising a family as a God-given obligation arising from the creation account in Genesis. Within this perspective, to be a celibate male is pejoratively equivalent to being a "eunuch," or not a man at all.

Furthermore, it must be stated that Jesus does not recommend celibacy out of contempt for sexuality, nor does he ever equate sexuality with sin. As Galot observes, "He has no obsessive preoccupation with carnal sins. When he disavows adultery, he stresses the guilty intention. He displays a greater severity when condemning hypocrisy, the refusal to believe, or lack of concern for one's neighbor."[3] Celibacy, Jesus says, is "for the sake of the kingdom of heaven" (Matt 19:12), which here is meant to include

---

[2] Jean Galot, SJ, *Theology of Priesthood* (San Francisco: Ignatius Press, 1985), 245.
[3] Ibid., 235.

not only finality but also causality. The kingdom grabs hold of one's life; it is the "treasure buried in a field" or the "pearl of great price" for which one "out of joy goes and sells all that he has" (Matt 13:44-46). The kingdom represents the grace of reconciliation and intimate communion with the Divine Source of life and love that brings about a new spiritual marriage and fruitfulness in love. Celibacy, moreover, bears witness to the eschatological nature of the kingdom, where in Jesus' words, "At the resurrection they neither marry nor are given in marriage but are like the angels in heaven" (Matt 22:30).

The gospels further attest that Jesus himself was celibate. Indeed, the link between priesthood and celibacy was first established by Christ himself. As Galot asserts, "The indisputable fact of Christ's celibacy shows that, in its most perfect realization, the priesthood entails the renunciation of marriage."[4] John A. Sanford, a married Episcopalian priest and psychologist, adds, "If Jesus was not married, it was not because he was averse to sexuality or to women, but because he was conscious of a unique mission he was to perform which precluded marriage, and also because he carried his marriage *on the inside.*"[5] Jesus, furthermore, frequently employed the symbolism of weddings to teach about the kingdom of God (see Matt 22:1-12; 25:10; Luke 12:36; John 2:1-11) and referred to himself as the bridegroom (Matt 9:15, 25:1; Mark 2:19; John 3:29). The conclusion left to be drawn then from Jesus' teaching and example is that "the supreme model of priesthood is the celibate model."[6]

In 1 Corinthians 7, St. Paul echoes Jesus' words about marriage and celibacy. He recommends continence and virginity but adds, "Indeed, I wish everyone to be as I am, but each has a particular gift from God, one of one kind and one of another" (v. 7). He too emphasizes the eschatological motive for celibacy when he says, "For the world in its present form is passing away" (v. 31). Paul does not intend to denigrate marriage, nor does he see it estranging one from God. In fact he writes to the Ephesians that marriage is "a great mystery, but I speak in reference to Christ and the church" (Eph 5:32). Paul primarily appreciates the apostolic and mystical value of celibacy; it allows for totally dedicating oneself to the things of the Lord and for a union with him which is unhampered by distractions (1 Cor 7:32-35). Jesus likewise extolled the ascetical practice and rewards, both eternal and temporal, of giving up everything—house,

---

[4] Ibid., 230.

[5] John A. Sanford, *The Kingdom Within* (Ramsey, NJ: Paulist Press, 1970), 166 with emphasis in the original.

[6] Galot, *Theology of Priesthood*, 230.

wife, brothers, parents, and children—"for the sake of the kingdom of God" (Luke 18:29-30).

Pope Paul VI writes that the patristic literature attests to the spread throughout the East and the West of the voluntary practice of celibacy by the ministers of the Church "because of its profound suitability for their total dedication to the service of Christ and of his Church" (SCael 35). He adds, "The Church of the West, from the beginning of the fourth century, strengthened, spread, and approved this practice by means of various provincial Councils and through the Supreme Pontiffs" (no. 36). The Spanish Council of Elvira (ca. 305), for instance, insisted that an ordained man who was married should thereafter live in permanent and unconditional continence. In the West these regional councils had mixed successes in their attempts to introduce the practice of clerical celibacy throughout the patristic era. Only with the Gregorian reforms of the eleventh and twelfth centuries did the discipline become widely established in the Latin Church. The Council of Trent in the sixteenth century then mandated clerical celibacy, and it declared all attempted marriages of bishops, priests, and deacons to be not only illicit but invalid. Galot thus points out that, "Celibacy for the sake of the kingdom has urged itself progressively upon the priesthood of the Church. It was an innovation ushered in by the gospel, and time was required for it to win recognition in all its scope and import."[7]

The above developmental approach to celibacy embraced by Pope Paul VI and numerous, mainline church historians and theologians has held sway for many decades, but more recently has been challenged by what Aidan Nichols, OP, refers to as a "movement of revisionist historiography." Thus he notes that, "The *history* of priestly celibacy is a controverted topic which still awaits its definitive chronicling, especially where the claim to an apostolic origin is concerned."[8] While discussion continues about the actual apostolic origin of clerical celibacy, there appears to be substantial evidence that clerical celibacy was not universally advocated in the great patristic era. How else can one explain St. Gregory of Nazianzus's touching portrait of the sanctity of a married bishop, which he presents in his

---

[7] Ibid., 239.

[8] Aidan Nichols, *Holy Order: The Apostolic Ministry from the New Testament to the Second Vatican Council* (Lancaster, PA: Veritas Press, 1991), 155–56 with emphasis in original. Among the revisionist historians of celibacy he cites Christian Cochini, SJ, *The Apostolic Origins of Priestly Celibacy* (San Francisco: Ignatius Press, 1990), and from the Ukrainian Catholic exarchate of Great Britain, Father Roman Cholij, *Clerical Celibacy in East and West* (Leominster, England: Fowler Wright Books, 1989).

funeral eulogy for his father?[9] Embarrassed by this ideal of a married episcopacy, some later writers tried to point out that Gregory's youngest brother was born before his father became a bishop, but the facts do not substantiate this.[10] Saint Basil the Great, father of Eastern monasticism, also allowed bishops, presbyters, and deacons to keep their wives, while he insisted on celibacy for monks.[11] Peter Brown, the Princeton historian of late antiquity, concludes, "Bishops and members of the upper clergy were frequently recruited from the desert, but village priests and minor clergy were usually married persons, who still slept with their wives."[12]

Moreover, Peter Brown maintains that the early Christian emphasis on virginity can never be limited exclusively to negative cultural and philosophical attitudes toward sexuality. These at best played only a secondary and minor role.[13] Rather, he writes, "virginity was frequently paraded as yet one further manifestation of the suprahuman origins of the Christian faith."[14] First of all, the life of the sexually continent represented on earth the "life of the angels." In ancient Mediterranean society it became a declaration of freedom from the conventional social expectation that all boys and girls, by the process of physical maturation, would marry and produce children. Thus, the body was no longer permeable to society's demands. Free from the demands of marriage, family, and kinship, the virgin state bears witness to the eschatological promise of Jesus to the "sons of God": "When they rise from the dead, they neither marry nor are given in marriage, but they are like the angels in heaven" (Mark 12:25). Great monasteries and nunneries were soon to spring up and provide alternative societies in miniature, "which pointedly lacked the one ingredient on which political communities had usually rested in the ancient world—the solid flesh and blood of family and kinship."[15]

By the end of the third century virginity was increasingly compared to martyrdom. Methodius of Olympus writes that virgins will be the first to follow in the Lord's train into the kingdom of heaven: "Their martyrdom

---

[9] See *Funeral Orations by Saint Gregory Nazienzen and Saint Ambrose*, vol. 22 of *Fathers of the Church* (New York: Fathers of the Church, Inc., 1953), 119–56.

[10] See J. Cummings, *New Catholic Encyclopedia* (New York: McGraw-Hill, 1967), vol. 6, 791.

[11] See *Epist.* 199.27.

[12] Peter Brown, *The Body and Society: Men, Women, and Sexual Renunciation in Early Christianity* (New York: Columbia University Press, 1988), 256.

[13] Peter Brown, "The Notion of Virginity in the Early Church," in *Christian Spirituality: Origins to the Twelfth Century*, ed. Bernard McGinn and John Meyendorff (New York: Crossroad, 1997), 433.

[14] Ibid., 427.

[15] Ibid., 431.

did not consist of enduring things that pain the body for a short period of time; rather it consisted in steadfast endurance throughout their whole lifetime, never once shrinking from the Olympian contest of being battered in the practice of chastity."[16] Other Fathers take up the same theme. Saint Ambrose holds that "virginity is not praiseworthy because it is found in martyrs but because it itself makes martyrs."[17] Virginity is seen as producing the same effect as martyrdom, namely, death to self bringing about a real participation in Christ's paschal mystery. With the end of state-sponsored persecutions virginity, like monasticism, succeeds to the martyr's mantle.

The virgin ultimately becomes characterized as the bride of Christ and, therefore, a symbol of the Church that alone is described as such in the New Testament: "For the wedding day of the Lamb has come, his bride has made herself ready" (Rev 19:7). Tertullian, therefore, admonishes virgins to wear veils that married women customarily wore.[18] Methodius of Olympus, in addition, demonstrates that the word "virginity" (*parthenia*) becomes "nearness to God" (*partheia*) simply by dropping one letter; this shows that virginity "alone makes divine the one who possesses it and who has been initiated into its pure mysteries."[19] Gregory of Nyssa also developed this theme of deification.[20] Although increasingly thought of in feminine terms, virgins in the first few centuries were spoken of as both masculine and feminine. Gregory himself thus emphasized the possibility of a spiritual marriage for both men and women, for as he pointed out, St. Paul taught "there is not male and female" (Gal 3:28), but "Christ is all and in all" (Col 3:11).[21]

There can be no denying that it was commonplace for the Fathers, when writing about virginity, to speak also about the disadvantages attendant upon marriage. Yet when marriage was actually attacked by Gnostic groups or extreme ascetics in the early Church, writers such as Clement of Alexandria, Gregory Nazianzen, and even Tertullian came to its support.[22] The mid-fourth-century Synod of Gangra in Asia Minor excommunicated

---

[16] *Symposium* 7.3 as cited in Boniface Ramsey, OP, *Beginning to Read the Fathers* (New York/Mahwah, NJ: Paulist Press, 1985), 136.

[17] *De Virginibus* 1.3.10.

[18] See Tertullian, *De virg. vel.* 16.

[19] *Symposium* 8.1 as cited in Ramsey, *Beginning to Read the Fathers*, 141.

[20] See *De virg.* 1–2.

[21] See *De virg.* 20.

[22] See Clement of Alexandria, *Strom.* 3; Gregory of Nazianzen, *Carm. In laudem virg.* 223–277 (PG 27.539-543); and Tertullian, *Ad uxorem* 2.9, written before his Montanist years.

a group of ascetics called Eustathians who condemned marriage, and it warned against pride on the part of virgins vis-à-vis marriage. Boniface Ramsey, OP, concludes that "despite such sentiments and precautions, it must be said that, by and large, marriage got short shrift in comparison with virginity in the ancient Church."[23] Marriage was seen by many of the Church Fathers as only a remedy for concupiscence. Also a number of the Fathers obviously inherited the demeaning attitude toward women that was so prevalent in classical antiquity. "A woman's overarching reason for existence was to bear children; for companionship it was usually assumed that a man would seek out the company of another man."[24]

While such negative attitudes toward marriage and women, along with a societal proclivity toward sexual license, colored many of the patristic writings exalting virginity, still other more substantial theological issues came into play. Fundamental Christian doctrines at the time were frequently attacked and ridiculed. "Christianity had rendered itself patently absurd to thinking pagans—and even more so to Jews, as to later Muslims—by its doctrine of the direct, unmediated joining of the highest God to human flesh in the person of Christ."[25] Furthermore, Christians professed that this event occurred in the womb of the Virgin Mary. While the Platonic school shared the Christian vision of the possibility of mediating antithetical categories, it considered humans to be too tainted with matter—in their earthly existence, at any rate—ever to rise to a mediating position. The ethereal *daemons*, sharing immortality with the gods and bodily emotions with the humans, filled the gap in pagan minds between heaven and earth. Peter Brown thus writes that, "behind the mounting fervor of the cult of the Virgin as Theotokos—she who gave birth to God—and as an intercessor for the human race, we can detect the final playing out of the half-conscious logic of the virgin state."[26]

God in Jesus Christ chose "to assert his solidarity with the human race in the most intimate possible manner, by taking his flesh from Mary's womb and then by nurturing that flesh through dependence upon her breasts."[27] The virgin state thus symbolizes this marvelous divine-human mediation, and along with martyrdom it bears witness to the self-sacrifice of Christ in the paschal mystery. The Fathers, furthermore, saw virginity pointing back to the original presexual state of Adam and Eve before the

---

[23] Ramsey, *Beginning to Read the Fathers*, 139.

[24] Ibid., 140.

[25] Brown, "The Notion of Virginity in the Early Church," 433.

[26] Ibid., 436.

[27] Ibid.

Fall and to their having come into being without sexual intercourse. Virginity thus gives witness to the true nature of human solidarity based not upon flesh and blood, but rather upon what Jesus said, "For whoever does the will of my heavenly Father is my brother, and sister, and mother" (Matt 12:50). And finally it points to the Resurrection where "they neither marry nor are given in marriage but are like the angels in heaven" (Matt 22:30). All these theological reasons can be found underlying the early Church's deep appreciation and admiration for virginity and the growing expectation that its clergy remain celibate.

However, pinpointing the exact roots of Christian thinking on celibacy for the clergy is difficult to determine. The combination of a number of factors, including a developing theological appreciation for virginity, all apparently had their role. Old Testament thinking about the priesthood also exerted a major influence. Levitical legislation, which placed marital restrictions on priests during their times of service, indicated a certain relationship between sexuality and the sacred. These laws were based upon the principle that he who touches holy things must be pure and holy, and that sexual activity, even within marriage, generates uncleanness and precludes participation in cultic functions. If the Old Testament required such sexual abstinence, then certainly the New Testament priesthood because of its greater dignity must require clerical celibacy.

Tertullian accordingly speaks of many men and women in ecclesiastical orders who through their continence "have preferred to be wedded to God."[28] Additionally, Eusebius of Caesarea focuses attention on the motive of spiritual fatherhood when he writes: "Those who proclaim and teach the Word of God must zealously renounce marriage in order to dedicate themselves to the performance of loftier deeds. They are fostering a divine and spiritual offspring. They do not rear just one or two children. Their concern extends to an endless multitude."[29]

Practical issues also came into play. As the Christian communities outgrew the early "house churches" full-time ministry was needed, and celibacy more readily allowed the clergy to give their undivided attention to ministry. Economic pressures and concerns in seeing that ecclesiastical property was not alienated also needed to be considered. In feudal times, for instance, dependence upon a manor lord for the financial stability of one's family could often prove to be a hindrance to apostolic activity. The universal discipline of clerical celibacy was only established finally in the

---

[28] Tertullian, *De exhortationis castitatis* 13 (PL 2, 930A).

[29] Eusebius of Caesarea, *Demonstration of the Gospel*, I, 9, 14-15 (PG 22, 81; GCS 23, 42, 1-12).

Latin Church by legislation and its enforcement under Pope Gregory VII and his successors. In his encyclical on celibacy Paul VI states that a different discipline was enacted in the Eastern Church by the Council of Trullo in 692, but he adds:

> Further, it is by no means futile to observe that in the East only celibate priests are ordained bishops, and the priests themselves cannot contract marriage after their ordination to the priesthood. This indicates that these venerable Churches also possess to a certain extent the principle of a celibate priesthood. It shows too that there is a certain appropriateness for the Christian priesthood, of which bishops possess the summit and fullness, of the observance of celibacy. (SCael 40)

The expectation that bishops be celibate in the East more than likely stems from their being the ones who normally presided at the Eucharist. Presbyters in the early centuries of the Church only did so on occasion when delegated by the bishop, and supposedly for this reason were not expected to remain permanently celibate. Early on it seems that celibacy was connected with the one who thus ordinarily represents Christ in leading the Christian community in the eucharistic sacrifice.

Just as the Church's theological understanding of ministry and priesthood has seen a gradual development over the centuries, so its perspective on celibacy proceeded in a similar way. Galot makes this very point when he states, "There has been a slow maturation: the realization of the ideal suggested by the gospel does not happen in one stroke. It requires a whole historical evolution."[30] Indeed, even after the Gregorian reforms, by the fourteenth century the nonobservance of celibacy by many of the clergy, including friars and monks, became fairly widespread. With marriage ruled out by legislation, the practice of clerical concubinage soon took its place. Moreover, what one fails to find during this period is anything that resembles a careful theological grounding for the discipline of celibacy. The dominant elements of such a theology found in sermons, hortatory, as well as in calls for clerical reform, merely repeated centuries-old argumentation. They included the notions that sexual relations somehow "soiled" one's bodily and personal integrity; that sexuality was an entangling force that drew one away from the realm of the spirit and from contemplation; that it was too closely allied with the profane and was therefore inappropriate for one so closely associated with the sacred as the priest was; and that a priest who offered sacrifice should himself live

[30] Galot, *Theology of Priesthood*, 242.

a life of sacrifice. All these reasons had first been proposed in the patristic era.[31]

The Council of Trent reconfirmed the Church's legislation regarding clerical celibacy. To reenforce it the Council, as already noted, declared all attempted marriages by the clergy to be not only illicit but also invalid. Trent, moreover, did not offer any new theological insights as a basis for the discipline, but it did proclaim that the state of virginity or celibacy is "better and more blessed" than marriage.[32] Galot insists that in making this statement "the Council intended to define a doctrine of faith."[33] And he adds that the opposite doctrine was qualified as "heretical" according to the theologians in attendance at Trent.

Paul VI in his encyclical notes at the outset that "matrimony according to the will of God continues the work of the first creation," and added that Jesus "raised it to the dignity of a sacrament and of a mysterious symbol of his own union with the Church." Then in reference to celibacy he stated that Christ "opened a new way, in which the human creature adheres wholly and directly to the Lord, and is concerned only with him and with his affairs" (SCael 20). In *Familiaris Consortio* Pope John Paul II, when speaking of virginity and celibacy, reaffirmed Trent's teaching; he noted that, "the Church, throughout her history, has always defended the superiority of this charism to that of marriage, by reason of the wholly singular link which it has with the Kingdom of God" (FC 16).

Celibacy: A Sign of Christ the Bridegroom's Love

After asserting the important need for the priest to understand the theological motivation of the Church's law on celibacy, Pope John Paul II writes in *Pastores Dabo Vobis*, "the will of the church finds its ultimate motivation in the link between celibacy and sacred ordination, which configures the priest to Jesus Christ the head and spouse of the church. The church, as the spouse of Jesus Christ, wishes to be loved by the priest in the total and exclusive manner in which Jesus Christ her head and spouse loved her" (no. 29). Invoking here the image of spouse to describe the relationship between Christ and the Church, John Paul II continued

---

[31] See Bernard Cooke, *Ministry to Word and Sacraments: History and Theology* (Philadelphia: Fortress Press, 1976), 582–583n112.

[32] Session 24, canon 10 (DS 1810).

[33] Galot, *Theology of Priesthood*, 250n55.

to employ the theological methodology of Vatican II, which turned to symbolic communication to present the mystery of the Church in *Lumen Gentium*. There, in fact, we can read: "In the Old Testament the revelation of the kingdom is often made under the forms of symbols. In similar fashion the inner nature of the Church is now made known to us in various images" (LG 6).

The renewal in biblical, liturgical, and patristic studies within the Church during the decades immediately preceding the Second Vatican Council brought to the fore once again the distinct revelatory role of image and symbol. Symbolic communication does not abandon concrete and historical realities but rather sees them as revelatory of deeper meaning. Images and symbols have the unique ability, as the Council Fathers confirmed, to make known the "inner nature" of things. Indeed, in the gospels Jesus employed the "kingdom of God" as the central image of his teaching when he wished to convey the immanent presence of a transcendent reality that defies definition or exact description. The parables of Jesus too are replete with picturesque images from daily life that caught his hearers' attention by their vividness and narrative color. We hear of farming and shepherding, of seeds, wheat and briars, of patched wineskins and household lamps, children quarreling in the marketplace, shady merchants, and wedding banquets. Through the use of symbolic communication Jesus not only unveils the mystery of the divine plan, the coming of the kingdom of God, but he at the same time invites us to enter into it.

Because symbols address the whole person—imagination, intellect, and will—and not just the intellect alone, they call not only for intellectual conversion, but for an even more fundamental affective and moral conversion as well. Such total conversion requires capturing first the imagination. This is the method Jesus employed when he taught the crowds and "spoke to them only in parables" (Matt 13:34). Jesus used stories and images to appeal to the listener's imagination. As Richard Gula, SS, explains, "Our imagination shapes what we see, feel, think, judge, and act because all thinking relies on images. We are guided and formed by the stories and images that dwell within us even more than we think ourselves to be. Our imaginations, shaped by stories and images involve a kind of felt knowing in which we hold together both what we know about something and how we feel about it."[34] Stories, symbols, and images involve the knower as a

---

[34] Richard M. Gula, SS, *To Walk Together Again: The Sacrament of Reconciliation* (New York: Paulist Press, 1984), 165.

person and have a transforming effect; they have a powerful influence on commitments and behavior.[35]

Affective conversion occurs with our appropriation of images and symbols. Under the aspect of the about-face that happens in this realm, we experience a change of values taking place within us as we with reason turn away from those images that express our self-centeredness and self-seeking to those that inspire self-giving and love of others. Embracing lifelong celibacy "for the sake of the kingdom of heaven" symbolizes our already having entered into an intimate communion of life (koinonia) with Transcendent Mystery, with the God who is Love. Therefore, by invoking the image of the Bridegroom to describe himself (cf. Matt 9:15), Jesus wished to present himself as the living symbol of the ever faithful and irrevocable marriage covenant between God and the entire human family. The Son of God, the Word-made-flesh, remains forever inseparably divine and human in the indissoluble union of the two natures, bearing ultimate witness to marital commitment and fidelity. Furthermore, the water changed to wine at the wedding feast of Cana prefigures the blood and water that poured forth from the pierced side and heart of Christ on the Cross (John 19:34). This at the same time consummates Christ's nuptial union with his bride, the Church, born from his side just as Eve came forth from Adam's side in Genesis 2:21-24.[36]

The role of marriage imagery in the Scriptures bears special import. From the Old Testament prophets onward God's offer of salvation to the human race has been depicted in terms of nuptial imagery (see Hos 2; Isa 54:4f.; 62:4f.; Jer 2:2; 3:20). Israel is seen as Yahweh's ardently loved spouse who will remain faithful even when Israel betrays his love. The

---

[35] In my earlier work, *Catholic Moral Tradition: In Christ, a New Creation* (Huntington, IN: Our Sunday Visitor, 1999; republished Eugene, OR: Wipf & Stock, 2006), I turned to the method of symbolic mediation to break open "the mystery of faith" that we are called to live as followers of Christ. For further reading on the role of symbolic communication in theology see Avery Dulles, *The Craft of Theology: From Symbol to System* (New York: Crossroad, 1992; expanded edition 1995), especially chap. 2: "Theology and Symbolic Communication"; also his earlier work, *Models of Revelation* (Garden City, NY: Doubleday, 1984), chap. 9: "Symbolic Mediation." Its particular application to the understanding of priestly celibacy may be found in my presentation "The Rediscovery of Symbolic Communication in Theological Methodology," in *Chaste Celibacy: Living Christ's Own Spousal Love* (First Annual Symposium on the Spirituality and Identity of the Diocesan Priest, held at Sacred Heart Major Seminary, Detroit, MI—March 15–18, 2001), ed. Edward G. Mathews Jr. (Omaha, NE: Institute for Priestly Formation, 2001), 65–79.

[36] See Hans Urs von Balthasar, *Church and World* (New York: Herder and Herder, 1967), 118–19.

deep intimate nature of this love is portrayed most clearly in the Song of Songs. This nuptial mystery ultimately reaches fulfillment in the New Testament where we find it present in the writings of St. Paul (2 Cor 11:2; Eph 5:22-23) and St. John (John 3:29; Rev 19:7, 9) as well as in the Synoptics. There the bridegroom's friends must not fast while Christ is still with them (Mark 2:19), and the kingdom of heaven is compared to a king who gave a wedding feast for his son (Matt 22:1-14; 25:1-13).

Pope John Paul II, moreover, maintained that *"the revelation of the spousal relationship between Christ and the Church* has particular significance" for clarifying the ultimate meaning of voluntary celibacy for the sake of the kingdom of heaven. He especially recommended Ephesians 5:25ff. as a decisive text in this regard stating that, "this text is equally valid both for the theology of marriage and for the theology of continence 'for the kingdom,' the theology of virginity or celibacy."[37] Within the context of his "theology of the body" John Paul II presents celibacy as a particular response to the love of the Divine Spouse. In this perspective love is a gift of self, spousal love is the paradigmatic gift of self, and the Trinity is the archetype of such a gift. Thus John Paul II in a number of his writings constantly referred to Vatican II's teaching on Christian anthropology, which holds that "there is a certain parallel between the union existing among the divine persons and the union of the sons of God in truth and love"; he then concludes that "man can fully discover his true self only in a sincere giving of himself" (GS 24). Both marriage and celibacy, therefore, bear witness to that spousal gift of love by which "Christ loved the church and handed himself over for her to sanctify her" (Eph 5:25).

This scriptural imagery of Christ the Bridegroom's love for his Church more easily discloses the true spiritual meaning of celibacy for the sake of the kingdom of heaven than any formulaic theological exposition or law. Chaste celibacy within the Christian tradition, furthermore, intends to prepare the soul for mystical union with Christ. This inner marriage, achieved in lieu of the outer marriage, is featured prominently in the writings of the great mystics, such as in *The Cloud of Unknowing*, in the mystical marriage of St. Catherine of Siena, and in the spiritual espousal of St. John of the Cross. Indeed, the latter's *Living Flame of Love* had a profound influence on Pope John Paul II's development of the "theology

---

[37] John Paul II, "Continence for the Kingdom—Between Renunciation and Love," General Audience of Wednesday, April 21, 1982, in *Man and Woman He Created Them: A Theology of the Body* (Boston: Pauline Books & Media, 2006), 79:8 with emphasis in original.

of the body."[38] Also Gerald May, MD, in his work on contemplative psychology explains that "the powers of genital and spiritual union are so strong and their similarities so great that it is not surprising to discover how heavily the mystics rely on marital and sexual metaphors to describe their experiences."[39]

In the wake of the theological *ressourcement* of the last century, the teachings of the Second Vatican Council, and the "theology of the body" of John Paul II, a true development in our theological understanding of the inner nature and reasons for the law of priestly celibacy has been taking place. Since New Testament times the Church has always had an innate sense that apostolic ministry and celibacy are somehow essentially connected. Yet while the Latin Church increasingly took legislative initiatives to enforce this discipline over the centuries, nevertheless, theological developments capable of providing a coherent and systematic understanding of the practice have been slow in coming. Indeed, it took John Paul II's philosophical and theological personalism, which lies at the core of his "theology of the body," to further the task.

The sense of personal subjectivity, which plays such a prominent role in the writings of John of the Cross, informed all of John Paul II's theology and led to a more in-depth systematic understanding of the genuine spiritual nature of virginity and celibacy for the sake of the kingdom. In *Pastores Dabo Vobis* he thus writes:

> In virginity and celibacy, chastity retains its original meaning, that is, of human sexuality lived as a genuine sign of and precious service to the love of communion and gift of self to others. This meaning is fully found in virginity which makes evident, even in the renunciation of marriage, the "nuptial meaning" of the body through a communion and a personal gift to Jesus Christ and his Church which prefigures and anticipates the perfect and final communion and self-giving of the world to come. (PDV 29)

This free gift of self, which constitutes the very essence of the marital covenant, is indispensably one with Christ's paschal mystery and reveals the inner nature of the Triune God who is Love. Likewise, the total and self-giving celibate love of the priest reveals the "nuptial meaning" of the body as it bears fruit in the fundamental priestly virtue of pastoral charity. Thus John Paul II states, "Pastoral charity is the virtue by which we imitate

---

[38] See "Introduction by Michael Waldstein" in ibid., 23–34.

[39] Gerald G. May, *Will & Spirit: A Contemplative Psychology* (San Francisco: Harper & Row, 1983), 149.

Christ in his self-giving and service. It is not just what we do, but our gift of self, which manifests Christ's love for his flock" (PDV 23).

At the same time that Vatican II, the Synod of Bishops, and recent popes have reaffirmed the law of clerical celibacy within the Latin Church and have endeavored to portray its deeper theological meaning, opposing views have come principally from those circles within the Church that have embraced a predominantly functional and pragmatic perspective on ecclesiology. Indeed, Father Robert Barron has challenged this point of view by writing that, "The issue of celibacy is not convincing when based on practical or even pastoral considerations."[40] Likewise, Gisbert Greshake contends that "it is becoming increasingly clear in recent years that the 'new' theological approach which seeks to define Church office 'from below', that is, on the horizontal level of the various charismata in the Church, is inadequate."[41]

Those today who argue against clerical celibacy, in addition, tend to exhibit a postmodern mentality that all too readily espouses the therapeutic approach of popularized humanistic psychology with its ethic of self-fulfillment. They appear hard-pressed to understand that self-donation, the total gift of self, and not self-fulfillment is what constitutes the heart of the Christian spiritual life. Thus they readily judge the Church's law to be impractical and unreasonable and even question the motives behind it.[42] Raniero Cantalamessa, OFM Cap, named Preacher to the Papal Household

[40] Robert E. Barron, "Priest as Bearer of Mystery" in *Church* 10, no. 2 (Summer 1994): 13.

[41] Gisbert Greshake, *The Meaning of Christian Priesthood* (Dublin: Four Courts Press; Westminister, MD: Christian Classics, 1988), 26.

[42] See, for example, Donald Cozzens, *Freeing Celibacy* (Collegeville, MN: Liturgical Press, 2006), who equates mandated celibacy with slavery: "And just as it is possible for a slave to know more true inner freedom than his master, it is possible for a priest to thrive spiritually and personally in the condition of mandated celibacy. But this does not justify the institution of celibacy any more than a personally liberated slave justifies the institution of slavery" (87–88). He even suggests that mandatory celibacy "raises the spectrum of injustice" and is a violation of an individual's right (88). It appears that the author here confuses "the freedom of the gospel" with individual autonomy. In the biblical perspective, as in St. Paul, for instance, Christian freedom is not an individualistic concept but a matter of the Spirit's presence (2 Cor 3:17), and from his point of view all human existence involves slavery. We are either slaves of sin, that is, selfishness, or we are slaves of righteousness (Rom 6:17-18). Indeed, St. Paul speaks of himself as a slave of Jesus Christ (Rom 1:1); for him freedom consists of being able to choose who our master will be. Thus, for the early Christians the ultimate freedom was exercised in choosing to become fully one with the Lord Jesus Christ by accepting even the self-sacrifice of martyrdom. By the end of the third century virginity itself was being compared to martyrdom.

in 1980 by Pope John Paul II, describes just this attitude when he writes, "We have let ourselves be influenced by all the talk raised against [virginity and celibacy] in the name of psychology and psychoanalysis. . . . In reality virginity makes sense precisely because eternal life and the risen state exist. It is a reality of the Spirit, and what Paul says about the things of the Spirit apply to it, namely, that 'the unspiritual person is unable to accept what comes from the Spirit of God, since for him it's foolishness. He's unable to understand such matters because they can only be evaluated spiritually' (cf. 1 Cor 2:14)."[43]

Cantalamessa furthermore adds, "Since it is not of divine origin, the compulsory celibacy of priests is open to discussion, but no one can honestly deny that despite all the difficulties and defections that are inevitable in a matter of this kind, the choice made by the Church has, overall, enormously benefited the cause of the Kingdom and of holiness and is a most effective sign among the Christian people today."[44] On the other hand, Donald Cozzens, for example, sees these same difficulties and defections as being the result of "the attempt by the Church to mandate a charism."[45] While he points out that "it took the church more than a millennium to recognize marriage as a sacrament,"[46] he seems to have a problem with accepting that the same developmental approach might be operative when it comes to understanding a vocation, or a gift-call, to the celibate priesthood.

The Church in coming to appreciate more and more its own essential sacramental nature, both in the West and East, has from its earliest centuries sensed a certain congruity between those it calls to preside at the Eucharist (both bishops and presbyters in the West; and principally bishops in the East, who even today must be celibate) and Jesus Christ, who was himself a celibate male and extolled celibacy for the sake of the kingdom of heaven. While allowing for occasional exceptions, such as married Anglican clergy seeking full communion with Rome, the Roman Catholic Church has increasingly over time come to see celibacy as integral to a priestly vocation. Thus a genuine vocation to the priesthood requires that one be, first of all, a baptized Roman Catholic male who, in addition, believes he is being called by God to give of himself totally in order to conform himself to Jesus Christ as both bridegroom and shepherd of the

[43] Raniero Cantalamessa, OFM Cap, *Virginity: A Positive Approach to Celibacy for the Sake of the Kingdom of Heaven* (New York: Alba House, 1995), 9–10.
[44] Ibid., 14–15.
[45] Cozzens, *Freeing Celibacy*, 2.
[46] Ibid., 38.

Church. In a very real sense, the sacramental ministerial priesthood is a wholly monogamous relationship demanding a total gift of self with an undivided heart and attention. The lived quality of this relationship, nevertheless, like every marital relationship depends upon the individual's willingness to continue to give himself completely to it. Continuing to allow oneself to be conformed to Christ's self-sacrifice is the indispensable key. Human failure in lived fidelity to one's commitments is attributable to the psychological, emotional, and spiritual maturity of the person involved and not to the value embraced.

"Celibacy is unreasonable, unnatural, and excessive," Father Barron writes, "which is why it has been chosen, across cultures and throughout history, as one of the ways in which lovers of God have traditionally expressed their love. To try to understand this self-gift or to explain it is to miss the point. Its very strangeness and incomprehensibility is the point. . . . People in love do strange things."[47] Thus as Pope John Paul II concludes, "Celibacy, then, is to be welcomed and continually renewed with a free and loving decision as a priceless gift from God, as an 'incentive to pastoral charity,' as a singular sharing in God's fatherhood and in the fruitfulness of the Church, and as a witness to the world of the eschatological kingdom" (PDV 29). Celibacy for the sake of the kingdom is like marriage in that it is all about the giving of oneself in love. Indeed, one may say that "celibacy keeps alive in the Church a consciousness of the mystery of marriage and defends it from any reduction and impoverishment" (FC 16). A society that has little or no appreciation for celibacy also tends to downplay the role of marriage.

Cultivating Affective Maturity and True Friendships

In *Pastores Dabo Vobis* Pope John Paul II points out that "affective maturity presupposes an awareness that love has a central role in human life" (no. 44). He then cites his first encyclical *Redemptor Hominis*: "Man cannot live without love. He remains a being that is incomprehensible for himself, his life is senseless, if love is not revealed to him, if he does not encounter love, if he does not experience it and make it his own, if he does not participate intimately in it" (RH 10). Such a love involves the whole person—physical, psychic, and spiritual—and is "expressed in the 'nuptial meaning' of the human body, thanks to which the person gives oneself

---

[47] Barron, "Priest as Bearer of Mystery," 13.

and takes the other to oneself" (PDV 44). Affective maturity results from an education in true and responsible love; thus John Paul II further states:

> Since the charism of celibacy, even when it is genuine and has proved itself, leaves one's affections and instinctive impulses intact, candidates to the priesthood need an affective maturity which is prudent, able to renounce anything that is a threat to it, vigilant over both body and spirit, and capable of esteem and respect in interpersonal relationships between men and women. A precious help can be given by a suitable education to true friendship, following the image of the bonds of fraternal affection which Christ himself lived on earth (cf. Jn. 11:5). (PDV 44)

Pope John Paul II, in this apostolic exhortation, identifies four essential pillars of priestly formation—human, spiritual, intellectual, and pastoral—which every priest must continually integrate throughout his entire life.

Seminary formation prior to Vatican II focused mainly on just two of these pillars—prayer and study. Prayer, moreover, was often rather formulaic and regimented; nevertheless, prayer and study basically constituted the entire seminary program. The pastoral, it was believed, would be learned after ordination—after priesthood ordination. Even diaconate was viewed as a mere stepping-stone and was usually exercised only within the seminary itself. Human formation—never referred to as such—would have been thought of in terms of growth in the natural virtues. It was not unusual for a young man to enter the seminary in the 1950s and 1960s at fourteen years of age. Many, however, did wait until they graduated high school. Discipline was very strict and rules were rigid. There were no women in the seminary, except perhaps religious sisters who staffed the kitchen and laundry. If a student were to visit another seminarian's room, he could be immediately dismissed with no questions asked. Vocations were plentiful, and dismissals were a regular occurrence.

If the author may be permitted to interject himself more personally into the text at this point, I remember that during my college seminary years in the mid-1960s we never had any formation sessions on issues of sexuality or sexual feelings. Spiritual and retreat directors on occasion warned us that all violations of the sixth commandment, including impure thoughts and masturbation, were mortal sins that needed to be confessed as soon as possible. Whenever we might experience sexual temptation we were advised to say a Hail Mary immediately, and if possible do physical exercise or take a cold shower. One spiritual director even warned that when we "visited home" for the summer we should never find ourselves alone in a room with one of our sisters because we cannot know "when the woman in her might come out." We were basically taught to look upon our sexuality as something "dirty" and as something to be feared, lest it lead us directly to eternal damnation.

Popular culture at the same time, the late 1960s and early 1970s, was proclaiming a sexual revolution. It was the time of the Vietnam War, student riots, and the "Woodstock generation" that touted "free sex" as healthy and normal. Within the Church, the Second Vatican Council had just ended after calling for a renewal in liturgy and theology, and especially moral theology (cf. OT 16). Yet not much was changing in the seminaries, and seminarians even staged protest strikes in some of the larger seminaries here in the United States. Some theologians too at the time—both Protestant and Catholic—were championing the "secular city" and situation ethics. There was loud opposition in 1968 to Pope Paul VI's encyclical on birth control, *Humanae Vitae*. Seminary faculties were often divided among themselves over these same issues. Most bishops and seminary rectors, furthermore, were highly suspicious of the new social sciences, especially psychology. Then too after the publication of Paul VI's encyclical *On Priestly Celibacy* in 1967, a number of younger priests began to abandon active ministry and attempt marriage.

The seminarians of my generation were left for the most part to sort it all out on our own. Some priest-psychologists were publishing articles and books exploring the realm of human emotions, feelings, and sexuality. I remember avidly reading a number of them, along with some contemporary spiritual writers, as I tried to understand my own feelings and desires. Although we continued to be warned about forming particular friendships, friendship groups and close friends did gather for prayer, conversation, meals out, recreation, and travel. Through close friendships and quiet prayer we began to learn about ourselves, how to relate and not relate to others, and how we might live out our vocations. By ordination an all-important lesson we had discovered was that we were by no means a finished product. Probably more than any previous generation of priests we realized that our formation would need to continue the rest of our lives.

In 1974 the Congregation for Catholic Education in response to a request made by Pope Paul VI in *Sacerdotalis Caelibatus* published "A Guide to Formation in Priestly Celibacy," in which affective or sexual maturity is described as

> not only accepting sex as a part of the totality of human values, but also seeing it as giving a possibility for "offering," that is, a capacity

for giving pure love, altruistic love. When such a capacity is sufficiently acquired, an individual becomes capable of spontaneous
contacts, emotional self-control and commitment of his free will. This
giving aspect of sex involves a feeling of being "one for another."
Therefore, self-giving is not entirely separate from receiving. Sex intro-
duces into life an aspect of relationship and, therefore, the capability
of both giving and receiving, a disposition to accept love that is offered
in order to let oneself be fully possessed.[48]

The document then adds, "Self-control really means self-discipline: impos-
ing order on mental activity and external behavior in such a way as to
produce joy, happiness, and well-being."[49]

Pope John Paul II in his "theology of the body" was really the first to
present us, on the highest official level of the Church, with a truly positive
acceptance of God's gift of human sexuality and love. Deeply rooted in
St. John of the Cross, he provided us with a vision of the mystery of love
that reaches from the Trinity through Christ's spousal relation with the
Church to the very bodies of men and women. Through the gift of sexuality men and women most fundamentally incarnate their relational nature
and give expression to the fact that they are created in the image and
likeness of God. Gerald D. Coleman, SS, writes, "Sexuality prompts each
of us from within, calling us to personal as well as spiritual growth and
drawing us out from self to interpersonal bonds and commitments with
others, both women and men. It includes the qualities of sensitivity,
understanding, intimacy, openness to others, compassion and mutual
support."[50]

Furthermore, many psychologists, beginning with Freud himself, make
a distinction between the affectionate and genital dimensions of human
sexuality. Affective sexuality precedes and goes beyond the genital aim
that begins with puberty. Affective sexuality expresses a move toward
intimacy, whether it be marital love, a close friendship, or just a warm
recognition of another human person, male or female. Such sexuality
means we want to get close to another, to "touch" another affectively. The
confusion of these two dimensions on the popular level in American

---

[48] Sacred Congregation for Catholic Education, "A Guide to Formation in Priestly
Celibacy" (April 11, 1974), in *Norms for Priestly Formation*, vol. 1 (November 1993), by
the National Conference of Catholic Bishops (Washington, DC: USCC, 1994), 167.

[49] Ibid., 167–68.

[50] Gerald D. Coleman, SS, *Human Sexuality: An All-embracing Gift* (New York: Alba
House, 1992), 10.

society today has led to false guilt and many missed opportunities for true friendship. As Dr. William Kraft points out:

> Affective sexual behavior can be an end in itself or can be in service of and part of genital behavior. For instance, a warm smile or a respectful caress can be ends in themselves, or they can lead to or be part of a genital encounter. Thus, affective sexuality can stand on its own as a way of relating to another person, or it can be a prelude to genital activity. When affective and genital sexuality are seen as identical or when affective sexuality is seen as leading to genital sex, unnecessary confusion and guilt can emerge. Consequently, some individuals might repress, unnecessarily suppress, or abuse affective sexuality—a healthy mode of sexual encounter. Intention is the primary dynamic in determining whether affective sexuality is an end in itself or a means to genital behavior.[51]

Living a happy and chaste celibate life requires first of all that one has a comfortable and positive attitude toward one's body, sexuality, and feelings.

Chastity does not mean to be sexless, but rather promotes and nourishes healthy sexuality as one relates to another person in an integrated and pure loving way. Repression of sexuality, on the other hand, is unchaste. Again Dr. Kraft states that, "simply because we do not behave sexually or indulge in genital relations does not mean we are chaste. To minimize ourselves as men or women, rigidly to control affective sexuality, and to repress genital sexuality are modes of unchaste behavior. Some frigid, rigid, and sexless people may be the greatest offenders against chastity."[52] Thus in writing about human sexuality and priestly formation Father Coleman points out that

> Celibacy demands a capacity for intimacy, i.e., an authentic awareness of oneself, of one's strengths and weaknesses, a willingness to risk engaging with others in a game-free relationship, and an ability to change and grow when relationships demand this. If the capacity-for-intimacy is not present in one's life, the seminarian becomes self-dependent, overly relies on authority, displays compulsive behaviors, is overly perfectionistic, sustains a rigid adherence to rules and forms of piety, and bears a true inability to love himself, others, or God.[53]

---

[51] William F. Kraft, *Sexual Dimensions of the Celibate Life* (Kansas City, KS: Andrews and McMeel, Inc., 1979), 96.

[52] Ibid., 130.

[53] Gerald D. Coleman, SS, "Human Sexuality and Priestly Formation," *Seminary Journal* 8 (Spring 2002), 19.

In the early 1980s, Jean Galot, SJ, wrote: "Today, we realize that the formation of priests has not been immune from profound inadequacies. The future priest has not been prepared to interact normally with the environment to which he is to minister; he has not been trained to achieve an adequate balance, nor have provisions been made for the affective fulfillment he needs."[54]

A number of psychologists maintain that human sexual desire is not simply the need for genital relations. Rollo May, for instance, holds that "for human beings the more powerful need is not for sex, per se, but for relationships, intimacy, acceptance, and affirmation."[55] Thus it may be said that, "The key to keeping the physical or genital dimension of a relationship in proper perspective is to develop the affective dimension of sexuality. It is possible to live fully, healthfully and happily without genital sexuality. It is not possible to do so without developed affective relationships."[56] However, the predominant schools of psychotherapy today tend to take a functionalistic "therapeutic approach" to resolving psychological problems and focus solely on the self and on the individual's self-realization. They basically deny all forms of obligation and commitment in relationships. In a society such as ours, where individualism reigns, personal and communal relationships including marriage, family, and friendship are constantly downplayed and even frequently come under attack.

Exalting the individual at the expense of the relational and communal has taken its toll and brought about a sundering effect on our social fabric. We witness it all about us in climbing divorce rates, domestic violence, abortion, child abuse, and the like. The affectionate dimension of sexuality has become almost totally identified with the genital, and the latter is then often engaged in for the purpose of finding the warmth and acceptance our hearts desire. But it never really happens in that way, and we thus become disappointed with love and relationships. Made in the image and likeness of God who is Love—*Relatio subsistens*—human beings are meant to be in relationships of love and friendship.

Perhaps the greatest gift the Church can give the world today, which is so fragmented by our cultural and societal individualism, is to teach and model the dynamics of genuine love-filled relationships. Family ministry and teaching the art of friendship need to become an integral part of the Church's evangelizing mission, the goal of which, as we have already seen,

---

[54] Galot, *Theology of Priesthood*, 243.

[55] Rollo May, *Love and Will* (New York: W. W. Norton and Co., 1969), 311.

[56] Vincent J. Genovesi, SJ, *In Pursuit of Love: Catholic Morality and Human Sexuality* (Wilmington, DE: Michael Glazier, 1987), 144.

is building up a "civilization of love" (see EIA 68). Chaste celibacy "for the sake of the kingdom" bears witness to the familial and affectionate love of brothers and sisters; it frees love from selfishness and aggression.

The art of true friendship (*philia*) is very much a part of biblical and Christian tradition. The Old Testament book of 1 Samuel tells of the friendship between Jonathan and David: "By the time David finished speaking with Saul, Jonathan had become as fond of David as if his life depended on him; he loved him as he loved himself" (1 Sam 18:1). Reflecting on this passage, Paul D. O'Callaghan, a married archpriest of the Orthodox Church, writes, "Again, although it shares some of the similarities, this is not an example of 'falling in love.' We have seen that the tendency to eroticize every form of attraction and deep connection between human beings is an unfortunate symptom of the modern American fixation on sexuality."[57] He adds that the common oath between Jonathan and David clearly demonstrates that their communion of friendship was rooted in God (see 1 Sam 20:23).

Some theologians have objected to the notion that friendship can be a Christian affection because philia by its nature is preferential, while the Christian ideal of love (*agapē*) is open equally to all. Yet the gospels attest that Jesus himself indulged in a number of preferential relationships. The Lord clearly had deep affection for Martha, Mary, and Lazarus, and among his disciples one stood out as "the one whom Jesus loved" (John 13:23). Indeed, at the Last Supper this beloved disciple "leaned back against Jesus' chest" (John 13:25). O'Callaghan comments, "This image is particularly striking to those of Western culture," and he adds, "The physical closeness between Jesus and this disciple is a manifestation of the closeness of their hearts."[58] It demonstrates the fact that certain persons are naturally drawn to other persons by a fundamental kinship of spirit. "Those who wish to malign engagement in preferential friendships as an unchristian practice are seeking to place themselves on a higher ethical plane than the Lord himself."[59] Nevertheless, it would be a mistake to conclude that the intensity of Jesus' love for his friends, even the Beloved Disciple, translated into exclusivity.

This genuine appreciation of friendship continued into the patristic age. Saint Gregory Nazianzen writes of the beginning of his friendship with St. Basil the Great while they studied together in Athens: "When, in the

---

[57] Paul D. O'Callaghan, *The Feast of Friendship* (Wichita, KS: Eight Day Press, 2002), 41–42.

[58] Ibid., 52–53.

[59] Ibid., 50.

course of time, we acknowledged our friendship and recognized that our ambition was a life of true wisdom, we became everything to each other: we shared the same lodging, the same table, the same desires, the same goal. Our love for each other grew daily warmer and deeper." He adds, "Our single object and ambition was virtue, and a life of hope in the blessings that are to come. . . . We followed the guidance of God's law and spurred each other on to virtue."[60] A core conviction that the origin of friendship is in God and that its orientation is toward the pursuit of God is found throughout the writings of the Church Fathers. Here too a friend is seen as a second self or as sharing the same soul.

For St. Augustine, Trinitarian love—the friendship God is—constitutes the source of human friendship; it is the love to which they must conform and the community in which they are perfected.[61] Caroline White notes:

> In the *Confessions* Augustine refers to the 'bright path of friendship' and writes that friendship is a delightful bond, uniting many souls into one (II.5.10). In Book IV he describes his close friendship (referred to as 'sweeter to me than all the pleasures in life') with an unnamed young man while teaching at Thagaste and explains how grief-stricken he was when his friend died prematurely, because the young Augustine had put so much energy into loving his friend and missed his companionship deeply.[62]

The most intriguing aspect of Augustine's understanding of friendship is his insistence that we do not choose our friends, God does. Every friend is both the gift and the work of God's love. Likewise, St. Paulinus of Nola, a contemporary of Augustine, maintained that the conviction God creates friendship is connected with the idea that God has predestined certain men to be friends from the beginning of time.[63]

As we have already noted, Pope John Paul II in *Pastores Dabo Vobis* most fittingly and wisely prefaces his treatment of affective maturity and its necessity for those called to celibacy with words from his first encyclical: "Man cannot live without love. He remains a being that is incomprehen-

---

[60] *Oratio 43, in laudem Basilii Magni* 15.16-17, 19-21; PG 36, 514–423, as found in the Office of Readings for January 2 in *The Liturgy of the Hours*, vol. 1 (New York: Catholic Book Publishing Co., 1975), 1286–87.

[61] See Paul J. Wadell, *Friendship and the Moral Life* (Notre Dame, IN: University of Notre Dame Press, 1989), 99.

[62] Caroline White, *Christian Friendship in the Fourth Century* (New York: Cambridge University Press, 1992), 186.

[63] Ibid., 155.

sible for himself, his life is senseless, if love is not revealed to him, if he does not encounter love, if he does not experience it and make it his own, if he does not participate intimately in it" (RH 10). We cannot live a life of virtue on our own. Friendship is necessary to live the virtuous life. Going all the way back to Aristotle in his *Nichomachean Ethics* we are presented with the truth that virtue can only be pursued in relationship with others. Wadell thus writes:

> No matter how worthwhile an activity might be, if we are forced to pursue it by ourselves we will likely tire of it. We tire of our projects not because their value lessens, but because left to ourselves we are incapable of appreciating what their value is; we require others in order to learn why the projects and concerns of our life actually are so important to us.[64]

The moral adage that values are more "caught" than taught readily comes to the fore here. Growth in virtue occurs when we personally appropriate and integrate what we have come to know through the intellect. Yet such personal appropriation and integration wholly depends upon our involvement with others who are close to us, who are attractive to us, who trust us and love us.

Western society and culture today present a number of difficult challenges for living a chaste celibate life. Prominent among these are a radical individualism, sexual obsession, and a rapidly growing secularism. Radical individualism looks upon human beings as isolated, self-sufficient, and fundamentally private. Our all-pervasive preoccupation with sex instantly casts doubts upon all affectionate relationships, presuming that they somehow must include genital expression. Then the positivistic mindset of our technological age considers the spiritual and transcendent as a leftover oddity from medieval times and relegates it to the strictly private sphere, allowing room only for the explicitly secular in the public square. A chaste celibate life, however, cannot be lived in isolation. Father Stephen J. Rossetti writes:

> We must work at our relationships. We must actively cultivate a network of real friends. Too many of us think of our acquaintances as friends. Most priests have a lot of acquaintances. . . . But friendship is more than that. Friends share their joys and their burdens. They speak of their sorrows and their hopes. Friends are vulnerable with

---

[64] Wadell, *Friendship and the Moral Life*, 59.

each other. And there is a nurturing and mutually supporting quality to their relationship.[65]

With the rapid growth of one-priest parishes in recent years, some dioceses are beginning to provide living arrangements whereby two or more priests serving the parishes of a given area may live in community, or even form a diocesan fraternity, such as the Companions of Christ started in the Archdiocese of Minneapolis–St. Paul, where they can pray together, share meals, and support one another.

A lack of affective maturity and not having one's affective needs appropriately met are nothing other than a prelude to a pastoral and professional disaster. Again as Father Rossetti points out:

> [C]elibacy cannot be lived in a kind of 'white knuckle' fashion, hanging on for dear life, hoping not to violate one's chastity. There are more than a few who do this. Some stay away from others, fearful that a loving relationship could not be controlled. Others hide behind their work, their position, or a search for power, never really becoming involved with others until they reach mid-life when they feel an overpowering emptiness. The latter are prone to dysfunctional behaviors of a myriad of kinds, including sexual compulsiveness.[66]

In his pastoral service the priest has only one concern: to meet the other's need for pastoral assistance. In such a pastoral relationship the priest's sexuality is a powerful relational energy supplying power for creativity, responsiveness, passion, and commitment. It is also a means for being tenderly present to those who are hurting. However, to mix a personal sexual agenda with this pastoral one is to cross the boundary into unethical behavior and is always wrong.[67]

The sexual abuse crisis within the ranks of the Catholic clergy in the United States, which exploded on the public media scene in 2002, has many things to teach us. First of all, clerical celibacy must be lived with renewed integrity. While moral lapses in the area of sexuality have afflicted all ranks of the clergy throughout the history of the Church, celibacy is not the cause, no more than one can say marriage is the cause of adultery. Rossetti accordingly writes that, "no self-respecting researcher in the field

[65] Stephen J. Rossetti, *The Joy of Priesthood* (Notre Dame, IN: Ave Maria Press, 2005), 95.

[66] Ibid., 89.

[67] See Richard M. Gula, SS, *Ethics in Pastoral Ministry*, chap. 5: "Sexuality" (New York/Mahwah, NJ: Paulist Press, 1996), 91–116.

of child sex abuse would suggest that celibacy is the cause for child sexual abuse. In fact, most child molesters in our society are, or will be, married. And for the few celibate priests who molest minors, their psychological problems were long in place before they promised to live a celibate life. Such clinical problems are etched into the psyche at an early age."[68]

It appears that the vast majority of horrible and tragic cases of the sexual abuse of minors by Catholic clergy, which came to light in recent years, either happened twenty to forty years ago or had been perpetrated by men ordained in the 1950s, 1960s, and early 1970s. Cases attributed to priests ordained in more recent years, after the psychological screening of seminary applicants was introduced and after priestly formation programs began to address more realistically the affective maturity of candidates, seem to be far fewer in number. While the absence of genital sex does not create a sex-starved clergy, bishops, diocesan vocation teams, and seminary formation programs need to be constantly vigilant about the applicants they accept. Furthermore, they need to help priesthood candidates understand better and accept their own sexuality as a God-given gift, as well as provide them with the psychological and spiritual resources that will help them mature ever more faithfully into happy, self-giving, and loving celibate males.

The primary sexual organ for human beings is not the genitals but the brain. Thus we can understand the genuine wisdom behind the Church's teaching regarding the gravity and necessity of avoiding "impure thoughts." The thoughts and images we allow to feed our imaginations have a powerful impact upon our feelings and motivations and upon the way we then choose to act. The Eastern Church Fathers referred to them as *logismoi*. As noted by George Maloney, SJ:

> Evagrius of Pontus, who lived in the Egyptian desert in the fourth century, taught that *logismoi* are images, sensible phantasms, that, dwelt upon, tend to draw us to that object existing outside ourselves. It is dealing with a reality that is not evil in itself, but, given our fallen nature and the distension introduced through the effects of original sin, we are easily drawn to those things. These are part of Paul's "unspiritual self" that wars within him, seeking to destroy him but enticing him to do the opposite of what his better self tells him is God's holy will (Rom 7:22-24).[69]

---

[68] Rossetti, *The Joy of Priesthood*, 84–85.

[69] George A. Maloney, SJ, *Gold, Frankincense, and Myrrh: An Introduction to Eastern Christian Spirituality* (New York: Crossroad, 1997), 104.

Negative feelings that arise from non-intentional states and trends, such as fatigue, anxiety, hunger, thirst, and sexual yearnings, tend to evoke images that motivate us in the direction of self-absorption and self-preoccupation. Our hormonal flow can also spark such images. Such natural concupiscence draws us in the opposite direction of grace, the Holy Spirit of love, moving us to self-giving and to relationships.

Our sex-obsessed culture spawns many who become compulsively sexual. It bombards us with the message: "Sex is my most important need." Fixated on sex, our society displays it incessantly and in often distorted ways, which in turn give rise to various sexual addictions. Rossetti observes, "There are millions of people in our society today who are caught up in sexually destructive, and often compulsive behaviors, such as internet cybersex, compulsive promiscuity, pornography, prostitution, and other sexual perversions."[70] Internet pornography has become in our society a multibillion-dollar-per-year enterprise and a major source of addictive behavior for many American males, because men tend to become more sexually stimulated by visual images than women. Coleman points out that, "Many individuals who become addicted to cybersex sustain low self-esteem, possess inadequate social skills, exhibit a suppressed sexuality, and have very little 'real' human connections (i.e., no authentic peer relationships)."[71] Additionally, addictive behaviors experienced from eighteen to twenty-five years of age will cause a chemical change in an individual's brain, which makes it virtually impossible to stop such behavior.[72]

Pope John Paul II states that affective maturity requires a clear and strong training in "responsible freedom" and education of the moral conscience. The person must be truly master of himself and capable of making the "sincere gift of self" (PDV 44). Conscience formation involves not only intellectual, fact-oriented knowledge about our traditions, doctrines, beliefs, moral principles, and rules, but also evaluative or affective knowledge, which flows from the way we see reality, our "philosophy of life," our worldview. Therefore, the cultivation of the Christian imagination is essential to the development of Christian virtue and character. Affective conversion requires the asceticism of self-control, a fruit of the Spirit (Gal 5:23), by which we turn away from those harmful images that motivate us to yield to selfish pleasure and self-absorption. We then intentionally fill our minds with positive images and symbols that motivate

---

[70] Rossetti, *The Joy of Priesthood*, 86.

[71] Coleman, "Human Sexuality and Priestly Formation," 22.

[72] See Gerald D. Coleman, SS, "Human Sexuality and Priestly Formation," *Summary Journal*, vol. 8 (Spring 2002): 22.

us in the direction of what Saints Augustine and Thomas Aquinas referred to in their writings as "the order of charity" (*ordo caritatis*), or in Jesus' teaching "the kingdom of God."

"Celibacy for the sake of the kingdom of heaven" focuses our attention with undivided hearts on God's plan, God's will. It constitutes our true consecration for continuing Christ's mission in our world. It requires that in communion with Jesus Christ on the Cross, we give ourselves in love for the salvation of the world. By continuing to bring his self-giving and reconciling love to the world, in word and deed, we transform it into a civilization of love. At the same time we bear witness to the world to come, to the heavenly Jerusalem and the marriage feast of the Lamb. Priestly celibacy must never be allowed to devolve into a clerical version of self-serving or self-isolating bachelorhood. Chaste celibacy thrives only when it bears witness of God's self-giving love, and it is sustained solely by continuing to cultivate affective, loving relationships—with the Triune God in prayer, and with others in true friendship. Priests and pastoral ministers, nonetheless, need to be extremely cautious in treating pastoral relationships as if they were friendships. Gula states that "trying to make a pastoral relationship a peer relationship only falsifies its real nature and puts us at greater risk of unethical behavior."[73] We should avoid all such dual relationships insofar as possible.

The Reservation of the Ministerial Priesthood to Men Only

The gospels attest that Jesus readily overstepped the bounds of Jewish customs in associating with women and welcoming them as his friends and disciples. The other New Testament writings tell of the outstanding contributions women made to the spreading of the Gospel and of their prominent place in some of the local churches. Yet we find that Jesus never called women to be apostles, nor did the apostles in their turn set them apart for apostolic ministry and the preaching of the Word of God. The *episcopoi* and *presbyteroi* of the early Church were all men. In fact, several New Testament passages categorically state that women should be excluded from both teaching and authority positions within the Church (cf. 1 Cor 14:34-35; 1 Tim 2:12) by reason of a command from the Lord (1 Cor 14:37). Yet over time, Jesus' attitude toward the religious equality of women had its impact upon the Church and society; it would lead St. Paul to write that among the baptized "there is not male and female; for you are all one in Christ Jesus" (Gal 3:28).

---

[73] Gula, *Ethics in Pastoral Ministry*, 76.

In the time of the Church Fathers, groups such as the Montanists, Valentian Gnostics, and Collyridians were judged heterodox partly because they allowed women to celebrate the Eucharist. The Fathers in addressing this issue point to the will of Christ as revealed in the gospels and to the fact that Mary was never assigned a priestly role.[74] Later in the Middle Ages, the Waldensians and the Cathari allowed women to preside at the Eucharist, but again the Catholic Church disapproved. A movement to admit women to the exercise of pastoral ministry spread among the Protestant churches in the twentieth century. In 1975 the Assembly of the World Council of Churches meeting in Nairobi clearly encouraged those churches that admit women to ordination not to allow ecumenical objections to hinder them along the way.

The Second Vatican Council in its Decree on the Apostolate of Lay People acknowledged that "since in our days women are taking an increasingly active share in the whole life of society, it is very important that their participation in the various sectors of the Church's apostolate should likewise develop" (AA 9). After the Council, a number of Catholic theologians along with others in the Church publicly raised the question of ordaining women. The magisterium responded in 1976 when the Sacred Congregation for the Doctrine of the Faith published its Declaration on the Admission of Women to the Ministerial Priesthood. The declaration's theological argument centers on the sacramental nature of the priesthood. In the celebration of the Eucharist the priest does not act in his own name but *in persona Christi*.

> The Christian priesthood is therefore of a sacramental nature: the priest is a sign . . . that must be perceptible and which the faithful must be able to recognize with ease. The whole sacramental economy is in fact based upon natural signs, on symbols imprinted upon the human psychology. . . . The same natural resemblance is required for persons as for things: when Christ's role in the Eucharist is to be expressed sacramentally, there would not be this "natural resemblance" which must exist between Christ and his minister if the role of Christ were not taken by a man: in such a case it would be difficult to see in the minister the image of Christ. For Christ himself was and remains a man.[75]

---

[74] See Galot, *Theology of Priesthood*, 260–61.

[75] Sacred Congregation for the Doctrine of the Faith, "Declaration on the Admission of Women to the Ministerial Priesthood" (*Inter Insigniores*), in *Vatican Council II: More Post Conciliar Documents*, ed. Austin Flannery, OP, vol. 2, 339 (Northport, NY: Costello Publishing Co., 1982).

Since the question of the ordination of women continued to be debated among theologians and other circles within the Catholic Church, Pope John Paul II in 1994 issued an apostolic letter *Ordinatio Sacerdotalis* in which he states:

> Wherefore, in order that all doubt may be removed regarding a matter of great importance, a matter which pertains to the church's divine constitution itself, in virtue of my ministry of confirming the brethren (cf. Lk 22–32) I declare that the church has no authority whatsoever to confer priestly ordination on women and that this judgment is to be definitively held by all the church's faithful.[76]

This teaching, he would later point out, "must be understood according to the particular criteria of the sacramental economy, i.e., the economy of 'signs' which God freely chooses in order to become present in the midst of humanity."[77] In its response to a question concerning the authority of the apostolic letter, the Sacred Congregation for the Doctrine of the Faith on October 28, 1995, maintained that the teaching that the Church cannot ordain women "has been set forth infallibly by the ordinary and universal magisterium (cf. *Lumen Gentium* 25)." Avery Dulles explains, "This reply was accompanied by an unsigned explanation to the effect that in *Ordinatio Sacerdotalis* the ordinary papal magisterium, by an act 'in itself not infallible,' was witnessing 'to the infallibility of the teaching of a doctrine already possessed by the Church.'"[78]

Important to note is that *Inter Insigniores* grounds its theological reflection not on the principle of representation, i.e., that a man is more appropriately able to represent Christ (the anthropological argument), but rather on the biblical theme of God's marriage with his people, which in the New Testament becomes the marriage between Christ and the Church. Thus Galot writes, "The Husband, the originator of the New Covenant, is male. It follows that the priest who assumes the role of Christ must be a male.

---

[76] John Paul II, "Apostolic Letter on Ordination of Women," *Origins* 24 (June 4, 1994), 51.

[77] John Paul II, "Letter to Women" (July 10, 1995), *Origins* 25 (July 27, 1995), 142.

[78] Avery Dulles, SJ, "Tradition Says No," *Tablet* (December 9, 1995): 1572. Because of a continuing handful of attempts every year to ordain women to the priesthood, the Congregation for the Doctrine of the Faith published a brief "General Decree Regarding the Delict of Attempted Sacred Ordination of Women" in the May 30, 2008, edition of *L'Osservatore Romano* declaring that "both the one who attempts to confer a sacred order on a woman, and the woman who attempts to receive a sacred order, incur an excommunication 'latae sententiae,'" i.e., automatically.

Sacramental representation calls for the bodily similarity implied in assuming the role of Husband."[79] For those who might say that the priest represents the Church, the Bride, and could therefore be more aptly represented by a woman, the declaration replies that the priest represents the Church because he represents Christ as Head and Shepherd of the Church.

Pope John Paul II in his 1988 apostolic letter *On the Dignity and Vocation of Women* further develops the symbolic dimension of spousal love as found in St. Paul's Letter to the Ephesians. There he writes:

> *Christ is the Bridegroom.* This expresses the truth about the love of God who "first loved us" (cf. 1 Jn 4:19) and who, with the gift generated by this spousal love for man, has exceeded all human expectations: "He loved them to the end" (Jn 13:1). The Bridegroom—the Son consubstantial with the Father as God—became the son of Mary; he became the "son of man", true man, a male. *The symbol of the Bridegroom is masculine.* This masculine symbol represents the human aspect of the divine love which God has for Israel, for the Church, and for all people.[80]

He then concludes:

> Against the broad background of the "great mystery" expressed in the spousal relationship between Christ and the Church, it is possible to understand adequately the calling of the "Twelve." *In calling only men as his Apostles*, Christ acted *in a completely free and sovereign manner.* In doing so, he exercised the same freedom with which, in all his behaviour, he emphasized the dignity and the vocation of women, without conforming to the prevailing customs and to the traditions sanctioned by the legislation of the time.[81]

It is obviously no mere coincidence that the Roman Catholic and Eastern Orthodox churches, whose ancient theological roots are anchored in a profound awareness of symbol and sacramentality, continue to maintain the tradition of ordaining only men. The Protestant tradition, a child of the Enlightenment, turned away at its inception from symbol to the rationality of the word and tended to equate the sacraments with magic and supersti-

---

[79] Galot, *Theology of the Priesthood*, 254.

[80] John Paul II, *Mulieris Dignitatem*, Apostolic Letter (August 15, 1988), no. 25 with emphasis in original.

[81] Ibid., no. 26 with emphasis in original.

tion. Ordained ministry in this latter perspective became just a functional service of preaching and pastoral care based upon the common priesthood of the baptized, both men and women. Fittingly, John Paul II reminds us that the apostolic ministry—and with it the ministerial priesthood—finds its source in "the Paschal Mystery, which completely reveals the spousal love of God." Thus at the Last Supper the Twelve "alone receive the sacramental charge, 'Do this in remembrance of me' (Lk 22:19; 1 Cor 11:24), which is joined to the institution of the Eucharist. On Easter Sunday night they receive the Holy Spirit for the forgiveness of sins."[82] Men only can be fitting sacramental signs of Christ the Bridegroom's love.

[82] Ibid.

Conclusion

"It is within the Church's mystery, as a mystery of Trinitarian communion in missionary tension, that every Christian identity is revealed, and likewise the specific identity of the priest and his ministry" (PDV 12). Pope John Paul II here is telling us that the identity of the priest, like that of every Christian, is found not in function but in mystery. He then adds, "As a mystery, the Church is essentially related to Jesus Christ. She is his fullness, his body, his spouse." This brings us now to the very core, to the heart of priestly identity: "The priest is a living and transparent image of Christ the priest" (PDV 12). The priest is called by God—a Trinitarian communion of Love—to be "a living and transparent image of Christ the priest." The very essence of a priestly vocation is to be a living and transparent image of the Good Shepherd who out of love for his sheep lays down his life for them (John 10:14-15). The pastor who does not know and love his people is nothing more than a functionary or hired hand. The priest only reveals Jesus Christ the Good Shepherd through the genuineness and depth of his pastoral charity.

The apostles saw themselves as having a vocation from God to make known the mystery of Christ. Thus St. Paul writes of being "a minister in accordance with God's stewardship given to me to bring to completion for you the word of God, the mystery hidden from ages and from generations past . . . Christ in you, the hope for glory" (Col 1:25-27). And the First Letter of John begins: "What was from the beginning, what we have heard, what we have seen with our eyes, what we have looked upon and touched with our hands . . . we proclaim now to you, so that you too may have fellowship with us; for our fellowship is with the Father and with his Son, Jesus Christ. We are writing this so that our joy may be complete" (1 John 1:1-4). The apostles understand that they have been called to proclaim "good news of great joy that will be for all the people" (Luke 2:10). Their ministry is a mission of evangelization, to make known by word and deed the Good News of Christ Jesus, the Truth of a Love that saves us from sin and death because it is stronger than death. Indeed, it is Life, eternal life.

Jesus at the Last Supper, the night before he lays down his life on the Cross as both priest and victim in that primary and ultimate act of pastoral charity, prays that his apostles and all those who believe in him through their word may be "consecrated in truth" (John 17:19). He prays that they may realize the truth that "you sent me, and that you loved them even as you loved me" (v. 23). To this end, Jesus consecrates himself for us in the love that leads him to the Cross. At the same time too he reveals the mystery of the God in whom "we live and move and have our being" (Acts 17:28). Indeed, Christ's paschal mystery reveals the God who is love (1 John 4:8). At every Mass then the priest leads the people ever more fully into the truth of this incredible mystery of God's love revealed by Jesus Christ on the Cross, when immediately after the words of the consecration he says: "Let us proclaim the mystery of faith."

The priest is first and foremost the bearer of the Mystery. Father Robert Barron writes, "The primary 'function' of the bearer of Mystery is to hold up to the people of God the great images, stories, and pictures of salvation that are at the heart of the Christian tradition. . . . [He] presents the truth which is God's love in Christ, and seduces, draws the worshipping community to share in it."[1] The priest does not make Christ present. God's love in Christ is present everywhere, but sin has blinded us to it. The priest is the one consecrated in this love and sent, as head and shepherd of the flock, to bear witness to it, to proclaim it, point it out and lead others into communion with it. Describing this Mystery, St. Augustine writes in his *Confessions*, "We come to you and go from you, but no place is involved in this process. In every place, O Truth, you are present to those who seek your help." And he adds:

> Late have I loved you, O Beauty ever ancient, ever new, late have I loved you! You were within me, but I was outside, and it was there that I searched for you. In my unloveliness I plunged into the lovely things which you created. You were with me, but I was not with you. Created things kept me from you; yet if they had not been in you they would not have been at all. You called, you shouted, and you broke through my deafness. You flashed, you shone, and you dispelled my blindness. You breathed your fragrance on me; I drew in breath and

[1] Robert Barron, *Bridging the Great Divide* (Lanham, MD: Rowman & Littlefield, 2004), 228–29.

now I pant for you. I have tasted you; now I hunger and thirst for more. You touched me, and I burned for your peace.[2]

Because we humans are incarnate beings, we live at one and the same time in both the spiritual and the physical worlds. However, because of original sin, we are mostly blind to the spiritual, to the Transcendent; yet our hearts remain restless for it. Human beings are so wired that we hunger for eternal Truth and infinite, unconditional Love. We long to touch and be one with the Mystery.

The Catholic priesthood today frequently finds itself divided according to generations. Indeed, the latest generation of priests and seminarians, sometimes referred to as the Pope John Paul II or millennial generation, more easily identifies with those priests formed in the pre–Vatican II seminary. This youngest generation is readily attracted to the more traditional forms of piety, worship, clerical dress, and the neoscholastic theology that was predominant prior to the Second Vatican Council (1962–65). The priests and seminarians of this Pope John Paul II generation also tend to be quite suspicious of those priests they consider to be of the Vatican II and immediate post–Vatican II generation. They feel that the priests, liturgists, and theologians of the Vatican II era, in effect, discarded the role of tradition and mystery. The Catholicism they learned as children consisted mainly of attitudes and feelings; it lacked substance. They thus react strongly to the overly horizontal and communal emphasis, and to the endless experimentation they often experienced in the parish liturgies of their youth.

There can be no doubt that doctrinal orthodoxy and the sense of Mystery were downplayed in the post–Vatican II period. The renewal called for by the Second Vatican Council very soon got caught up in the "spirit of the age" marked by a pervasive skepticism of traditional authority and institutions—religious, governmental, and educational included. A general movement toward secularism, pluralism, and moral relativism ruled the day. Many of those in the Church—theologians, clergy, and laity—were not immune to this rapidly growing cultural phenomenon. A positivistic and scientific mindset, which recognizes only facts and data, soon swept philosophy, theology, and the liberal arts into the far corners of higher education, as the social sciences expropriated the role of the humanities.

---

[2] St. Augustine, *Confessions, Lib.* 10, 26.37-29, 40: CSEL 33, 255-256) as found in the Office of Readings for Wednesday, Eighth Week in Ordinary Time in *The Liturgy of the Hours*, vol. 3 (New York: Catholic Book Publishing Co., 1975), 273.

The emphasis on the scientific method and technology in contemporary higher education, moreover, does not teach students to think in metaphysical and transcendent categories, which alone are capable of exploring the inner nature of reality.

The native capacity for theological discernment is rarely developed today, and seminarians consequently are inclined to seek certitude in the clear-cut formulas of the Catechism. I have seen this trend develop over the last twenty years I have spent in seminary formation work. While each new edition of the U.S. Bishops' *Program of Priestly Formation* increased the required number of credit hours in philosophy from a minimum of eighteen in its 1981 third edition to a full thirty in the 2005 fifth edition, I have attended meetings of college seminary rectors where comments were made that credits in psychology and sociology would suffice. At the same time, the Roman pontifical ecclesiastical universities regard a PhB (approximately sixty-five hours) as the only proper philosophical preparation for theological studies, although they still reluctantly accept the number of credits established by the norms of individual episcopal conferences, such as the *PPF* in the United States. From my own recent working with U.S. seminarians in Rome, I have witnessed firsthand their struggles with theological and spiritual concepts because of the lack of proper philosophical preparation. Their expectation of concrete, "black-and-white" doctrinal formulas flows much less from any ideological preference than from their inability to think and discern in anything other than scientific and technical terms. Some of them seem almost surprised that a theological text cannot be read like a computer manual.

The interpretation and application of the documents of Vatican II has taken two basic directions in the years and decades that followed the Council. One has sought primarily to update Church teachings and pastoral practices by adapting and changing them to fit basic contemporary philosophical and utilitarian categories, which in turn lean toward exalting the freedom of the individual above familial and communal relationships and toward promoting better societal, political, and organizational design and functioning. The other direction continued to embrace the "return to the sources" movement, which began before the Council, in an endeavor to explore more fully the inner depth and meaning of the Christian tradition. Those who have taken the former direction are inclined to view the priesthood in more functional terms and argue against the requirement of celibacy in today's Church. The latter, conversely, have delved into the biblical and patristic sources to trace the developing theological understanding of the inner nature of the Church, the sacraments, the ministerial priesthood, and celibacy. The fruits of these labors we find in the recent documents of the Church, the theological writings of Wojtyla/John Paul II, Ratzinger/Benedict XVI, and other theologians who have followed this same approach, such as Galot, von Balthasar, Greshake, as well as Dulles and Barron in the United States, to name but a few.

Diocesan presbyterates today often find themselves polarized along any number of lines—theological, generational, and formational—as well as by ministerial focus. The sexual abuse scandals, the dwindling number of vocations, and the increasing number of foreign-born clergy further complicate the current climate in which priests live and serve. Relationships between bishops and priests have also been strained by the way cases of sexual misconduct have often been addressed and handled. Every priest and seminarian today is well aware that he is but one accusation away, whether true or false, from being barred permanently from active ministry. We can only admire and respect those young men who continue to come forward in response to a vocation from the Lord to present themselves for priestly service. Their faith, generosity, and courage need to be applauded and supported, especially by those of us who entered seminary formation in the Vatican II and immediate post–Vatican II eras.

The priests of my generation who entered seminaries in the 1960s and early 1970s entered in a time that seemed to us to be the Catholic Church's new Pentecost. The energy and excitement of the Second Vatican Council was palpably felt. In the United States especially, seminaries were filled to capacity, new and larger parish plants were constantly being built in the suburbs and rural areas, and our country had its first Catholic president. Vocations to the priesthood and religious life were gladly supported by families and friends. But as I have told the seminarians whom I have had the privilege to work with in recent years, "If I and my generation entered the priesthood in what appeared to be the Catholic Church's Easter Sunday, you are entering on the Church's Good Friday." Despite the scandals of sexual abuse, despite the dwindling numbers of Catholics actively practicing their faith, and despite sometimes very vocal opposition from parents, siblings, and friends, young men—and even men of more mature age—continue to come forward to enter priestly formation. Their prior formational experience in the faith may have been very different and even much less extensive than what my generation experienced, but their hearts are ever more on fire with love of the Lord and with the desire to evangelize.

Pope John Paul II has written, "The ordained ministry has a radical 'communitarian form' and can only be carried out as 'a collective work'" (PDV 17). Through his ordination a priest becomes a member of the diocesan presbyterate in communion with the bishop. What every diocesan priest of any given diocese shares in common far surpasses intergenerational differences. Priests must communicate and celebrate what they do have in common. Presbyteral unity is instrumental in bringing faith to the world, in carrying out the Church's evangelizing mission. As Father Stephen Rossetti has observed:

> Today we priests face a divided Church and divided parishes. We have Hispanics and Vietnamese, Poles and Italians, Filipinos and Haitians. We have the 'liturgical police' watching our every moment on the altar and conservatives screening our words for orthodoxy. We have liberals complaining about our pro-life homilies and our support for *Humanae Vitae*. We work side-by-side with homosexual people and heterosexual people, priests who wear cassocks and those who yearn for the "glory days of Vatican II." We have old people in nursing homes who nostalgically remember the Latin Mass and vehemently reject removing the communion rail, and young people who have never received communion on their tongues and think that the communion rail is a decoration. It will be easy for a priest, and very tempting, to align himself with one group or the other. Inevitably, some of this naturally occurs since our predispositions will make us more sympathetic with some stances rather than others. But our vocation is to be a shepherd, a pastor of souls to all, regardless of their theological or cultural makeup, orientation, or age. The priest should be a 'man of communion.'[3]

With the source of his identity being found in Trinitarian communion and mission, the priest of Jesus Christ cannot rightly be anyone other than a "man of communion" and a "minister of reconciliation."

Many priests and seminarians operate out of a distorted image of God. This reality impacts negatively upon their spirituality, self-image, and ministry. Intellectually they know that God is all-loving and forgiving, but in fact they live as if God were harsh and demanding. Seminarians, especially, often believe that they must first become perfect in order to be ordained. Such perfectionism can lead to self-condemnation and to their even backing away from a priestly vocation. As a seminary formator, I have frequently told seminarians, "We are preparing you for ordination, not canonization—at least not immediately!" Christian charity, chastity, and all the virtues require daily practice and effort. Being formed in Christ is

---

[3] Stephen J. Rossetti, *The Joy of Priesthood* (Notre Dame, IN: Ave Maria Press, 2005), 120–21.

a lifelong process that involves ongoing conversion and cooperation with God's grace, i.e., his presence and love.

Feeling and accepting our limits is an asceticism we must embrace. As God is always patient with us, we must learn to be patient with others, with where they are at in their faith journey, and with ourselves. Saint Gregory the Great in his *Moral Reflections on Job* phrased it so well:

> The dawn intimates that the night is over; it does not proclaim the full light of day. While it dispels the darkness and welcomes the light, it holds both of them, the one mixed with the other, as it were. Are not all of us who follow the truth in this life daybreak and dawn? While we do some things which already belong to the light, we are not free from the remnants of darkness. In Scripture the Prophet says to God: *No living being will be justified in your sight*. Scripture also says: *In many ways all of us give offense*.[4]

It was Aristotle who introduced the idea of "measure" when discussing virtue. The two extremes of "too little" and "too much" in relation to virtue became referred to as a "vice." Thus we have the Latin saying: *In medio stat virtus*. Perfectionism is a vice, which afflicts many a seminarian and priest with anxiety and the fear of never being able to measure up, and it, in turn, vexes those they encounter and are called to serve.

Saint Gregory the Great, consequently, warns against the arrogance and harshness to which perfectionism can lead:

> The teaching of the arrogant has this characteristic: they do not know how to introduce their teaching humbly and they cannot convey correctly to others the things they understand correctly themselves. With their words they betray what they teach; they give the impression that they live on lofty heights from which they look down disdainfully on those whom they are teaching; they regard the latter as inferiors, to whom they do not deign to listen as they talk; indeed they scarcely deign to talk to them at all—they simply lay down the law.[5]

Such arrogance or "rigidity" is not a matter of commitment to orthodox teaching. Liberals and conservatives can be equally arrogant. It is a clear

---

[4] *Lib.* 29, 2–4; PL 76, 478–480 as found in the Office of Readings for Thursday, Ninth Week in Ordinary Time in *The Liturgy of the Hours*, vol. 3 (New York: Catholic Book Publishing Co., 1975), 308–9.

[5] *Lib.* 23, 23–34: PL 76, 265-266 as found in the Office of Readings for Wednesday, Ninth Week in Ordinary Time in ibid., 303–4.

and fundamental lack of pastoral charity. Love is the form and essence of Christian perfection. Writing to priests, Archbishop Fulton J. Sheen maintained that "authority without love is tyranny."[6] Luke's parallel to Matthew's phrasing of Jesus' teaching "So be perfect, just as your heavenly Father is perfect" (Matt 5:48) is "Be merciful, just as [also] your Father is merciful" (Luke 6:36). Christian perfection finds its expression in mercy and compassion. It differs radically from the classical Greek notion of perfection, which aims for the attainment of a harmonious personality, morally faultless and self-contained. Many a seminarian, I have found over the years, unfortunately pins his self-image to the latter definition rather than aspiring to genuine Christian perfection.

Tied to the vice of priestly perfectionism is the inability to say no. Most priests are "pleasers"; they want to be liked, but ministry is a bottomless pit. Rossetti writes, "It is painful to say no or not to respond to valid human needs when there is no time. It is an asceticism to say no. Each day the priest makes a difficult discernment of deciding which needs he can fulfill and which ones he cannot. Frankly, some are not doing this well and many are overextending themselves in the process."[7] He adds, "The one who is constantly and forever on duty denies himself necessary personal time for rest, recreation, study and spiritual regeneration."[8] The then-Cardinal Ratzinger addressing this same issue wrote: "He who acts on Christ's behalf, knows that it is always the case that one sows and another reaps. He does not need to bother incessantly about himself; he leaves the outcome to the Lord and does his own part without anxiety, free and cheerful because he is hidden within in the whole. If priests today so often feel overburdened, tired and frustrated, the blame lies with a strained pursuit of results."[9]

There are also instances of the opposite phenomenon in the priesthood. As I once heard a bishop several years ago remark, "The priests of this diocese will not burn out; they will rust out." Archbishop Sheen too has observed, "The lazy priest will always work the 'hardest' to finish his Mass as quickly as possible."[10] While priestly ministry is often emotionally rich and intense, it can also be draining, as Rossetti writes:

---

[6] Fulton J. Sheen, *The Priest Is Not His Own* (New York: McGraw-Hill, 1963), 187.

[7] Rossetti, *The Joy of Priesthood*, 15.

[8] Ibid., 98.

[9] Joseph Cardinal Ratzinger, *Called to Communion: Understanding the Church Today* (San Francisco: Ignatius Press, 1996), 129.

[10] Sheen, *The Priest Is Not His Own*, 266.

People do not call us when everything is going fine. They call us when they are troubled or when there has been a tragedy. Or they will call us when there are great joys, someone is about to be married, or they are celebrating the birth of a child. It is not uncommon for the parish priest to preside at a funeral Mass and burial, and then go directly to witness the wedding vows of a young couple followed by a joyous reception. The priest in public ministry lives life in its intensity.[11]

The greatest challenge to priests today is perhaps not celibacy but permanent commitment. It is not at all uncommon to hear a seminary applicant or a seminarian ask, "Can I really be happy as a priest for the rest of my life?" Our culture and society does not value permanent commitments. In the professional and business worlds there is a constant turnover in jobs and positions; one needs to have his personal portfolio ever at hand. More than half the marriages today end up in divorce. A large number of priests too in recent years have left active ministry. A recent study of newly ordained priests shows that the first five years of priesthood are the most likely period in which one will leave. Yet it was not ministry itself, which most found to be very satisfying, nor celibacy. Rather, the resigned priests felt lonely, isolated, unappreciated, and disconnected. Such personal difficulties made them very vulnerable to seeking out a coupled relationship.[12]

Priests beyond question constantly need to cultivate their relationships with God through prayer and with others, especially other priests, through healthy friendships. Once again, Father Rossetti offers sage advice:

Suffering and pain are the lot of every human life. . . . This is true of our lives as well. At times, we priests suffer and may even question our vocations. . . . Does this suffering mean that we have necessarily done something wrong? No. Suffering is a part of every life: married, single, and celibate. Questions arising about our vocation can be an invitation to move even deeper into this life and commitment. Most of all, we priests ought to take comfort and strength from the life of Jesus, who was a suffering servant.[13]

The cultivation of the Christian imagination by means of prayer, contemplation, and *lectio divina* counters the negative images and feelings that arise in our day-to-day lives and ministry and that draw us to objects outside of us and tempt us to self-absorption and self-pity.

---

[11] Rossetti, *The Joy of Priesthood*, 14–15.
[12] See ibid., 91.
[13] Ibid., 17–18.

At this time in the life of the Catholic Church, especially after all the negativity generated in the wake of the sexual abuse scandals by members of the clergy, we must never lose sight of the Church's raison d'être and mission to bear witness to the Gospel mystery. Jesus Christ was "consecrated and sent" by God to save the world from sin and death by revealing the depth of God's love for sinners. Indeed, at the Last Supper on the night before he embraced the Cross out of love for us Jesus tells his apostles, "Amen, amen, I say to you, you will weep and mourn, while the world rejoices; you will grieve, but your grief will become joy" (John 16:20). Thus St. Peter could later write to the first Christians dispersed by persecution, "But rejoice to the extent that you share in the sufferings of Christ, so that when his glory is revealed you may also rejoice exultantly" (1 Pet 4:13). Also in the midst of the daily grind of ministry and his many trials—rejection by the majority of his Jewish brothers and sisters, internal disputes within the Christian communities, and his own mood swings, tiredness, and overwork—St. Paul would write in his Second Letter to the Corinthians: "I am filled with encouragement, I am overflowing with joy all the more because of all our affliction" (2 Cor 7:4).

The Church that was born from the wounded side of Jesus Christ on the Cross as the spouse of the new Adam cannot expect to be kept free from suffering, trial, and persecution. We may not forget too that among the Twelve there was Judas Iscariot, and that scandals have involved all ranks of the clergy down through the centuries, including the papacy. We should not be surprised then that sin continues to rear its head anew in every age. What should surprise us, though, is the continuing joy that is ours in Jesus Christ. As Pope Benedict XVI reminded us before his election to the See of Peter:

> The history of Christianity begins with the word χαίρε: Rejoice! . . . For Luke, this word, which inaugurates the history of Jesus and, with it, the history of Christianity, is a comprehensive programmatic designation of what Christianity is by nature. . . .
>
> The content of the Christian *evangelium* reads: God finds man so important that he himself has suffered for man. . . . But if God so loves us, then we are loved in truth. Then love is truth, and truth is love. Then life is worth living. This is the *evangelium*. . . .The promise of love that makes our own life worthwhile remains firm even if the messengers are themselves unprepossessing, even if the priest is far from being an entertaining speaker—although it is not a bad thing if he is one, because deep joy of the heart is also the true prerequisite for a sense of humor, and thus humor is, in a certain sense, the measure of faith.

> [W]e might formulate this basic rule: where joylessness reigns, where humor dies, the spirit of Jesus Christ is assuredly absent. But the reverse is also true: joy is a sign of grace. One who is cheerful from the heart, one who has suffered but not lost joy, cannot be far from the God of the *evangelium*, whose first word on the threshold of the New Testament is 'Rejoice!'[14]

After receiving their evangelizing mission of reconciliation from the Risen Lord immediately before his ascension (cf. Luke 24:47-48), St. Luke tells us that thereupon, "They did him homage and then returned to Jerusalem with great joy" (Luke 24:52). Sharing in the one priesthood of Jesus Christ, i.e., his self-sacrifice of reconciling love on the Cross, and living out a vocation to continue the threefold ministry of the apostles in the local church remain the great joy of the diocesan priest.

---

[14] Joseph Cardinal Ratzinger, *Principles of Catholic Theology* (San Francisco: Ignatius Press, 1987), 75, 81, and 84.